FIXING FRANCE

HOW TO REPAIR
A BROKEN REPUBLIC

With best wishes,

NABILA RAMDANI

Nabila

HURST & COMPANY, LONDON

For my Parents

CONTENTS

INTRODUCTION

Rebuilding the Dream

I am trying to give France the appearance of a solid, firm, confident and expanding country, while it is a worn-out nation. . . . The whole thing is a perpetual illusion.

—CHARLES DE GAULLE (1890–1970)

France is a very easy place to idealize. Even if—like me—you grew up in one of the less salubrious suburbs of Paris, there is much to be positive about. Those of us whose earliest memories are of concrete residential blocks and run-down community centers surrounded by vandalized street furniture certainly have the myths drilled into our heads at a very early age.

We learn about the Belle Époque, when France represented not just peace and prosperity for the elite, but incredible technological breakthroughs that benefited everybody. The medieval slums that had bred disease and discontent in my home city were replaced by a golden, modern Paris with wide avenues, parks, and aqueducts. World's fairs showed off icons of the industrial era: there were escalators and futuristic conveyor-belt pavements that moved at three different speeds. Up went the Eiffel Tower, and the Paris Métro was inaugurated down below.

1

Belief in the Belle Époque can apply to France today, if you really want it to. The country is the most visited in the world, attracting close to one hundred million admirers from every corner of the globe each year. They come to do business and to study, but predominantly to relax, to eat, and to fall in love. Many even aspire to live in France, or at the very least they like to mimic its joie de vivre in their own countries. Beyond the culture—from the language of Molière to Impressionist paintings—an extremely generous welfare state, including universal access to education and health care, is a source of envy around the world. France's capital is an Olympic city and an epicenter of ecological hope, one that lends its very name to the United Nations Paris Climate Accords of 2015.

Yet the modern Republic is failing to live up to its once-exalted reputation. Nostalgists hark back to a time when Gallic civilization was exported with pride. They resent that very little has replaced the glory days, and that all they have left are rapidly fading shadows. There is a profound fear that all that Frenchness—a universal *mode de vie*—is being swallowed up by bland multinationalism. France's lost grandeur manifests itself domestically in ancient institutions that are no longer fit for purpose. Corruption, civil strife, industrial decay, and globalist standardization are all part of the crisis. This sense of downgrading—*déclassement*—is also reflected in foreign policy; France is no longer the great world power it once was.

The Republic is built on dissent, and the French still revere a Revolution that saw every privileged rank, including that of King and Queen, replaced with the category of Citizen, which is what everybody with a French identity card is today. It is meant to provide great advantages, not least of all the warm feeling of belonging that comes from the highest principles known to humanity, enshrined in our tripartite national motto: *Liberté, Égalité, Fraternité*—Liberty, Equality, Fraternity. Such ambitious language has inspired supremely optimistic innovation, and indeed genius, in every field. It also empowers citizens to keep on dissenting, while aspiring to that sacrosanct motto.

France's National Day is July 14, commemorating 1789, when a mob stormed the Bastille prison in Paris and commoners—the Third

Estate—rose up against the absolute monarchy of Louis XVI. They were enraged by unjust taxes, debt, and a series of terrible harvests. Most of the aristocracy was killed off, but the fighting by no means stopped there. On the contrary, radical expressions of discontent went on and on, through the Terror, the Napoleonic Wars, and numerous other rebellions, right up until today. The bloodshed has been horrific, but it has never succeeded in killing the fantastical dreams of an evolving nation.

This book continues in this disruptive tradition. It focuses on ten key themes: Politics, Society, the Far-Right, Protest, Terrorism, Education, Identity, Feminism, Economics, and Foreign Policy. I'll be assessing the fault lines in France's approach to all of them, and how they might be rectified. *Fixing France* does not suggest magical solutions; there are already too many Gallic illusions, and we do not need more of them. A crucial step is to accept reality and deal with it appropriately.

What makes France especially interesting is that it is overwhelmed by idealism. It goes back to those who created a Republic based on sacred texts concentrating on Enlightenment values that are impossible to apply to real life. Freedom and equality for one group of French citizens usually means the suppression of another group.

I consider myself particularly well qualified to examine such a dichotomy, because my North African background often excludes me from France's national story. I was born in Paris to Algerian parents, I was educated in Paris, I have a French passport, and I can think in French ("Being French" is very much a mode of thought and expression). Yet there are many French people who do not acknowledge that I am French, because of my origins and because of my appearance. Many like me are pushed into lives on the periphery.

As with numerous young French people in recent years, I had to go abroad to further my life chances. Fortunate meetings and a lot of reading inspired me to move to the United States. I secured a position as a Lecturer at the University of Michigan in Ann Arbor, and my first journalistic experience was as a host on WCBN-FM, the student radio station. I was free to chat about a range of subjects of my own choosing, and listeners responded enthusiastically. I enjoyed all the lofty clichés about the US, reveling in a dream powered by can-do ambition and energy, rather than an increasingly blurry history. There was adventure everywhere, no matter what my background.

Britain was next. I studied at the London School of Economics, taught at Oxford University, and was welcomed into similarly prestigious organizations with the minimum of fuss. Comparable elite institutions in France were certainly not interested in signing me up. While the US and UK media offered me paid assignments and contracts, French companies did not allow me a look-in, not even as an unpaid intern. Rejection was sometimes for boorish bureaucratic reasons, but there was also prejudice. A significant part of the exclusion process involved never being told about the most rewarding opportunities in the first place. Jobs weren't just unavailable to people like me—we simply didn't know about them.

Those of us from Algerian backgrounds are still viewed by many as being "French Muslims of Algerian origin," an administrative term that became very popular among authority figures when Algeria was the "Jewel in the Crown" of Empire. This remained so during the war of resistance, one that ended in an Algerian victory over France in 1962 and then independence. The Algerian War, more than sixty years after it finished, is absolutely crucial to any understanding of modern France, partly because the Fifth Republic itself—the present iteration of the French ideal—was created by Charles de Gaulle to deal with the growing threat posed by Algerian nationalists. The Constitution of 1958 produced a Republican Monarch who continues to rule with an absurd amount of power and resources. De Gaulle—a devout Roman Catholic who firmly believed in a supernatural universe—celebrated an Eternal France, but also recognized the hollowness of many of its supporting myths.

There have been fewer than ten Presidents since De Gaulle, and all—including the current incumbent Emmanuel Macron—have been white men from pretty much the same background. They regularly use flowery rhetoric, and quasi-religious references, to express their version of the national will. All can rule by presidential decree, allowing them to bypass Parliament, as happened when Macron raised the pension age by two years to sixty-four in March 2023. It was a measure that appeared innocuous enough, but it led to nights of rioting, as even teenage students objected to seeing their retirement plans challenged. Macron retreated to his palace, safe in the knowledge that his hyper-privileged position was also guaranteed by a ruthless security state that includes a nuclear arsenal.

In France, everybody is *technically* entitled to a fair share of national joy. There is no American-style "pursuit of happiness" clause in the French Constitution, but Louis Antoine de Saint-Just, an especially prominent revolutionary, did set out the French variation in a speech to the National Convention in 1794 when he said: "Let us teach Europe that you do not intend there to be one unhappy man or one oppressor on French soil. Let this example bear fruit throughout the world, and let it foster love of the virtues and of happiness. Happiness is a new idea in Europe!"

Sadly, the French are certainly far less content than their reputation for running the world's most popular tourist destination might suggest. Pessimism is written into the French language. Pervading gloom gave rise to Existentialism, one of the most influential philosophical movements of our times. Sighing is a national pastime.

The French think their politicians are corrupt and useless, and that the sluggish judiciary and traditionally fawning media do not hold them to account. The government performed disastrously during the COVID-19 pandemic. Many public hospital workers were on strike when the virus arrived from Wuhan, China, in January 2020, and—as in neighboring countries such as Britain and Italy—there were huge shortages in tests and protective equipment. Economically, France has yet to reform its unsustainable social model or to work out how to make modern capitalism benefit all citizens. There are worries about purchasing power, inflation, and jobs disappearing because of new technology and the democratization of knowledge online, even before the shared nightmares of global warming, rogue states, and a European war in Ukraine contribute to a feeling of impending doom.

Alienation descends like a cloud, especially among those living in rural areas and on suburban council estates. An endemic problem is that these people are not even recognized as being disadvantaged, because officially there is no such thing as a separate community with its own grievances. The French universal model is about equality in everything, including suffering. The principal victims of this systematic fault are instead ignored. French leaders talk about avoiding ghettoization, but it has already happened. Millions of citizens are isolated in their homes, in their schools, in their hopeless search for quality jobs, and in their overall sense of detachment from a fast-changing world.

People like me are certainly not meant to write state-of-the-nation books like this one, nor to suggest ways of mending a broken republic. Thoughtful expression about France, including its deep-seated issues, is supposed to come from members of a class who inhabit the upper-floor apartments in the Haussmann buildings on either side of the River Seine, and who also spend much of their time in Paris's historic bistros and bars. They have usually enjoyed a comfortable, bourgeois upbringing, having attended not just a university but also a graduate school that gave them a sense of what it feels like to be part of a narrow ruling class. They like to agonize—French philosophies are frequently a direct product of lived café culture experience—but generally they think their homeland is doing pretty well and they are very glad to be a part of it, despite the ennui. Such privileged voices pontificate languidly about beauty and truth and revere the romanticism of their City of Light—a city they consider to be filled with people who are just like them. This is not a literal perception—of course they are aware that greater Paris is a metropolis full of social diversity—but they like to imagine that everyone is striving to become an educated, articulate French citizen who can fantasize about expressing themselves to a like-minded audience. They embrace conformism.

The myth of an impossibly romantic, magical city inhabited by bookish aesthetes has as much to do with the area of suburban Paris where I grew up as Marie Antoinette, France's last proper Queen, had to do with five-a-side football. The Essonne department, south of the capital, is known as the 91 and contains the sprawling housing configurations that the authorities and the media call "troubled." Sensitive Urban Zones (ZUS) is the official jargon. The *grands ensembles* were built to deal with a huge population explosion after the Second World War. The 91 also includes Orly Airport, which is still an entry point for thousands of immigrants every year.

Many of the original towns in the 91 were bombed to pieces by the Allies, so planners effectively starting from scratch were given carte blanche. Rather than conveying a sense of utopian splendor—that was the objective of the architects—these housing developments are chronically underfunded and bleak. The fallacy is that creativity among their sizeable populations does not extend far beyond aggressive rappers aiming crude insults at politicians and their oppressive forces of law and order. Snarling lyrics highlight unemployment, discrimination, and the outrageous hypocrisy of the Paris establishment writing their ponderous books a few miles away.

Growing up in the 91, I very soon became aware of the enormous potholes in my country's national story and the myths that sustain French identity. It all started when teachers at my infant school, following the national curriculum, told me and my classmates that, no matter what our heritage, we owed a large debt of gratitude to fair-skinned, red-haired tribesmen from the Iron Age and early Roman period.

"Our Ancestors, the Gauls" remains a legend that is integral to "Being French." There is particular emphasis on Vercingetorix, chieftain of the Arverni tribe who led heroic resistance against Julius Caesar before surrendering to him and then being executed in Rome in 46 BC. Beyond formal lessons, we were introduced to such Gauls through the Asterix and Obelix comic strip series, about an indomitable Gallic village that was the last to stand up to the Romans. The settlement is unnamed, undoubtedly so that it has a universal feel to it. Residents gorge on wild boar roasted on spits, in between beating up those trying to subjugate them. As with the fantasies about Paris, there is a supernatural element to the success of these cartoon Gauls: they have a druid's magic potion that makes them indestructible. The important point is that they are quarrelsome, very tough, and also rather brilliant. Asterix and Obelix, like Vercingetorix, personify the greatness of an ancient, troubled nation.

Marshal Philippe Pétain, the Nazi collaborator, put the Vercingetorix story to what he thought was particularly good use during the war, when he compared the Gauls' capitulation to the Romans to France's humiliating defeat following the German Blitzkrieg in 1940. The idea was that Vercingetorix had submitted to a superior Roman culture, and thus modern France should bow to a new European order organized by the Aryan master race. Vercingetorix, the "first resistance fighter in our history," became a symbol of the defeated French—but the happy, proud defeated French. Submission was encouraged.

Having to look up to Vercingetorix is hard for a brown-skinned Muslim who does not eat pork (and certainly not spit-roasted boars). My family background is the North African city of Annaba; my parents were economic immigrants from a country that was once run by French colonizers who exported war and destruction and acted in a manner that was even crueler than the Romans. We just don't connect with Vercingetorix.

France's revolutionary tradition involves frequent outbursts of violence by the discontented. However, there is now a significant distinction between types of dissenters. While anti-government protesters such as students and rural workers might be viewed as legitimate political agitators, ethnic minority members rebelling against discrimination and underfunding on the estates are regularly described as savages (*sauvages*) and scum (*racaille*). Such words have gone mainstream. White demonstrators might smash up the Arc de Triomphe, blockade the Sorbonne, break windows on the Champs-Élysées, and set fire to branches of the Bank of France, yet such rioting is considered quirkily democratic. Some destruction draws public sympathy, no matter how much it costs to repair or how many people are hurt. Opinions change when the perpetrators are non-white, however. "Terrorism"— the most extreme manifestation of dissent in the Republic and a word that was invented in France—is used to demonize entire communities of French citizens. Collective guilt is routinely spread by those who think there are too many "foreigners" in France.

Such manipulations are the specialty of the most consistently successful political dynasty in recent French history—a grouping currently known as the Rassemblement National (RN) that can trace its roots right back to the Waffen-SS and specifically the Third Reich's Charlemagne Division. The RN attracts a huge vote at elections, largely because it is focused on a hatred of immigrants and anyone linked to them. The Nazi connection, and the RN's association with those who still believe that the Occupation of Algeria was a good thing, is one of

France's worst failures. Two Le Pens—father and daughter—have used the family party, which was formerly called the Front National (FN), as a springboard to the highest office in the land. They have not quite succeeded, yet.

The RN's fixation on populist nationalism—which excludes any deep thinking—benefits from an education system designed under Napoléon Bonaparte. It encourages pride in the nation: its institutions, its history, and its military. Overwhelming conformity and a sense of civic dignity lead to a glorification of the past—not just battles won, but also colonies gained. You hear terms such as "Republican model" and "French values" as if they should not be questioned. While America and Britain are full of inquisitive students, the French learn by rote. Young people are convinced that they are part of a great state and want to perpetuate it.

This reactionary view extends to modern French philosophy, which is dominated by populist pessimists: angry men (as with Presidents, they are almost always white males) who are certain that the country's fall is due to forces that should have remained outside France. Stated facts are scant, but hatred is deep. The French are very good at seeing national problems in terms of betrayal, and they are quick to blame everyone except themselves.

I intend to add to this cacophony of outrage, but always in a manner that is backed up by evidence—which, in many cases, I've uncovered myself—and that offers solutions. I've interviewed plenty of powerful people, as well as listened to voices who are not normally given a chance to express themselves. These voices include disillusioned women who complain about France's abysmal gender equality record and rising rates of sexual violence. Meanwhile, France's secular tradition—*laïcité*—is routinely weaponized to criminalize Muslim women for wearing the "wrong" type of clothing.

For all these reasons, *Fixing France* is first and foremost a constructive critique, but it can also be read as a contemporary guide. There are many aspects of the country that I admire, even if they might sound idiosyncratic at times. France produces the greatest footballers on the planet—Les Bleus are recent World Champions—and the best players by far come from the same areas of Paris as me, the outer suburbs (many of them have Algerian blood coursing through their veins too). Some say these players become so good because they hone their talent on cramped artificial pitches rather than the full-sized grass ones used by members of more prosperous communities. Taking part in smaller games develops close control and the skills needed to dribble around an opponent. Deprivation does not come with many advantages, but you always have to look on the bright side.

It is often said that Paris is now like a permanent museum or an ornate garden like the ones at Versailles. Complacent technocrats fiddle around at the margins, but no change is substantial, let alone able to capture the imagination. *Liberté, Égalité, Fraternité* are on postage stamps and government posters—often alongside a depiction of Marianne, the female firebrand in a Phrygian bonnet who embodies the triumph of the Republic—but it increasingly all feels very shallow and tokenistic.

The writer James Baldwin summed up how important dissent is in his short story "This Morning, This Evening, So Soon," which is primarily set in Paris.[1] He describes a Black American jazz musician returning from France to the United States, where he had suffered extreme bigotry. He lampoons the Statue of Liberty as "an ugly joke for me." The Stars and Stripes meant even less to him, and he said he "had seen the French flag drive the French into the most unspeakable frenzies."

For the narrator of the story, the state of Alabama, where he grew up, was a place of oppression and danger. Paris was his salvation, because he was viewed as a glamorous visiting artist there, rather than a marginalized Black man. In turn, the colonized North Africans he mixed with—people just like my parents—experienced nothing but prejudice. Just as pertinently, Baldwin wrote in *Notes of a Native Son*: "I love America more than any other country in this world, and, exactly for this reason, I insist on the right to criticize her perpetually."[2]

France's "perpetual illusion" has locked it into glorious myths, recalling legendary moments that have little hope of being repeated. French elites are joining an increasingly powerful transnational global class, while those left behind settle for bland conformity. France is undergoing an identity crisis, and those of us who care have every reason to highlight failures that are both inherited and new. What is needed to change all this might be nothing less than a radical overhaul of the republican model—including bringing about a progressive Sixth Republic. I hope my book will explain exactly why, while also suggesting how France might be fixed.

1

POLITICS

The King Is Dead, Long Live the President

I'm proud of my immaturity and political inexperience.
—EMMANUEL MACRON (1977–)

On a surreal Friday evening in 2017, I witnessed firsthand the elation of a young Frenchman who was about to be elevated to one of the most powerful positions on earth. It was May 5, and Emmanuel Macron and I were in the open-plan office of *Mediapart*, the Paris online news and investigative outlet, sipping from glasses of water as we discussed the absolutely bizarre situation he found himself in.

Macron had just beaten a range of candidates from established political parties in the first round of elections to choose France's twenty-fifth President. Opponents included one from the sleaze-ridden Gaullist conservatives—hubristically calling themselves Les Républicains—who was already an indicted criminal suspect. Another was a despairing Socialist from a party that had achieved next to nothing during five years in power. This meant that the two major political parties in France would not be providing a President for the first time since the Second World War. Instead, all Macron had left to do on the following Sunday was get more votes than Marine Le Pen, the current representative of a far-right dynastic organization whose founding members had included Waffen-SS veterans who had sworn an oath to Adolf Hitler and defended a Nazi France.

The brutal simplicity of Macron's task was hardly a cause for optimism. On the contrary, it was an indictment of a system capable of quickly turning any determined individual into a quasi-dictator who might accurately be portrayed as an elected King (there has never been a female President of France). Hardly anybody had heard of Macron a few years before. The first election he ran in was for the presidency. He had no traditional constituency, no partisan supporters who had stood by him through thick and thin. Like everywhere else, French politics can be extremely tribal, but Macron had no tribe. His En Marche! (On the Move!) party was less than a year old and had a flash-in-the-pan novelty feel to it, not least of all because it shared Macron's EM initials. It appeared to represent nothing except for Emmanuel Macron.

Yet there he was, not yet forty and bracing himself to take charge of the third-largest economy in Europe, along with the codes to a nuclear arsenal. More than that, the former banker and civil servant would become the principal representative of his country on the world stage, ready to be welcomed as an honored guest from the White House to the Kremlin.

Macron was relaxed and affable, a clean-cut, boy-next-door type with sideburns in the same light-brown color as his Caesar-style hair. Wearing a conventional business suit and tie, he fixed his bright blue eyes and gap-tooth smile on anyone who showed an interest in him. I was certainly fascinated, and he responded to my first approach with an outstretched right hand. When I took it, he used his left hand to perform a warm double shake.

Macron was open to all kinds of questions, listening intently before replying with a slight but noticeable lisp. I was working for a British newspaper, so I asked him to answer as much as he could in English. He laughed nervously—he had just spent two hours being interrogated about anything and everything in his own language—but he quickly rose to the challenge. Macron came across as an aspiring actor keen to be seen as a precise statesman, but there was plenty of hesitancy. He would say something quite coherently and then clarify it, as if he was somewhat ashamed of what he had just said. I was drawn to this at the time, as it suggested vulnerability and honesty. The boy wonder did not just have an answer to everything; he had three or four.

Macron was a bit older than me but very much of the same generation. Apart from his wife, Brigitte, everybody in his entourage was a thirtysomething go-getter who had grown up in a world dominated by small screens and instant communication. Brigitte had just turned sixty-four, making her a quarter of a century older than Macron.

"We're being watched and filmed all the time," Brigitte told me, as one of my colleagues shot a video of us chatting. "It wasn't like this in the past, but it is something everybody has to adapt to. It's hard. We have to be ready for everything. People are always recording."

Brigitte knew that modernization was integral to her husband's future, so her comments were not complaints. She was aware that the age gap with her husband was indicative of the rapid societal changes of the last few years, not least of all in the way politics was done. Pompous, untrustworthy old men had run France for years. They had often been able to keep the cameras away, ensuring all kinds of behind-the-scenes manipulations, from diverting taxpayers' money for private or party use to discreet second families.

Macron had been a Rothschild investment banker—hardly the kind of job that instills love and affection in anyone—but there was no hint of financial impropriety around him. He did not boast about being a classically trained pianist, instead expressing his fondness for golden oldies: Jacques Brel, Charles Aznavour, and Édith Piaf were all favorites. His karaoke choice was Johnny Hallyday's "Que je t'aime."

The Macrons highlighted their unflashy provincial background; they were clearly very proud of it. Both were from Amiens, the capital of the northern Somme department, one historically associated with cataclysmic warfare. Amiens was destroyed while being fought over repeatedly during both world wars. Much of it had to be rebuilt, and the countryside around it is full of memorials to humanity's abject failures. Macron told me that he was only too well aware of how quickly relations between nominally civilized nations can descend into bloody chaos. The old ways needed changing, he said.

I tried to push Macron on policy details, but he was more interested in discussing ideals, the kinds that are crucial to any understanding of

France. By law and tradition, everyone is meant to be in the service of the Republic's ambitious declaration championing Liberty, Equality, and Fraternity. These high principles have had global influence. The works of great French Social Contract philosophers certainly had much to do with the American Revolution against British colonialists. The Founding Fathers looked to France for new ideas about independence and freedom. Thomas Jefferson's "All men are created equal" owed much to Jean-Jacques Rousseau, for example. Macron—who studied philosophy at university—appreciated such antecedents as much as anyone else set to become President of France.

The *Mediapart* event—Macron's last effort before election campaigning stopped—was broadcast online and given the title "Beat Le Pen, and Then What?" This was very appropriate. The good news was not that Macron had some brilliant new program for France, but that he was not a Républicain, he was not a Socialist, and—best of all—he did not belong to Le Pen's party, which was then called the Front National.

The implication was that Macron was a safe alternative on a ballot form full of beasts. The worry was that, having fulfilled his principal job of keeping the vile creatures at bay, he might do what elected monarchs do best, which is not very much at all beyond posturing in flowery, ambiguous language.

Being President of France comes with executive jets, fleets of limousines, and a detachment of bodyguards—from cavalrymen to secret servicemen. There are no less than seven magnificent residences available, including country homes designed exclusively for leisure. It was hoped that Macron would not spend his time trying to enrich himself or attempting to replace his wife with somebody else—something that all his immediate predecessors had done during their terms of office. Once elected, any new President becomes the most powerful figure by far in French politics, a supreme leader who underpins the entire republican system.

Soon after guillotining King Louis XVI and Queen Marie Antoinette, the French elevated Napoléon Bonaparte to Emperor. It was as if they longed to return to the mysticism of royalty and the sense of enduring certainty it provided. The Fifth Republic has continued with this tradition, creating a mighty role at the heart of a highly centralized nation. France functions not just by the administration of law but on the force of an individual's personality, even though such a concentration of power is anathema to democracy and undermines the very principles of *Liberté, Égalité, Fraternité* that hold France together.

Common Criminals

As well as Macron, I've met all of France's other twenty-first-century heads of state: the late Jacques Chirac, Nicolas Sarkozy, and François Hollande. They not only appeared flawed but in two cases were provably deeply flawed: Paris courts found them guilty of corruption.

Both Chirac and Sarkozy—who were once firm allies—were convicted following highly publicized trials after they left office. Their indictable offenses had not prevented them from being given access to the codes of the French nuclear arsenal or from having a pivotal role in world affairs. Chirac and Sarkozy's ultimate shame and humiliation said everything about a system of government that has been in crisis since the very foundation of the Fifth Republic in 1958, at a time when France was coming close to civil war.

A semi-presidential system was then created. It *technically* involves a dual executive, which is to say a President working alongside a Prime Minister and Cabinet. Articles 20 and 21 of the Fifth Republic Constitution state that the Prime Minister and his administration govern, but the reality is that the President is very much in charge. He selects his own Prime Minister—one who, like all ministers, does not have to be an elected politician—and can dissolve Parliament at any time. In fact, he can bypass Parliament altogether and rule by decree. For good measure, the President has a suspensive veto on all legislation: if he's unhappy that Parliament has agreed on a bill, he can request another reading. This gives him effective control of the National Assembly, France's lower house, which sits in the Bourbon Palace in Paris and comprises 577 deputies drawn from single-member constituencies via two-round elections. The upper house is the Senate, which is inside the capital's Luxembourg Palace. It is made up of 348 Senators chosen by around 150,000 officials during indirect elections. The Senate is mainly concerned with constitutional and foreign affairs. However, "in the event of a serious crisis," both houses of Parliament become redundant as the President can exercise emergency powers.

Crucially, the President is free from prosecution while in office and can pardon wrongdoers. A new measure introduced in 2007 means he can *technically* be removed in cases of "breach of his duties," but such a move requires an initial two-thirds majority vote in the National Assembly, which he is likely to control, so it would be extremely difficult to achieve, especially at short notice. The President chairs the Council of Ministers, the equivalent of an American or British Cabinet. He appoints three out of nine judges on France's Constitutional Council, which adjudicates on the constitutionality of legislation, and judges serve nine-year terms on the court. The President also negotiates and signs all foreign treaties, and can call a referendum on any contentious issue. The President can convene the Congress of the French Parliament, which is when both National Assembly and Senate members meet at the Palace of Versailles, the former stately home of the French monarch.

Unlike the British model of parliamentary democracy, where the head of state is largely a ceremonial figurehead—an actual King or Queen—the President of France has an electoral mandate all to himself, and this helps make him stupendously powerful. Thus, the nature of those who become President is crucial to any understanding of France's system of government. Bearing in mind that the American Constitution gives Congress the authority to impeach and remove a serving President of the United States—and that this has been attempted in recent years—there is an argument to suggest that the French President is in an even stronger position than the American one. The President's finger is on the nuclear *force de frappe*, and he is the commander of all of France's armed forces.

I've noted an immense flunky count during all my visits to the Élysée Palace. They come at you from all angles. As well as civil servants engaged in political and administrative work, they include uniformed staff serving vintage wines and cordon bleu food, plus those who can help the President with his fitness, his holiday plans, his moneymaking, or any other private interest, including his love life.

François Hollande used to meet his mistress in an apartment in Rue du Cirque (Circus Street, appropriately), just around the corner from the Élysée Palace. The *Chef d'État* would get there by hopping on to the back of a scooter driven by one of his many plainclothes heavies, who would wait outside the building while the President cheated on his *Première Dame*. Sometimes, the officer would buy croissants for Hollande and the *Deuxième Dame*. This was by no means an unusual example among the thousands of taxpayer-funded public servants who attend to the President. Sarkozy, Chirac, and—probably worst of all—François Mitterrand were all known for their affairs while in office.

There is certainly a profound sense of unreality among the gilt decor, Louis XIV furniture, and endless mirrored salons of the Élysée Palace. There, I heard Nicolas Sarkozy admit that he had started bombing Libya before getting approval from the United Nations in 2011. He announced this grotesquely cynical news in a matter-of-fact manner as his butlers handed out petits fours and glasses of Bordeaux to correspondents from around the world.

It was around the time when Sarkozy and his third wife, the former supermodel turned pop singer Carla Bruni, had been pilloried for running up an annual bill of €275,809 on fresh flowers. The figures were part of the first state audit of a French leader's expenditure since the reign of Louis XVI. The King's outrageous spending with Marie Antoinette was one of the causes of the 1789 French Revolution. Following his own audit, Sarkozy immediately asked for the receipts for any undisclosed items to be returned to him, so that they would not create a public outcry. This attempt at secrecy failed, as did an effort to keep quiet about the fitting of two €75,000 bread ovens on the presidential Airbus A330. It is a cliché to keep comparing modern French Presidents and their partners to the two most famous guillotined royals in history, but it is never wholly inappropriate.

Algerian France

Those of us from an Algerian background are particularly well qualified to analyze the failings of France's President-King because of his historical links with our oppression. In May 1958, the Algerian War of Independence was at its height when European settlers, supported by the French Army, launched a putsch against the Governor-General in Algiers and called for the dissolution of the government in Paris, so that it could be replaced with one explicitly and robustly committed to the survival of the North African colony. They argued that General Charles de Gaulle, who had been in the wilderness for twelve years after leading the Free French through the Second World War, was the only leader capable of preventing the abandonment of Algeria.

European settlers loyal to Paris—known as *pieds-noirs* ("black feet" literally, but referring to the black shoes or boots invariably worn by the colonists)—organized themselves into "vigilante committees" to fight Algerian revolutionaries from the National Liberation Front (*Front de Libération Nationale*, FLN), who were demanding freedom. France had pulled out of Vietnam after almost a hundred years of colonial rule following defeat at Dien Bien Phu in 1954. Shaken by this catastrophe, France was ill-equipped to deal with the Algerian crisis. The National Assembly approved the restoration of De Gaulle—the war hero sexagenarian—to take charge. This followed an 82 percent majority vote backing the new Constitution in a constitutional referendum. "Vive De Gaulle!" was the rallying cry of French patriots, while he insisted, "Who honestly believes that, at the age of sixty-seven, I would start a career as a dictator?"

Despite De Gaulle's initial caution, paratroopers and other elite military units were prepared to take control in mainland France if he was not reinstalled as leader. President René Coty told Parliament that the nation was "turning towards the most illustrious of Frenchmen." De Gaulle said he would accept his new role under the precondition of a new Constitution that would end the Fourth Republic—the unloved one (*la mal aimée*)—and include the all-powerful President. The first head of the Fifth Republic would naturally be De Gaulle himself. More than that, he wanted extraordinary powers to deal with the security threat posed by the increasingly successful Algerian nationalists. This opened the way for more savagery against indigenous Algerian Arabs and Berbers and the subjugation of their human rights. Algeria was administratively part of France at the time; it had its own *départements* and representatives in the Paris Parliament. Despite this, those living in

Algeria were treated as appallingly as the Algerian Muslim diaspora on the mainland.

De Gaulle certainly tried to present himself as a King-like figure who was above the fray. He kept well away from Paris on the day in October 1961, when up to three hundred pro-FLN demonstrators were murdered by police in the center of the city, for example. De Gaulle's new Republic was to remain profoundly influenced by the Algerian disaster, long after the Algerians won their War of Independence in 1962.

De Gaulle wanted the new presidency to embody the nation. There was a mystic quality to this. It was as if he envisaged France always being ruled by a modern Joan of Arc, someone imbued with so much unearthly power that all resistance, no matter how determined, could be crushed. Instead, more worldly Presidents survived various insurrections using France's ever stronger security state.

De Gaulle was from a devout Roman Catholic family. He took comfort in a supreme commander, centralization, and unquestioning faith. An omnipotent ruler, safe in a walled palace and surrounded by the Republican Guard, fitted in perfectly with his vision. As De Gaulle is said to have told a confidant, "In reality, we are on the stage of a theater where I have been keeping up the illusion since 1940. I am trying to give France the appearance of a solid, firm, confident and expanding country, while it is a worn-out nation . . . the whole thing is a perpetual illusion."

Fallen Gods

François Mitterrand, Socialist President of France between 1981 and 1995, certainly worked hard to mythologize himself. He was considered so haughty that he was dubbed "God," but not necessarily in an admiring, or morally affirming, way. His duplicitous life included creating a personal dirty tricks unit to keep a second family hidden. His long-term mistress, Anne Pingeot, was a state secret throughout Mitterrand's fourteen-year presidency, as was the couple's child, Mazarine.

All kinds of dark arts were employed, including the wiretapping of journalists, lawyers, and political rivals. There were criminal trials and convictions of operatives—foot soldiers in the security services who carried out illegal missions—long after Mitterrand's death in 1996, and judges ruled that he was the "instigator and essentially the controller of the operation." When news about Mazarine finally leaked out toward the end of his presidency, Mazarine felt she was "the shame of the French Republic, and an affront to morality."

Mitterrand's successor, Jacques Chirac, was not as Machiavellian as his immediate predecessor, but he was nicknamed "the Bulldozer" for good reason. As far as corruption in French public life was concerned, Chirac's criminal conviction in December 2011 was highly significant. He was allowed to skip the trial because of ill health, including memory loss, but did not appeal the verdict. When found guilty in the most historic court in France, he became the first former head of state of the Fifth Republic to be publicly exposed as a common criminal. Less than five years after stepping down from office and losing immunity from prosecution, he was found guilty of embezzlement and abuse of trust.

Chirac's trial at the *première chambre civile* of the Palais de Justice related to his time as Paris Mayor from 1977 until he was elected President in 1995, but it threw light on every aspect of Chirac's character—and on the kind of person who inevitably ended up in the Élysée Palace. Institutionalized sleaze was the focus, and action was finally taken against a decaying system that has produced an extraordinarily decadent and ineffective political class. Chirac's punishment—a two-year suspended prison sentence—was measly considering he misspent millions in taxpayers' money, but the impact of his conviction could not be underestimated. In a pertinent twist, Chirac was tried in the same Paris courtroom where Marie Antoinette was condemned to death by guillotine.

Chirac had introduced a law preventing serving Presidents from being prosecuted. This meant that nobody could touch him when, as head of state between 1995 and 2007, the corruption allegations first surfaced. It was eventually proved that as Mayor of Paris he had created fictitious jobs and diverted money to his conservative party, in part to reward supporters. Put in simple terms: Chirac spent twelve years as President thanks to dirty money. Yet Georges Kiejman, Chirac's defense lawyer, said on his client's conviction, "What I hope is that this ruling does not change in any way the deep affection the French feel legitimately for Jacques Chirac."

Chirac's crimes were a symptom of a country that has been in denial for years. The French Foreign Minister Alain Juppé had already received a fourteen-month suspended prison sentence over the same allegations in 2004. If this kind of scandal had happened in any other democracy, there would have been a public outcry, but strict French privacy laws and a fawning Paris media had originally ensured that such matters were relegated to a protracted magistrates' inquiry that few showed much interest in.

One of the reasons successive administrations got away with so much was because of the deferential attitude the French had toward the institution of the presidency. Economic stagnation, bureaucratic incompetence, foreign policy catastrophes, and street riots didn't seem to inhibit the opulent lifestyles of presidential couples.

Nicolas Sarkozy's term of office became another textbook case of what was wrong with the system. Sarkozy had considered himself to be the most original French leader in the postwar era, but he also did much to expose the absurdities of the presidential institution. His energy saw him tagged *le hyper-président*, as well as a "Gallic Thatcher." Margaret Thatcher had destroyed her own country's suffocating post-war consensus, taking on the Left in a hugely divisive move aimed at wealth creation. Sarkozy said he wanted to use similar liberal econom-ics to boost growth and employment by cutting taxes, reducing deficits, shrinking government, and loosening labor laws.

Soon, all the Sarkozy propaganda fizzled out. As far as reform was concerned, he was not the *hyper-président*; he was the president of hype. Sarkozy's much-vaunted "rupture" with all the outdated aspects of French public life simply did not happen. Rather than a frenetic dash into the modern world, the pace of the Sarkozy government was more like the tired limp of yet another wizened old man—the kind who had been letting France down for years.

Just over a decade after his election to the presidency, Sarkozy was playing out a very different drama—still taking place in the full glare of publicity, but this time within the French criminal justice system. On March 21, 2018, Sarkozy was indicted over millions of laundered dollars he was said to have received from Colonel Muammar Gaddafi, the late Libyan dictator, to illegally finance his successful 2007 presidential campaign. The charge was particularly alarming because Sarkozy had been behind the Western attack on the North African country in 2011, one that ultimately led to Gaddafi being hacked to death by a mob.

Following the announcement of Sarkozy's indictment, his third wife, Carla Bruni, responded on her Instagram account in three languages—French, Italian, and English—posting the words: "I'm proud of you my love. You are righteous, clear and strong. I'm proud of your dignity against all odds and of how you always stand straight no matter how low the strikes can be." An endearing photograph of the politician accompanied Bruni's declaration of enduring love.

The mounting evidence against Sarkozy would see him become the first former head of state in the history of modern France to be tried for corruption linked to his time in office as President. Beyond Libya, Sarkozy had also attempted to obtain classified information from a judge by offering him a prestigious legal position in Monaco, the Riviera principality and tax haven. The judge, Gilbert Azibert, had details about a criminal investigation into Sarkozy's alleged acceptance of bribes from Liliane Bettencourt, the L'Oréal heiress who was once France's richest woman.

Sarkozy was also found guilty of a range of offenses in the so-called Bygmalion affair, named after the PR firm that handled Sarkozy's appearances during his failed 2012 reelection campaign, many of them made with Bruni. The company was said to have used a vast system of false accounting to conceal illegal funding for his campaign. Sarkozy was sentenced to prison for exceeding expenditure by more than $20 million, subject to appeal. The legal onslaught had started when Sarkozy lost his presidential immunity from prosecution when he was ignominiously voted out of office after just one term in 2012. The Paris home he shared with Bruni was raided by fraud squad officers.

Despite this, the Sarkozy-Bruni couple tried to revive the fantastical world they had lost, acting as if they were still VIPs entitled to vast wealth and influence. Sarkozy pressed on with his political career, even standing and failing to become President again in 2016. Bruni maintained her rictus smile at all times, while continuing to record AC/DC and ABBA covers in a bid to be thought of as a stylish crooner, rather than the despairing wife of a busted chancer.

The feel-good façade was impossible to sustain. After multiple failed appeals, Sarkozy was finally placed in the dock. His appearance in Court 32 of the Tribunal de Paris was the first of many, as judges and juries prepared to try him for some of the gravest executive crimes in the history of the Fifth Republic. Their verdicts would not just apply to Sarkozy, but to the increasingly rotten system that allowed him to come to power.

On March 1, 2021, Sarkozy was found guilty of trying to bribe a judge and sentenced to three years in prison, with two suspended. It related to the so-called wiretapping affair, when police investigators listened in on burner phones belonging to Sarkozy and Thierry Herzog, his lawyer. The bug tapes—which were played in the public court for the first time—picked up Sarkozy and Herzog discussing ways of obtaining confidential information about other inquiries that were being handled by judges at the Court of Cassation in Paris. Prosecutors said Sarkozy aimed to garner intelligence from Judge Azibert, including by getting him the Monaco job. Azibert did not take up the post in Monte Carlo, but under French law prosecutors do not have to prove that anybody benefited from a corrupt deal to secure a conviction.

The conviction for corruption and influence peddling meant Sarkozy became the first President of the Fifth Republic to be sentenced to actual jail time, rather than a suspended sentence. He immediately appealed, which began another lengthy delay, and he was also given the chance to serve his sentence using an electronic tag at home. Nevertheless, the judges had made a statement of intent. (The last French head of state to go to prison was Marshal Philippe Pétain, the wartime Nazi collaborator. He was given a death sentence, but because of his age and First World War record, this was later commuted to incarceration.) Carla Bruni, who had been in court for some of the Sarkozy trials, posted the message "The fight goes on" on her Instagram account, and also "The truth will emerge." She did not specify when or what version of the truth she had in mind.

During his time as Interior Minister and then President, Sarkozy had also built up a reputation as an unreconstructed authoritarian, somebody who believed that tougher jail sentences were necessary to deter criminality. More than that, *le Top Cop*—another one of Sarko's varied nicknames—believed that truncheons and tear gas were as important to maintaining France's social fabric as the deportation of immigrants who "failed to integrate." He was obsessed with increasing the power of the security state, not least of all to protect the assets of his key constituency: the superrich.

In the summer of 2020, before Sarkozy's conviction the following spring, his former Prime Minister, François Fillon, and his British wife, Penelope Fillon, were also given prison sentences after being found guilty of fraud. Judges sitting at the Paris Correctional Court ruled that the couple had created fake jobs that paid Mrs. Fillon more than €1 million in public funds. Fillon was given a five-year sentence, with three years suspended, while his wife received a three-year suspended sentence. Both appealed.

Before his conviction, Fillon had been a shoo-in to become the next President of France. There is absolutely no doubt that he had viewed the 2017 presidential election as a chance to escape jail. If he had won the contest—and he gained an impressive 20 percent of the first-round vote, even after having been charged—then he could have evaded prosecution for at least five years and potentially ten. The Fillons were devout Catholics who prided themselves on their moral compass. Fillon was a member of Les Républicains, the latest incarnation of the Gaullist party that was meant to represent the upright politics of Charles de Gaulle.

Supporters of indicted politicians always raise conspiracy theories, suggesting that miscreants like Sarkozy and Fillon are the victims of dark plots. Both claimed their original problems with the judiciary were engineered by left-wing magistrates and police working for a Socialist government. During his first TV appearance after leaving office in 2012, Sarkozy said the justice system was being used as a "political instrument" against him.[1] Speaking after being taken into custody by the fraud squad for the first time, Sarkozy said, "In our country, the country of human rights and the rule of law, there are things that are being organized to present an image of me that is not the truth." Despite such attempted mitigation, the sentencing of a former President of France and his Prime Minister caused shockwaves.

Small wonder that France has some of the highest levels of political mistrust in Europe. In a survey carried out in January and February 2021 in France, Germany, Italy, and the United Kingdom, French citizens were the most damning of their political class. Some 65 percent thought that elected members and leaders of political parties were "mostly corrupt." This compared to 42 percent who took that view in Germany and 52 percent in the United Kingdom. Moreover, only 16 percent of the French trusted their political parties, versus 17 percent in Italy, 32 percent in the United Kingdom, and 39 percent in Germany.[2]

The most significant consequence of the François Fillon embezzlement scandal, and the collapse of the fatally divided French Left, was the presidential runoff between Macron and Le Pen. Macron might not have run in any election before April 23, 2017—the first round of voting for the presidency—yet he shot to power following the second round on May 7 with relative ease.

Beyond a ludicrously powerful President, the Fifth Republic has an electoral system that is profoundly undemocratic. The President is under no obligation to put elected officials in the highest offices of state. On the contrary, he can appoint anyone he likes. Government ministers are nominally chosen by the Prime Minister, but only after consultation with the President. Even prime ministers are frequently nonelected officials. Jean Castex, who was brought in as Prime Minister by Macron just before the COVID-19 pandemic struck, had no democratic mandate. Nor did Macron himself when he started his ministerial career in Hollande's single-term administration. Macron regularly rules by decrees. Over fifty-three days from the end of October until the start of December 2022 alone, his government used Article 49-3 of the Constitution nine times to pass legislation without a parliamentary vote. The most controversial use of 49-3 came in March 2023, when Macron pushed through a rise in the retirement age from sixty-two to sixty-four. It was his big chance to shake up France's ruinously expensive social system, he argued, and he was ready to weather nationwide dissent, including riots and strike action. Such behavior at a time of war in Europe, galloping inflation, and post-COVID-19 exhaustion prompted comparisons with the Bourbon Kings.

The De Gaulle model presidency undoubtedly corrupts. The strange Constitution encourages all of the lofty arrogance, sneakiness, and sinister backstabbing of monarchy. The President is entitled to too much of a fairy-tale lifestyle, and abuse is all but inevitable.

Emmanuel Bonaparte

Amiens, Macron's hometown, is just ninety miles from De Gaulle's birthplace of Lille. The two northmen naturally shared a fascination with warfare, given the crucial role their area of France played in two world wars and numerous historical battles before that. They were educated at schools founded by Catholic monks, including Jesuit ones, and revered Christian icons such as Joan of Arc, as well as the great French philosophers.

"The history of my family is one of republican ascent in provincial France," Macron writes in his autobiography, *Révolution*. Like De Gaulle, he focuses on duty to his country. He may have been born seven years after *le Général*'s death, but Macron's devotion to the mysteries of ancient France is every bit as strong as De Gaulle's.

Despite the appalling records of his immediate predecessors, Macron certainly believes in the presidency and the Gaullist dynamic upon which it is based: that of a commander guiding the state using the power of his personality and glorious national myths. Within six months of his coming to power, *Libération* used an editorial to describe the new President as "Emmanuel Bonaparte." *Libé* said Macron was "an imperious character" combining authoritarianism, youthful energy, and hurried reform. "Like Bonaparte, Macron sleeps little, works constantly, speaks in a piped and cutting voice, and decides on everything."[3] Macron also became the youngest head of state since Bonaparte.

Storytelling and symbols are essential to Macron. On the night of his election victory in 2017, he chose to celebrate at the Louvre, surrounded by emblems of old imperial glory. Macron walked slowly and solemnly across the Cour Napoléon toward the glass Pyramid, which had been part of Mitterrand's Grand Louvre plan aimed at projecting France as a forward-thinking nation. As Macron followed in the footsteps of his predecessors, thousands of supporters waved blue-white-and-red tricolor flags. Rather than "La Marseillaise," the music blaring out of speakers was Beethoven's "Ode to Joy"—the EU anthem. Here was a new leader firmly tied to ancient Kings and Bonapartism but also modernity and a European project that he would now be guiding. "Europe and the world are expecting us to defend everywhere the spirit of the Enlightenment which is under threat in so many places," he declared.

It was *Challenges* magazine that first gave Macron his "Jupiter" nickname in 2016, in the run-up to his presidential win. Macron said Hollande, his predecessor and former boss, "does not believe in a Jupiterian leader, but I don't believe in a normal president. The French aren't waiting for that. On the contrary, such a concept makes them feel insecure." Macron added, "I think the president of contemporary, democratic France needs to be someone who leads society by the force of his convictions and actions and offers clear direction."

Like De Gaulle, Macron spoke as if he was somebody who embodied France, echoing Louis XIV's apocryphal boast: "L'État, c'est moi" (I am the state). Cultivating the image of the all-powerful military man from day one of his presidency, Commander-in-Chief Macron appeared on the Champs-Élysées after his election in a military jeep instead of the traditional limousine. Favored publicity stunts included being lowered by winch into a nuclear submarine or posing in his *Top Gun* French Air Force fatigues. He relied on secret "defense councils," particularly when dealing with crisis issues such as the COVID-19 pandemic, terrorist crimes, and the Ukraine War. Being in charge of the *force de frappe*, France's independent nuclear strike capability, also appealed to Jupiter's sense of omnipotence.

Macron relocated his own court to the Palace of Versailles three times in less than a year of office: to receive Russian President Vladimir Putin, to address both houses of Parliament, and to host a "Choose France" business summit for the heads of multinational companies. Macron also celebrated his fortieth birthday at the Château de Chambord, François I's Renaissance hunting lodge in the Loire Valley.

On April 5, 2018, Macron even paid a nocturnal visit to the Basilica of Saint-Denis, where many of the former Kings and Queens of his country, including Louis XVI and Marie Antoinette, are buried. He lingered at the tomb of King Dagobert, the first monarch to be interred there, and at the graves of François I and Henri II.

Macron is a superb actor, and his theatrical choreography is perfectly suited to being President of France. The bill for paying a makeup artist called Natacha to powder his face during his first three months of office came to €26,000. An Élysée Palace spokesman admitted that the cost was "a little bit high," and that future bills would be "significantly reduced." Previously, the near-bald Hollande had been accused of shampoo socialism after spending almost €10,000 a month for a personal barber.

Macron says "En même temps" all the time. It literally translates as "At the same time," but the best English-language equivalent is probably "On the other hand." "It will not be on the Right, not on the Left," said Macron in 2016 while discussing his new movement and disingenuously ruling out a crack at becoming head of state. "I took time, I reflected, I consulted, I associated," he waffled. "This is not a movement aimed at producing yet another umpteenth presidential candidate. This is not my priority today. My priority is the situation in the country." *L'État, c'est moi*, in other words.

Macron's well-scripted modesty was designed to place him above squalid and selfish ambition, to turn him into a universal figure focused solely on the future of France, but in the vaguest way possible. The mysticism of the presidency suited Macron. On May 8, 2016, a month after the launch of EM!, Macron was in Orléans for the anniversary of France relieving the English siege of the city in 1429. Paying tribute to Joan of Arc—the Maid of Orléans—Macron filled his speech with allusions to his own career trajectory, an extraordinary conflation. Both Joan and Macron came from provincial backgrounds, but "like an arrow," fulfilled their destinies, Macron said.

There was no martial glory involved in Macron's own rise to power, least of all against the English. After coming fifth in his class when graduating from the civil service school ENA (*École Nationale d'Administration*) in 2004, Macron started with the elite Inspection

Générale des Finances—a fast track to some of the biggest jobs in the French technocracy. (The combined local and overseas government system that Macron skipped over is vast. There are some thirty-five thousand communes, all with a council and a Mayor, while 101 departments are headed by a general council and President, as are eighteen regions. Despite all of this administration, it has not been reformed since Bonaparte's time.)

Macron joined François Hollande's presidential office aged thirty-four as a civil servant and became the Socialist President's personal envoy at the Group of Eight (G8), Group of Twenty (G20), and European Summits. Macron had briefly been a member of the French Socialist Party years before but was not during his period of service with Hollande. The Socialists offered to set Macron up as a member of Parliament in an easily winnable constituency, but he showed no interest. This did not stop Hollande from making Macron Minister for the Economy, Industry, and Digital Affairs. Socialist policies were failing, so a bright specialist who understood real-world capitalism was needed. Macron had spent four years from 2008 working for the merchant bank Rothschild & Co. in Paris.

When told about Hollande's plan to tax high incomes at 75 percent, Macron likened it to "Cuba without the sun." Macron is a free-market capitalist with a self-professed social conscience, like Bill Clinton or Tony Blair. He approves of someone making lots of money but, like many French, is suspicious of the excesses of Anglo-American commerce.

Macron was a highly polished, technocratic graduate of ENA, and yet, according to the mythmaking, both he and Joan of Arc had been chosen for greatness.[4] Macron continued to articulate like a Jupiter should. Speaking about the void in national life since the 1789 Revolution, Macron said, "In French politics, this absence is the presence of a King, a King whom, fundamentally, I don't think the French people wanted dead. The Revolution dug a deep emotional abyss, one that was imaginary and shared: the King is no more!" France has tried to fill this void, most notably with Napoléon Bonaparte and then Charles de Gaulle, but "the rest of the time," said Macron, "French democracy does not manage to fill this void."[5] Of course, Macron did not literally want a King back. Just somebody like the King would do. Somebody like Emmanuel Macron. Macron projected himself as a man-of-the-hour hero who would heal his country.

In addition to artfully choreographed images, modern PR tools—endless selfies, bilingual tweets, and the catchphrase "France Is Back"—are a big part of the Macron package, exploiting emotions over intellect. He wants to be one of the most visible statesmen in the world, a guardian of democratic values who will go anywhere and everywhere to support justice and truth.

An early indication of just how close Macron felt to Jupiter was the strange Benalla affair of 2018. A video released on May Day that year, captured by a journalist called Taha Bouhafs, showed Alexandre Benalla, a key Macron security aide, wearing a police helmet and identification tag as he beat up a woman demonstrator on the streets of Paris. He then dragged her away to be arrested. Following public outcry, Benalla was suspended on full pay for two weeks but then welcomed back into the President's inner circle. Benalla carried a gun for "personal security" and said he had secured a National Assembly pass so as to use its gym and library. He was not officially entitled to any of these rare privileges.

Benalla had been Macron's chief of security during his presidential campaign. The pair often went biking and on skiing trips. They jogged and played tennis together. Perhaps unsurprisingly, the attack on the woman did not end Benalla's cosseted position. He was still regularly pictured with Macron afterward. He helped organize the triumphant return of France's World Cup–winning football team to Paris following their victory in Moscow in the summer of 2018.

Prosecutors eventually started investigating, and Benalla was charged with assault and impersonating a police officer, but Macron was by no means happy about this. "You're the only ones who are interested in this," he told journalists.

Macron joked, "Benalla has never had the nuclear codes." Then he changed his tune to "I am to blame" and dared his opponents and the press to "come and get me—I will answer to the French people." He first acted as if he was above the law, and then made out that he was the law. Despite this, Benalla was sentenced to three years in prison, with two suspended, subject to appeal, in November 2021.

De Gaulle started his own father-of-the-nation act on radio and then became a master of television. During the emergency intervention in Algiers in 1958, De Gaulle was feted as a savior figure, as he appealed to both sides—the French nationalist settlers and the indigenous Arabs and Berbers who wanted an end to French colonialism. His speech in Algiers on June 4 was broadcast live on radio and also recorded for newsreels and TV. It lasted nine minutes, and the most memorable phrase reassured everyone: "I have understood you!" This could have meant anything. Academics are still arguing over it to this day. *En même temps* is in the same school of political vocabulary.

De Gaulle's priority was for the President to become the key decision-making office in France, effectively taking control of foreign and defense policy so that his country might once again achieve great power status. The illusion of authority crumbled a few years later when France lost the Algerian War, following regular attempts by nationalist terrorists of the Secret Army Organization (OAS) to assassinate De Gaulle as part of their campaign to keep Algeria French.

More than sixty years later, a President of France was again telling Algerians one thing and the French quite another. Macron visited Algiers during his 2017 campaign and said that 132 years of colonization had been a "crime against humanity," adding, "It's truly barbarous, and it's part of a past that we need to confront by apologizing to those against whom we committed these acts."

Four years later, Macron's administration released a new report on the "Memory of Colonization and the Algerian War," and a spokesman for the President was adamant that there would be "no repentance, nor apologies" for what had happened.

A Sixth Republic?

Before considering the possibility of a new political arrangement based on a continuity model—a Sixth Republic—let us recall how we got to where we are today. The First Republic was proclaimed in 1792, during the Revolution, but beyond glorious ideology (notably the Declaration of the Rights of Man and of the Citizen), it was underpinned by carnage. *Madame Guillotine* and *la Terreur* were creations of an intensely violent period that lasted until November 9, 1799, when Napoléon Bonaparte launched a coup d'état called 18 Brumaire after the eccentric republican calendar system. In 1804, Bonaparte crowned himself Emperor of the French under the First French Empire. The French largely feign indifference toward Bonaparte nowadays, but there is no doubt that his legacy is enormous. The Napoleonic Code remains the basis of the country's system of civil laws. Bonaparte wanted to micromanage his entire empire, and he did this through a "Code" that, more than two hundred years on, is still hugely influential—it has shaped the legal systems of more than seventy countries around the world.

After Bonaparte's defeat at the Battle of Waterloo in 1815, Bourbon Kings ruled France until 1848. The Second Republic followed the 1848 Revolution, one of many that spread across Europe. Bonaparte's nephew, Louis-Napoléon Bonaparte, was elected President, and in 1851 he, too, staged a coup and proclaimed himself Emperor Napoléon III of the Second Empire. He ended up being captured during the Franco-Prussian War in 1870, and a Third Republic was proclaimed following France's crushing beating. The new republic was focused on a parliamentary system of government and lasted for seventy years until the Nazi Occupation during the Second World War. All power was then handed over to Marshal Philippe Pétain and his Vichy collaborators.

Charles de Gaulle, who had run the Free French while in exile, returned to France after the war, when, in 1946, a Fourth Republic was created. A system of proportional representation led to instability, as multiple parties competed in the decision-making process. By the time the Fourth Republic ended in 1958, there had been sixteen prime ministers in just twelve years.

Given its turbulent start in 1958 during the Algerian War, there was no guarantee that the Fifth Republic would last more than a few years. Michel Debré, the author of the new Constitution, originally wanted a UK-style prime ministerial government, but Article 5 set the President up as the "arbitrator" of pretty much everything. In 1965, there was the first direct election of the President, giving him even more legitimacy. Debré described De Gaulle as a "Republican Monarch," while De Gaulle himself referred to a "popular monarchy."

The decision to reduce the French President's term from seven years to five in 2002 might sound as though it would have weakened the President's power, but it in fact made him stronger. It meant that the focus of political debate would almost always be on the incumbent in the Élysée Palace.

France's two-round election system for President and Parliament is also of great use to the monarchical President. Changes to the electoral calendar in 2001 saw parliamentary elections moved from the midterm—when they acted as a check on the head of state—to a couple of weeks after the presidential election. This pretty much guarantees a repeat of the election result and, with it, a pro-President Parliament, with no midterm challenge to the head of state.

Macron was only too aware of the extra power this gave him, saying after his 2017 election, "You have elected me, now give me an Assembly that allows me to govern." He got exactly what he wanted. Macron's fledgling En Marche! movement easily won the National Assembly elections in June 2017. A party that did not exist a year and a half before took 308 seats to add to the 42 won by its allies, the Democratic Movement (MoDem), giving the coalition a vast majority in the 577-seat National Assembly. Le Pen's Front National won just eight seats.

The 2022 legislative election that followed Macron's second presidential victory was not as successful for him as 2017, but he got by. There was a hung Parliament for the first time since 1988, but Macron's Ensemble (Together) bloc still secured the most seats: 245 out of 577. Macron was able to make Élisabeth Borne the second female Prime Minister in France's history, so there was no fear of another period of cohabitation—that is, when a President must work with an opposition Prime Minister. Le Pen's Rassemblement National, however, won eighty-nine seats—the most in their history.

As usual, millions had turned out to oppose the RN. The two-round electoral system is meant to prevent instability, but in fact it encourages tactical voting. People use the first round as a protest vote and then work together to keep a detested candidate out. Thus, we end up with an "anyone-but-*X*" candidate like Macron.

Despite the RN's relatively limited success in parliamentary elections (they do a bit better at the local and regional level, and in the European Parliament), the fear of a Le Pen becoming President has become routine. A single representative of a populist movement opposing immigration and globalization, while promising traditional left-wing welfare and protectionist policies, has millions of supporters, despite the party's overtly racist antecedents. In other parliamentary systems, such individuals can be tamed for good through centrist grand alliances, but not in France.

The straitjacket of the presidency prevents France from establishing a stable parliamentary coalition of the kind that governs other countries such as Germany. The mainstream parties do not come together to pass commonsense reforms, as they are too obsessed with who is going to win the next presidential election.

Disillusion has translated into a steady decline in turnout at elections, to the extent that the largest voter bloc is made up of nonvoters. A dismal 46 percent turned out to vote in the second round of the legislative elections in 2022. In mainland France, Seine-Saint-Denis—the poorest suburb of Paris—held the apathy record: 63 percent of registered voters failed to appear. Turnout in the second round of the 2022 presidential election for the whole of France was 72 percent, the lowest in such a runoff since 1969.

A new Constitution should, at the very least, abolish Articles 8, 12, and 15 of Title II of the current one, removing the President's right to appoint the Prime Minister, call new elections, and serve as Commander-in-Chief of the Armed Forces. Making it essential for the Prime Minister to be elected would certainly strengthen democracy, as would an end to the President ruling by decree. More efforts to spread real power away from Paris and across the whole country would also help enormously. Focusing an entire system on a kingly President is failing, and changes to the October 4, 1958, Constitution can be achieved through Article 89: "The President of the Republic, on the recommendation of the Prime Minister, and Members of Parliament alike shall have the right to initiate amendments to the Constitution."

One leading early critic of the reactionary presidential system enshrined in the Fifth Republic Constitution was François Mitterrand, the future Socialist President. In 1964, he published a pamphlet called *Le Coup d'État Permanent* (The permanent coup d'etat). The essay said De Gaulle had betrayed France by replacing a sovereign Parliament with a single leader who enjoyed unbridled powers. Mitterrand argued that the Algerian crisis that ensured De Gaulle's return from the wilderness had been staged in order to put an elected dictator in place. It was one of numerous conspiracy theories that alleged that the Fifth Republic might be illegal. Mitterrand compared the events of May 13, 1958, to those of Louis-Napoléon Bonaparte's coup of December 2, 1851. Mitterrand's opinion about the Fifth Republic naturally changed when he spent a full fourteen years as head of state under the system that De Gaulle had created, but his original insight remains compelling.

Macron's highly classified "defense councils" are a prime example of presidential manipulation. He has relied on them to tackle all the big issues facing France in recent years. Meetings take place in the Élysée Palace every week, and all participants are bound by "defense secrecy." "The Defense and National Security Council is a French specificity," according to the Élysée. "It is a select Council of Ministers, chaired each week by the President of the Republic to coordinate defense and national security policy." It was enshrined by Article 15 of the 1958 Constitution, to allow the Commander-in-Chief of the Armed Forces to mainly deal with military matters. Sure enough, Macron expanded its powers with a decree in December 2019 "to address internal security, economic and energy issues and respond to major crises." In other words, Macron can bypass Parliament or any conventional Cabinet any time he likes, so as to deal with any problem as if he were *le Général* himself.

When Queen Elizabeth II died on September 8, 2022, all the living French Presidents paid emotional tributes. Macron said we "all feel an emptiness" at her passing, as he told the British people, "To you, she was your Queen. To us, she was *the* Queen. She will be with us all forever." Macron was once again alluding to the hollowness in the French system caused by the absence of a blood monarch, and specifically the

constitutional monarchy that works so well in Britain. Yet he has gradually moved France's own presidential monarchy toward becoming an
absolutist one.

A crucial factor in the reform of France has always been a cataclysmic event, usually a war. It took defeat in the Franco-Prussian War to
bring about the Third Republic, Allied victory in the Second World
War to create the Fourth Republic, and the chaos created by the Algerian War for the Fifth Republic to emerge. Unsurprisingly, there are
now numerous failings with the Fifth Republic—born as it was in a
reactive moment of national crisis and colonial collapse—and plenty
of dissenting voices. Yet it will take a lot more than France's traditional street anarchism or leftist coalitions in Parliament to bring about
a Sixth.

2

SOCIETY

Free Falling

Architecture is what makes beautiful ruins.

—AUGUSTE PERRET (1874–1954)

We all have vivid memories of childhood. In one of mine, I'm sitting in a packed classroom full of eleven- and twelve-year-olds, many of whom feel that life has already turned against them. One boy is very bored—let's call him Mehdi. He has little interest in what's being taught, so he fidgets and stares idly out of the window, making it clear that he would rather be somewhere else, even if he's not sure where.

As in all schools in France's public education system, the teacher is a civil servant, there to impose republican values, so she thinks a morality lesson is in order. She points to a man in blue overalls pushing a broom along the pavement just beyond the school gates. He looks as disillusioned as Mehdi, only older. The municipal worker wears a brown beanie and neat black beard. His skin is dark; he is of North African Arab origin, as is Mehdi. "Carry on in the way you are, and you'll end up like him," says the teacher. "I know him," says Mehdi. "He's my dad."

The truth, of course, is that Mehdi was likely to end up like his father whatever happened. That is the nature of many of the *cités*, the architectural monstrosities that surround French cities. Those who live there, and especially those who can trace their roots back to France's former colonial empire, are put in their place constantly. Authority figures from teachers to police officers perpetuate a generational cycle of mediocrity, and even humiliation. The rite of passage put-downs increase the sense of futility.

Ask anyone in France from an ethnic minority background when they first experienced a robust police document check, for example, and they will not say it was during the COVID-19 lockdowns. Most of us were brought up on decrepit estates where brutal interference in day-to-day life remains the norm. Tellings-off, curfews, home arrests, beatings, and other gratuitously violent restrictions on movement are all regularly deployed in the *cités*, not just in times of crisis.

The kind of "controls" that became common during the global health emergency start extremely early in life for many. I can well remember people running away after the warning *Keufs!*—street slang for police officers—was shouted out. The armed patrols were always looking for dark-skinned targets because they were perceived as a far greater threat to public order than anyone else. They were also unlikely to be legally represented, or to be of much interest to journalists looking for sob stories.

Capture could be a horrible experience: body searches were intrusive, and it was not unusual for even young children to be forced to lie on the ground before they were handcuffed. Quite apart from any physical injury, the mental suffering never ended. The jargon was *contrôle au faciès*, racial profiling. Enduring this sort of scrutiny made you feel part of an underclass, forever under suspicion. We all had neighbors and friends who had been manhandled for no other reason except their physical appearance. At best, the checks were deeply uncomfortable; at worst, they could end in a suspect being killed. This is why people fled.

Those left to suffer in the *cités* are known as *banlieusards*, which can loosely be translated as "suburbanites" but in fact the term is a lot spikier. It really has come to suggest brown, immigrant, and—increasingly—Muslim. In the popular imagination, *banlieusard* life is played out to a soundtrack of hip-hop, gangsta rap, and Bob Marley's "Burnin' and Lootin'." There is an entire genre of French cinema known as *film de banlieue*. The first was *La Haine* (Hate) in 1995. Its title implies ferocious rage—the kind associated with the Black Lives Matter protests a quarter century later—but in fact estate life is more about aimlessness. Repetitive music blares out of tower block windows while some youngsters play football and others lounge about, talking garbage and smoking marijuana—or *shit* as it's called in France. Some of the kids stare into mobile devices all day, playing X-rated video games and watching violent Hollywood-style police dramas, not thinking about anything most of the time and doing even less. The standing joke in *La Haine* is of a determinedly optimistic man who leaps out of a high-rise building. As he passes each floor, he tells himself, "So far, so good." The pay-off line is: "It's not how you fall. It's how you land."

Les Misérables, a more recent *film de banlieue* directed by greater Paris suburbanite Ladj Ly, also conveys this bland angst: the sense that people are just hanging around waiting for doomsday. Again, there is plenty of violence in *Les Misérables*—much of it perpetuated by the police—but the overwhelming dreariness of normal life is what stands out. Residents grow up in tiny spaces accessed by elevators stinking of cannabis. Rat and cockroach infestations are common in buildings that are far too hot in summer and freezing cold in winter. Police cars, fire engines, and ambulances appear in the middle of the night, which is when heavy-duty drug dealers are active, but for the most part life is mundane. The electro score by Pink Noise builds up the tension in *Les Misérables* to what often turns out to be nonevents.

It is not just physical running away that I will be discussing in this chapter, but rather the way the French establishment has largely retreated from its political, economic, and social responsibilities to millions of French citizens—especially those who are the primary victims of the planning and administration of the *cités*.

Immigrant *Cités*

The suburban estates were originally designed as modern utopias for a rapidly expanding postwar population, so their disintegration into centers of crime and social isolation causes particular angst to both their residents and all those involved in running them. France is obsessed with social justice and the need to redistribute wealth toward those who really need it, so critics used to attacking America about the failures of capitalism are made to look pretty hypocritical by the intense unfairness of the *cités*. The chaos there is by no means just a race issue, but ethnic minorities certainly get the roughest deal—to such an extent that senior politicians talk about an unofficial system of apartheid.

There is a profound problem with discrimination in France, but also a universalist model that does not recognize prejudices that apply to specific communities or individuals, so making them very difficult to assess, let alone remedy. The assumption is that Mehdi and his father are just like anybody else. The very first article of the Constitution states: "France is an indivisible, secular, democratic, and social republic. It ensures equality of all citizens without distinction of origin, race, or religion." The claim is that everybody is free and equal and enjoys a fraternal relationship with other French citizens, but in fact this is nonsense. Beyond the politicians, human rights monitors and other respected commentators concur that racial discrimination is rampant in every field of life, from policing to employment and housing.

The overlap between such bias and those from disadvantaged, foreign backgrounds is huge. There are plenty of employers who refuse to hire anyone who is Black, Arab, or Muslim, for example. Police, meanwhile, adopt law enforcement strategies that would be better suited to war zones. People like Mehdi and his dad are massively held back by their North African heritage, but nobody in France can discuss the problem using statistics. The collection of data pertaining to ethnicity, race, or religion is not allowed in any kind of official context. This goes back to the collaborationist Vichy regime, when such information about citizens was freely handed over to the Nazis when they were selecting victims for the Holocaust.

There are times when representatives of the French suburbs come into direct contact with the Paris establishment to try to deal with their grievances. Hundreds of guests, including *cité* residents and their mayors, roll up at the Élysée Palace to discuss the latest hopeless social reform strategy. It may be a financial plan involving very little money or an attempt to get the private sector to employ thousands of young *banlieusards* on zero-wage internships. Who knows? Mehdi and his dad may have attended one of these pointless meetings by now, but they will still be in their *cité*, as disappointed and agitated as ever.

Those I grew up with in the *cités* were mainly described by our fellow French citizens as Arabs and Blacks. We were born and brought up on the literal and metaphorical fringes of the most mythologized city in the world, and we knew we were different. The greater Paris region—the Île-de-France—contains around twelve million people. Our department was the 91, the administrative number for Essonne in the south. Unofficial estimates suggest it has a population of around 1.5 million people including unregistered immigrants. According to a 2017 census, those born abroad and living in towns across Essonne included thirty-three thousand from Portugal, nine thousand from Turkey, and six thousand from Senegal. I was part of an Algerian diaspora that included twenty-four thousand actually born in Algeria, including my parents.[1]

The pejorative French word for segregating by group identity is *communautarisme*, but—despite the media myths and politicking—there was no question of us living separately. On the contrary, the vast majority of people from different ethnic groups mixed well, helping each other out when asked, and making friends. It was routine for a group of children from different backgrounds to be walked to school by one mother in the morning. Family flats needed revolving doors—neighbors were coming in and out all the time. French *banlieues* are certainly more diverse than their American equivalents. Beyond those from North African origins—including Algerians, Tunisians, and Moroccans—in Essonne, I grew up with Chinese, Indians, West Africans, Kosovans, and dozens of other nationalities.

Close to the *cités*, there are relatively wealthy areas, with big houses and top marque cars in the driveways. Residents from older waves of white, Christian, European migrants—Portuguese, Italian, and Spanish—are the most likely to have succeeded economically, along with indigenous French families.

It is the poverty-stricken estates that are overwhelmingly Arab and Black. Those living there get small flats in blocks with ambitious names celebrating high French culture: Matisse, Debussy, or Monet, for example. There are also bucolic appellations such as Les Mimosas or Les Rosiers, particularly incongruous for concrete jungles. The roads on which their buildings are set are called Avenue Charles de Gaulle or Rue de la République. This is all about reminding everybody they are in a France to be proud of.

"Visible minority" (*minorité visible*) is the politically correct term in France for those who are discriminated against because of features that are easily noticed—skin color and dress, for example—but more unpleasant bureaucratic abbreviations include "non-BBR," for *non-Bleu-Blanc-Rouge*. This means that a person is not representative of the blue, white, and red of the French tricolor and therefore not considered ethnically French. The acronyms BBR and non-BBR are secretly very common in councils' and employers' concealed databases.

The original non-BBRs arrived in large numbers after the Second World War, when France needed to rebuild its shattered infrastructure. Itinerant workers were placed in *bidonvilles* (shantytowns) in the suburbs of cities such as Paris, often with the help of charities. Abbé Pierre—the Roman Catholic priest and French Resistance veteran—founded the Emmaus movement, which called for "an uprising of kindness," especially during the freezing winter of 1954, when homeless people were dying in the streets.

Successive Fourth and Fifth Republic governments responded to such calls for social action with housing projects. They were originally financed by the Marshall Plan, America's European Recovery Program, which saw more than $13 billion (some $115 billion in today's money) transferred across the Atlantic for the whole of Europe for four years starting in 1948. US interests at the time included preventing countries falling to Communism, so there was some irony in funds being poured into the kind of concrete monoliths favored by totalitarian regimes during the Cold War.

The French Communist Party (PCF) won more votes than any other party in national elections in France in the decade up to 1956. They were hugely boosted by the part leftists had played in the wartime Resistance, and hence became known as "the party of the seventy-five thousand executed people." PCF membership was five hundred thousand in 1945, and the 1946 parliamentary election at the start of the Fourth Republic saw the party win 182 seats, with just over 28 percent of the vote. By the end of the year, membership had risen to eight hundred thousand.

Americans of the era—including Dean Acheson, the Secretary of State—feared there could be a Communist takeover of France. The Americans made the expulsion of Communists from government a condition of Marshall Plan cash, and PCF ministers were thus excluded from Prime Minister Paul Ramadier's administration in May 1947. The PCF responded with strikes and industrial sabotage.

Much of the Marshall aid was also used by the French to try to sustain disastrous colonial legacies in Indochina and Algeria, but the new *cités* on the site of the *bidonvilles* became essential for accommodating laborers from former colonies. They were mainly Arabs and Berbers who arrived from North Africa to fill staff shortages. Work was plentiful during the so-called *Trente Glorieuses*, the three decades of "glorious" economic success fueled by mass consumerism from the end of the war up until the mid-1970s oil crisis. This period was overlapped by *le baby boom*, when couples who had been put off starting families by the Great Depression and Second World War began to have lots of children.

Housing all these new arrivals meant there was an explosion in government building programs. The biggest projects were in greater Paris, the Île-de-France, where a particularly large workforce was needed. Entire new towns near the capital appeared, including at Sarcelles and Marne-la-Vallée. Thus, a mainly rural France of cows, cottages, and cabbage patches transformed into one full of state-sponsored, urban settlements that remain eternally fascinating to social scientists.

The early estates were built on idealism. New residents coming from inner-city slums enjoyed clean, well-designed spaces for the first time in their lives. The air was fresher—most of the sites were on former farming land well away from factories—and there were recreational grounds for children to play. The tall towers were meant to represent security, light, and inspiring views. Those leaving the working-class areas such as the 13th and 19th Arrondissements of Paris had their own inside toilets and bathrooms—something they were denied in their old homes—as well as safe kitchens that were not continually at risk of going up in flames because of faulty gas and electricity supplies.

The *cités* were originally based on the vision of the French-Swiss architect Charles-Édouard Jeanneret, better known as Le Corbusier, which roughly means "the crow-like one." Born in 1887—when Queen Victoria was on the throne in Britain and Jules Grévy was President of France—he became associated with some of the most aggressively modern creations ever. They eventually extended all over the globe, including to Britain and America (Le Corbusier completed Harvard University's Carpenter Center for the Visual Arts in Cambridge, Massachusetts, in 1963).

Le Corbusier's emphasis was on geometric starkness and lots of reinforced concrete. He wanted estates to be seen as a "machine for living." He believed that high-quality industrial architecture could make the masses feel happy and thus avoid the need for revolution, even in a traditionally turbulent country like France. Le Corbusier said, "The materials of city planning are sky, space, trees, steel, and cement—in that order and in that hierarchy."

Despite so clearly underplaying his reliance on concrete, Le Corbusier devised a dream living space in 1924 that he called the Radiant City (*Ville Radieuse*), built in a garden. Identical tower blocks would house thousands in so-called *unités*—living areas supported by laundries and shops on the ground floor and swimming pools and kindergartens on the roof. Zoning within the Great Park would allow for a central Capitol Complex to include courts, councils, and universities, while fast underground trains and cars could speed residents to where they wanted to be. Perfect geometry was meant to correspond to equality and justice. There was certainly no conception of people throwing themselves off the high-rises while passing every floor and thinking, "So far, so good."

The first ever Le Corbusier–inspired modernist estate was the Cité de la Muette (the Silent City) which went up in the early 1930s in the Paris suburb of Drancy. Its architects, Eugène Beaudouin and Marcel Lods, built it by Drancy-Le Bourget rail station, ensuring an easy commute into central Paris or out to towns in northern France.

Steel frames and prefabricated concrete panels were used to create a mix of fifteen-story buildings and lower ones, including a distinctive U-shaped structure. The construction was well ahead of its time and attracted worldwide attention, as it was ambitiously presented as an urban utopia. Anybody visiting the remains today and knowing nothing about it always wrongly dates it to the 1960s or, at the very earliest, the late 1950s.

Perhaps appropriately, the French turned the Drancy *cité* into a prison camp at the start of the Second World War. German and Austrian nationals were interned in it before Paris fell to the Nazis in 1940. Then Drancy became a holding center for Jews and other "undesirables" before their transfer by train to concentration camps, especially Auschwitz, during the Holocaust. The Drancy camp was under the control of the collaborating French police until 1943, when the SS took over command. The U-shaped block in the *cité* was requisitioned and was originally intended to hold seven hundred people, but at its peak there were more than seven thousand men, women, and children considered enemies of the Third Reich crammed inside, all of them in horrific conditions. In less than a decade, the Cité de la Muette had become a terrifying example of the totalitarian potential of the new estates.

Despite this, the building went on. Another of the big suburban Paris estates was the Cité des Quatre Mille (the Four Thousand), which comprised four thousand homes in La Courneuve, to the northeast of the capital. This translated into a population of seventeen thousand people and floors in the tower blocks went up to twenty-six.

Le Corbusier's star projects also included the Unité d'Habitation in Marseille. It was an early example of the Brutalist style that ignored the ornate beauty of so much earlier French architecture. It became known as the Maison du Fada (the Madhouse); the fear was that all the residents would soon start to feel mentally ill. As the progression of history revealed, the Radiant City was a ludicrous pipe dream. A new jargon developed around the estates: ZUPs, for Priority Zones for Urban Development (*Zones à Urbaniser en Priorité*), was coined in 1958, but by this time the dream was already fading. Nobody calls Le Corbusier–inspired creations utopias anymore.

The *cités* were becoming vast poverty traps: places where isolation, boredom, and a general sense of hopelessness thrived. The schools were terrible. Planners and academics began to draw a correlation between concrete-dominated environments and severe social problems. The term *sarcellite* was used in the early 1960s to describe the depression associated with living on the Lochères estate in Sarcelles, north of Paris. Disorder was a consequence; outdoor spaces that were difficult to secure were no longer viewed as desirable playgrounds but as uncontrollable crime zones.

It was clear that much of the new housing had been rushed. Apartments were piled on top of each other, or in grim rows like cages in factory farms. The buildings looked temporary, as if they were designed to last a few years before being demolished and the residents sent packing. Materials were cheap and often not fit for purpose. They were homes for losers, people who were made to feel worthless.

Utopian Prison

Housing projects in the 91 include La Grande Borne, which was built in a style described as "utopian" in the 1960s but is now one of the most notorious council estates in France, plagued by poverty and crime. It is next door to Fleury-Mérogis prison, the largest in Europe. The two institutions—prison and estate—exchange inhabitants on a regular basis.

My father helped with extension construction work on Fleury-Mérogis, which looks just like a *cité* itself, complete with five concrete blocks full of people who don't want to be there. Fleury-Mérogis was described as being "more than a prison" in an AFP report when the first stone was laid in 1964. A government handout said it was "a complex of clear, harmonious and functional buildings" installed in the middle of fields in Essonne. Does this kind of language sound familiar? Of course, it does—it's classic early *cité* hyperbole.

France's Justice Department described Fleury-Mérogis as an institution built "in the spirit of new judicial concepts," which aimed to transform the "traditional prison universe" of "high forbidding walls and thick metal bars" popularized by filmmakers and novelists.

Instead, the new panopticon "all-seeing" masterpiece was all about low walls and relatively discreet surveillance. The Fleury-Mérogis architects said they were inspired by the British philosopher Jeremy Bentham, the founder of Utilitarianism who lived at the time of the French Revolution and who wanted guards to be able to monitor their charges without the prisoners' knowledge.

The blocks at Fleury-Mérogis were in the shape of a three-blade propellor, leading out from a central control post. A system of electric doors and intercoms covered the entire building, including cells, meaning the number of guards was originally very small. Toughened glass replaced bars, ensuring light and views, and cells were individual ones. This particular utopia was meant to replace La Santé, the sinister central Paris prison that dates back to 1867, and which once included a section for convicts waiting to be guillotined. It was as recently as 1972 that two inmates had their heads chopped off inside the jail.

Fleury-Mérogis was meant to turn a corner on such barbarity, but it didn't. The "prison from which there is no escape"—in the words of its original architects—soon turned into a squalid, violent mess. Escapes included one by helicopter in 1981. By 2020, Fleury-Mérogis was blighted by suicides, gang fights, and overcrowding. "It's a monster, a juggernaut, it's hell to manage," said prison warden trade unionist Thibault Capelle. Penal reformers were by now talking about building smaller, more open structures in city centers, so as to help reintegration.

Many of the 4,100-plus prisoners inside Fleury-Mérogis are from the nearby *cités*. They pick up first convictions for possessing illegal drugs, and then the number of brushes with the forces of law and order increases. They lift weights and listen to rap, hoping they will at least be feared and respected through physical strength and a firm identity. Once inside, the sense of alienation intensifies. They take more drugs and make contacts who will keep them resupplied once they are released.

A tiny but horribly significant minority—ones known as *fragiles*— find themselves drawn to jihadism. These psychologically weak inmates notice that most other prisoners are Muslims just like them, branded as enemies of *laïcité* (secular) France. Pushed to the bottom of the social order, they see an escape in global terror groups. Hollywood has taught them about killing and other forms of violence, and this is exploited by organizations such as the so-called Islamic State and Al-Qaeda.

Despite the propaganda, there is zero evidence of mass radical movements developing within Muslim communities. The prison experience—involving both acute alienation and drugs—is the main cause of radicalization of lone-wolf misfits who commit obscene acts of their own volition.

Rather than a model of liberal incarceration, Fleury-Mérogis is now a dehumanizing monster. Its buildings are decaying and surrounded by litter. Former residents include the late swaggering "Public Enemy No. 1" and Algerian War veteran Jacques Mesrine. He served as a low-ranking soldier during the conflict and, after two years, was in 1959 decorated with the *Croix de la Valeur Militaire*. Mesrine learned how to use weapons in North Africa, and later recounted how he was ordered to summarily execute prisoners, including civilians. Multiple psychologists made the very obvious link between Mesrine's barbaric conduct in Algeria and his later career as a murderous armed robber and kidnapper. Salah Abdeslam, the only surviving suicide bomber of the terrorist attacks on Paris of November 2015, is in solitary confinement in Fleury-Mérogis. Abdeslam is said to have first been radicalized while serving time for various offenses in Belgian prisons.

Even for those who manage to stay out of prison, the achievement level on the estates is notoriously low. Most young people end up going into cheap labor at best, unemployment at worst. If you were asked to name a famous French-Algerian, you wouldn't mention a politician or businessperson. It is almost certain that you would choose an elite sportsman, and probably a footballer like Zinedine Zidane, whose goals won France the World Cup in 1998.

Zizou was born in La Castellane, the modernist council estate in Marseille originally built for refugees from Algeria. Riyad Mahrez, the Manchester City midfielder who captained Algeria to their Africa Cup of Nations victory in 2019, was born and raised in the Paris suburb of Sarcelles (the one that gave rise to the term *sarcellite*) and spent most of his summer holidays in Algeria. Zizou and Mahrez became multimillionaire superstars, but the vast majority from the same back-ground will remain trapped.

Nicolas Anelka, also one of the most successful footballers in recent years and whose parents are from Martinique, told me how growing up in the suburban towns of Le Chesnay and Trappes helped forge his personality as he converted to Islam. Describing the institutional problems in the *cités*, Anelka said, "French people of North African and African background try to make things work for them, but French society keeps them in check. There are a lot of obstacles in the way. For example, if you send a CV with the 'wrong' postcode and a Muslim-sounding name, then you won't be considered for a job. You need to hide your name and picture in the hope of getting work. That level of discrimination is unacceptable."

Sofiane Feghouli, who captained the Algerian national team and played for a range of top clubs including West Ham United, was born in Levallois-Perret, around five miles from the center of Paris, and then grew up in nearby Saint-Ouen, in the Seine-Saint-Denis department bordering the capital. He chose to play for Algeria instead of France because of "history, and where my heart wanted me to be," he said when I interviewed him.

Ring Road to Nowhere

Go-ahead Parisians living within the confines of the *périphérique* ring road that circles the old city embrace high tech, finance, culture, and tourism. Inside the *périph'* largely represents privilege, while outside often signifies neglect. To ring road insiders, the outer suburbs have a Third World feel that they would rather ignore. The ring road acts as a dirty, congested, fume-filled barrier between civilization and what lies beyond. Manuel Valls, the former French Prime Minister who built his career in the Socialist Party in the 91, described his country's bitter social divide as a "territorial, cultural, and ethnic apartheid." He spoke of a "fractured" country of "second-class citizens" living in "ghettos," where "social misery is added to daily discrimination because one does not have the right family name, the right skin color, or because one is a woman." Such descriptions become particularly startling when we consider that the greater Paris region contains more than twelve million people living across eight *départements*—easily making it the most populated area in France—while there are only around two million people inside the *périphérique* in what might be described as traditional Paris.

There are transport links with the center of Paris from the 91, but they do not work very well, despite being full of cleaners and manual workers from the estates in the very early morning. The TGV high-speed trains can get you from Paris to Marseille in under three and a half hours, or to London in not much more than two, but nobody wants inhabitants of the estates sneaking into Paris at any kind of speed. All they get is dirty, unreliable old trains on lines like the RER D, which is nicknamed the "D-for-Delinquent" line.

Banlieusards do not go to the €5-a-coffee pavement cafés and restaurants of the Latin Quarter or Champs-Élysées. Instead, they are herded into the shopping malls and concrete recreation areas where large formations of police keep an eye on them.

Many *cité* residents, and especially the older ones, do not even think about going into "traditional" Paris. The psychological difference between the 91 and the Champs-Élysées is far greater than that between north and south of the river in London, or between the Bronx and Wall Street, for example. Visitors to tourist attractions such as the Eiffel Tower and the Louvre have little idea that spending a few more minutes on their trains and buses would take them to stops designed for *cité* dwellers.

The *banlieusards* presence in the city proper prompts commentators to prattle on about the underclass, the lack of investment, and how cowboy politicians want to lock everybody up or even blow them away. The crassest portrayal is of gangs of Arab-looking youths linking up with *les noirs*—the Blacks—to pillage sport shops. The government policy is always to send the riot police in, with their truncheons, water cannons, and rubber bullets, even before anybody has done anything illegal.

Just before the nationwide suburban riots of 2005, the then Interior Minister Nicolas Sarkozy—*le Top Cop*, as he was nicknamed—

referred to troublemakers as *racaille* (rabble or scum). The previous summer, the diminutive Sarkozy had vowed to expunge anyone wearing baggy jeans, reverse baseball caps, or speaking *verlan* (an imaginative youth language that mainly involves transposing syllables) with a Kärcher pressure cleaner. One of his initiatives was to put mounted police at school gates. Adolescents would know who was boss when they saw a massive stallion every time they headed to lessons. On the plus side, Sarko suggested it would be nice for the better-behaved children to have a horse around.

What Sarko chose to ignore is that plenty of Americanized, middle-class French youngsters were using *verlan* and wearing baseball caps. These included his son, Pierre Sarkozy, who styled himself as a rap producer called Mosey. According to Sarkozy's caricature, Sarko Junior was as likely to fit the image of the unpatriotic, disaffected kid as any young Muslim, yet he avoided being targeted simply because he was a well-off member of the white bourgeoisie.

It is not just the major cities where there are problems. There are towns in the south of France like Béziers, where Robert Ménard, the far-right mayor, received a conviction for inciting racist hate against Muslims around the time of the 2017 presidential campaign. During a TV appearance in September 2016, he said, "In a city center classroom in my hometown, 91 percent of the children are Muslim. Obviously, this is a problem."

Ménard frequently referenced the "Great Replacement" theory, which warns that the indigenous French population could be replaced by Muslims who have bigger families. For his hateful rhetoric, Ménard was fined just €2,000 and damages of €1,000 to be paid to the anti-racism campaigners who complained about him. Such punishments are little more than a badge of honor for the bigots who dominate extremist discourse in the mainstream media. In Ménard's case, the conviction was quashed on appeal.

Ménard was first elected as Mayor of Béziers in 2014 as an independent but with the backing of the Front National. Like the far-right party, his focus was on immigration, security, and French identity. He wanted more handguns for police and to stop those escaping the war in Syria from squatting in Béziers. Ménard campaigned for a local referendum on the whole question of refugees because he rejected national government orders to look after them.

During the COVID-19 pandemic, I spent a lot of time in an area of Paris renowned for its beauty and history. Police were notably absent in the residential squares and boulevards around popular tourist spots. There were hardly any police checks, while the big estates in Seine-Saint-Denis—which has three times fewer intensive care places in hospitals—were swarming with officers "controlling" ethnic minorities. This was France's two-tier residential system at its most stark.

Drug trafficking became a particularly serious problem on the estates from the 1960s onward. Illegal substances were used by residents to briefly forget the circumstances they found themselves in, while the estates' menacing concrete warrens were ideally suited for dealers selling their wares. Cannabis came in from North Africa, while harder drugs including cocaine and heroin were imported from European cities such as Amsterdam. Beyond *cité* residents, there was a rich bourgeoisie living in more prosperous parts of greater Paris that required a constant supply, but these kinds of customers are rarely troubled by the law.

The scale of the problem is perfectly illustrated by the "drugs supermarket" Boullereaux estate in Champigny-sur-Marne, southeast of Paris. It was also referred to as Dopeland because of its role in the mass supply of cannabis, which became a pillar of the local economy. Many of its inhabitants, from gardeners to supermarket workers, ended up before judges at Créteil criminal court in 2013 after it emerged that they were controlled by the dealers.

Those living in top floor flats in the Boullereaux twenty-story blocks were paid up to €2,000 a month to stock the cannabis. Lookouts, mostly teenagers, were given €300 a month and walkie-talkies to keep an eye out for police patrols. Windows were painted black to hide what was going on inside, while oil was regularly poured over bannisters and steps to delay any officers who might rush into the buildings at the wrong time.

There were more than 5,500 people living at Boullereaux, and it became one of the biggest drug-dealing zones in greater Paris. *Bienvenue à Shitland* (Welcome to Dopeland) was painted on a prominent wall. Relatively polite written instructions for arriving clients included: "Get your banknotes out and unfold them." A less polite notice read: "Anyone who pays with a forged note will be tied up in a cellar for punishment."

The cannabis arrived from Malaga in high-performance BMW and Mercedes cars known as *les go-fast* because they could outrun the police Renaults and Peugeots. Dealers had names like Snoopy and Top Cat and wore the classic uniform of baggy sports apparel and equally massive Nike trainers. At the end of the Créteil trial, nineteen people were sentenced to up to seven years in prison, while twenty-five others were convicted in another process. So-called nannies—ordinary residents who had agreed to store the drugs—got off with suspended jail terms. The president of the judges' bench told them, "This is a warning—the court has been extremely lenient and hopes never to see you again."

After Le Corbusier's death in 1965, the artist Salvador Dalí described the architect's buildings—the place where these "nannies" became employees of the dealers—as "the ugliest and most unacceptable buildings in the world." Dalí said Le Corbusier's death was an "immense joy" and called him a "pitiable creature working in reinforced concrete."

Building the Republic

My Algerian father did not apply to become a French citizen on principle—too many people close to him had been killed or wounded during the struggle for Algeria's independence—but he was expected, according to eager administrators and contract managers, to continue with the construction of the still burgeoning Fifth Republic in the 1970s. The number of migrants to France was rising, and a majority were being directed to greater Paris.

By 2021, seven million immigrants lived in the republic, 10.3 percent of the total population of 67.6 million. Of these immigrants, 2.5 million of them—36 percent—had acquired French nationality after arrival. Just under 48 percent of all immigrants living in France were born in Africa, the largest portion from Algeria (12.7 percent), then

Morocco (12 percent). This is followed by newcomers from other coun-tries: Portugal (8.6 percent), Tunisia (4.5 percent), Italy (4.1 percent), Turkey (3.6 percent), and Spain (3.5 percent).[2]

Dad mainly worked on the estates in the 91, the ones that were originally shantytowns designed for colonial workers. Such slums had no electricity or running water, and outside toilets were shared. It was a time when—as now—an Arab appearance was enough to provoke a truncheon beating, arrest, and torture. (If you looked even vaguely Mediterranean—Spanish or Italian, for example—you also got a hard time.) You did not even have to be in custody to be killed. Up to three hundred Algerians were massacred on a single day—October 17, 1961—when many were tossed off landmark Seine bridges by Paris policemen and left to drown. Like those attacked during the COVID-19 pandemic, the victims' nominal offense was breaching a curfew—in this case, a selective one that only applied to Algerians who were protesting peacefully, calling for France to concede defeat in the Algerian War of Independence. (I'll discuss this outrage at length in Chapter 5, along with other acts of state terrorism.)

There were constant attempts by the French to socially engineer radicalism out of its North African laborer communities. In the 1960s, Algerian children were bused out to camps in the Alps, the Côte d'Azur, and the island of Corsica, where it was hoped they would develop "Frenchness." The camps were nominally apolitical and focused on fresh air and recreation, but non-Algerian youths joined them on the holiday and Gallic values were championed at all times. This system—known as *brassage*—was meant to create a feeling of unity.

The reality was that police regularly used these social action schemes to crack down on FLN activity in France. Surveillance was common, especially of young men. Counselors were told to make notes on how they reacted to French films shown at the holiday camps, for example. As a device to forge France and Algeria into one big happy nation, *brassage* failed miserably. The sinister methods employed have by no means disappeared from the modern estates either.

A key feature of the *cités* today is Islam. France is home to the larg-est number of Muslims in western Europe. There are no precise figures, because the French do not compile them, but the Pew Research Center put the figure of Muslims in France at 8.8 percent of the population—just under six million people—compared to 6.3 percent for the United Kingdom.[3] Most French Muslims can trace their heritage to Algeria, Morocco, or Tunisia, all once part of France's empire. The aim of the French throughout this colonial period was to suppress Muslims, especially if they rejected the *mission civilisatrice*—the civilizing mission imposed by Gallic invaders.

Anti-religious prejudice in France is not solely against Islam. The 1789 Revolution was against an absolutist state firmly linked with Roman Catholicism, and *laïcité*—the French version of secularism—is designed to keep all religions out of public life. However, Christianity remains a cornerstone of traditional French values, and non-Christian faiths, especially Islam and Judaism, are regularly discriminated against. Both Jews and Muslims have at times been portrayed as a threat to the Republic. Thus, *laïcité* is used as an ideological weapon to attack both.

It is for such reasons—religious and historical—that many Algerians in particular feel alienated from modern France. Even those who were born in the country often have more loyalty toward Algeria. When, in October 2001, the Algerian national football team played in Paris for the first time since independence in 1962, the game had to be called off as thousands of French youths of North African origin booed the "Marseillaise" and invaded the field.

When trouble starts on the estates in the 91 or neighboring departments today, journalists turn up in flak jackets and combat helmets to film trash bins and Peugeots being set on fire. The reporters occasionally try to track down the cousin of an English Premier League footballer (plenty of Arsenal, Chelsea, and Manchester United players have rogue family members in suburban Paris). Some come in for just a few minutes, get their money shots, and then cut to an anchorman standing on the balcony of an upmarket hotel in the center of the city, gravely announcing, "And as Paris burns, I fear that this is the end of French civilization as we know it." This is undoubtedly how Fox News got its "hundreds of French no-go zones" headlines in 2015. The hyperbolic news channel spoke of "neighborhoods where neither tourists nor cops dare enter," making greater Paris sound like Kabul or Basra.

As always, the truth is far more mundane, but there is no doubt that there have been devastating periods of rioting. Many of them have followed racial abuse by the police. The first mass, nationwide anti-racism demonstration was in 1983, following a surge in violence and crimes against ethnic minorities. Riots broke out in Les Minguettes, in the Lyon suburb of Vénissieux, in the summer of that year—dozens of cars were burned as part of an anti-government protest on the estates.

A police raid in Les Minguettes that saw a community leader called Toumi Djaïdja wounded by gunfire provoked fury. Then, Habib Grimzi, an Algerian tourist on his way back to his home country, was stabbed to death by three Foreign Legion recruits who then threw their victim out of a window of an express train traveling out of Bordeaux. Grimzi, aged twenty-six, was targeted because he was a North African, and his murder emboldened the demonstrators.

Inspiration for the historic *Marche des Beurs* (the March of the Arabs; *Beurs* is slang for Arabs) came from the American Civil Rights Movement and particularly the kind of peaceful demonstrations favored by Reverend Martin Luther King Jr. The "March for Equality and Against Racism," as it is more formally known, left Marseille on October 15, 1983, and arrived at the Place de la Bastille in Paris on December 3, seven weeks later. A few dozen people started, but by the end more than one hundred thousand had joined, most of them the children of Algerian immigrants who had arrived in France after the Second World War. The significance of the protest was that the Paris establishment and media began to take huge interest in the problems of a second generation with links to the Maghreb (the term used to describe the Arab region of North Africa bordering the Mediterranean Sea, mainly encompassing Algeria, Morocco, and Tunisia). President François Mitterrand invited eight marchers to the Élysée Palace and pledged a range of new measures, including harsher punishments for convicted racists and ten-year residence permits for new arrivals from former French colonies.

A film called *The Marchers* about this *Marche des Beurs* between Marseille and Paris was released in 2013 and centered on a teenager called Mohammed being shot by the police. Director Mathieu Kassovitz's motivation for *La Haine* was also the shooting of an immigrant by police. In April 1993, seventeen-year-old Makomé M'Bowolé, who was from Zaire, was accused of shoplifting in the 18th Arrondissement of Paris before being handcuffed to a radiator in police custody. An inspector was trying to get a confession out of the terrified M'Bowolé. The police officer claimed that he thought his gun was unloaded before shooting his victim in the head. Three days of rioting followed as youths took to the streets to protest against what they saw as a racist execution. Judges later ruled that the death was accidental, but the policeman was sentenced to eight years in prison for intentional violence leading to an unintentional killing.

The 2022 Disney+ miniseries *Oussekine* dramatizes the murder of Malik Oussekine, an Algerian student aged twenty-two, in late 1986. He was beaten to death after being chased by police during a university protest in Paris that he was not even involved in. Following an inquiry and trials, the police officers responsible were found guilty of minor charges and got off with suspended prison sentences. Oussekine's death took place almost twenty-five years to the day after the October 1961 massacre by police of hundreds of Algerian nationalists.

It was a *contrôle au faciès*—the police stop and search of suspects singled out simply because they had dark-colored faces—that led to three weeks of rioting across France in 2005. The *cités* exploded after Zyed Benna, seventeen and from a Tunisian background, and Bouna Traoré, fifteen and from a family originally from Mauritania, died in horrific circumstances in Clichy-sous-Bois, one of the most isolated Paris suburbs. Soon after 5 p.m. on October 27, police arrived at a building site to investigate a suspected burglary. The innocent Benna and Traoré were on their way home after a game of football to break their fast with their family during the holy month of Ramadan, and did not want to go through a *contrôle*. Half an hour later, lights in the area flickered, and many went out. The teenagers had run away from the police and hidden in an electricity substation, where they had been electrocuted.

The boys' deaths were soon widely publicized. They became a symbol of all that was wrong in the fundamentally unequal and discriminatory French Republic. Thousands of *cité* residents empathized with the need to avoid the *contrôles*. These institutionalized racial police checks

were a throwback to the days of French colonialism when a Black African or Arab appearance was considered enough of an excuse for police
persecution and brutality. It was this lingering reality in a society full of
powerful bigots that had led to the eruption of protests. Beyond repression, *cité* dwellers were also rallying against high unemployment and
the general lack of opportunities.

Police were going into the estates to impose order with extreme
force. There was no concept of neighborhood policing; community
associations and social workers were sidelined. In response, people
wanted to highlight the profound malaise at the heart of society using
a traditional method of gaining attention that went back to the French
Revolution.

The anarchy that followed the deaths of Benna and Traoré was so
intense that a state of emergency was declared on November 8, 2005.
Measures including curfews were enforced using legislation introduced
in 1955, at the height of the Algerian War. As human rights groups
complained about such colonial-style subjugation and other racism at
the root of the disturbances, the French government moved to deport
foreigners convicted of involvement in nighttime rioting. Nicolas Sarkozy, who was then the conservative Interior Minister, claimed that
illegal migrants were among those spearheading attacks on the police.

The turmoil spread across France and particularly to the Sensitive
Urban Zones. It was pretty much self-harm: rioters were destroying
their own estates, including their community halls and their neighbors' cars. Extra police were bused into the worst-hit *quartiers*, and
courts held trials and dispensed immediate punishments, including
prison sentences, around the clock. There were almost three thousand
arrests—half of them minors—over the three weeks.

The fast-track system that allowed unruly youngsters to be criminalized in record time was—astonishingly—still in operation in
lockdown France. So-called *audiences de comparution immédiates* put
suspects up before a magistrate within hours of an alleged misdemeanor
so they could be incarcerated straight away. With many lawyers choosing to stay away in self-isolation, defendants were threatened with pre-
ventative detention until a trial date could be set. Prisons that were
already full of ethnic minority *cité* dwellers, meanwhile, were among

the highest-risk spaces for contracting coronavirus. In contrast, pretty much everything possible was done to keep establishment convicted criminals such as Sarkozy and his Prime Minister, François Fillon, out of a cell, despite their sentences for very serious offenses, during the months when the COVID-19 crisis was at its peak.

A criminal inquiry into Benna and Traoré's deaths lasted for almost a decade. In 2015, two police officers finally faced trial on charges of "non-assistance to a person in danger"—an offense that comes with a sentence of five years in prison. It was billed as one of the most important criminal trials in years because it could expose the inequalities and other injustices suffered by those condemned to life in the *cités*.

Unsurprisingly, there were no convictions. There seldom are when the police are in the dock. Even though the 2005 riots underlined how negative stereotypes from the colonial era were as strong as ever and continued to dictate policing strategy, there was no change.

This is why twenty-two organizations, including Human Rights Watch, called for an end to excessive police checks during the COVID-19 lockdown. Francesco Rocca, a Red Cross chief, warned that coronavirus was a "social bomb" that could trigger "social unrest," but we did not need a global health pandemic to tell us this. In the case of the treatment of ethnic minorities in France, profound and radical change cannot come soon enough.

Spaceman Gaga

In August 2019, the Cité Gagarine, a red brick estate southeast of Paris in Ivry-sur-Seine, was slowly torn down. It was a fascinating place because it was dedicated to the first man in space, Russian cosmonaut Yuri Gagarin. The naming took place in 1961, the year of Gagarin's successful Vostok 1 flight, when he launched the Space Age with the words "Let's go!" The Soviet pilot actually arrived in Paris in person in September 1963, in the uniform of a Lieutenant Colonel on a scheduled flight from Moscow. Gagarin mainly stayed out in the *banlieue*, where everyone called him "comrade." He was showered in rose petals and hugged enthusiastically by residents when he visited the *cité* named after him.

The French Communist Party had particularly high hopes
for the Cité Gagarine; they were convinced its 382 apartments in a
fourteen-story T-shaped block would be a workers' paradise. In line
with Le Corbusier thinking, "Gaga" provided stunning views of Paris
and its outer suburbs. Local Communists paid for Gagarin to enjoy a
tour of the so-called Red Belt of greater Paris, which they celebrated as
an achievement of the Soviet era.

The dream had died by 2015, however. A Cité Gagarine rehous-
ing project got underway after the decision was made to raze the
entire place to the ground. Soon, husks of asbestos-blighted buildings
were all that was left of Gaga. They were riddled with bullet holes,
and their windows were covered by wooden boards and wire meshes.
Security guards with German Shepherds were in place to prevent
squatters, and entrances were also sealed. This kind of grim reality
aptly summed up immigrant France going nowhere, let alone shooting for the stars.

What was promised in the place of the destroyed Cité Gagarine
was an eco-project encompassing 1,429 new homes, shops, schools, and
an urban agriculture program. The estimated cost approached €100
million, but only 30 percent of the homes (428) would be social housing ones. The new name was the Gagarine-Truillot project (it involved
rebuilding the Gagarine blocks and renovating the Truillot ones), and
it was a ZAC (Concerted Development Zone, *Zone d'Aménagement
Concerté*). This effectively meant gentrification: bringing in business
and the prosperous middle classes, while reducing space for those in
need of support.

Before work started on the Gagarine-Truillot eco-project, all that
remained of interest on the original estate was a giant mural promoting
the rappers Tarik and Nabil Andrieu, brothers of Algerian origin who
formed a group called PNL. They had lived in Building C of the Cité
Gagarine as teenagers, so included it in the clip for their song "Deux
Frères" (Two brothers). Their hugely popular music video—which
had already been viewed up to two million times on YouTube within
twenty-four hours of its release—made the estate as popular as it had
been at the time of Yuri Gagarin, but for very different reasons. The *cité*

thus ended its days as an ephemeral backdrop, one that had outlived its promises before being reduced to dust.

Living Together

Emmanuel Macron was smiling broadly when *banlieue* residents arrived at the Élysée Palace on May 22, 2018. Six hundred guests had come to learn about the President's latest policy approach for the priority zone *cités*. The only tangible blueprint for reform was an aging €48 billion plan by Jean-Louis Borloo, one of Jacques Chirac's old ministers. It was called "Living together, living large, for national reconciliation," but Macron was not impressed by the Borloo proposal, calling it "a strategy as old as me." He said it was an "umpteenth Marshall Plan" backed up by platitudes.[4] "Somehow it wouldn't make any sense for two white males [Macron and Borloo] who don't even live in these neighborhoods to even produce a report," said Macron. "It doesn't work like that anymore."

The President made no apology for his administration cutting social housing benefits. He did promise thirty thousand internships for young people from the *banlieue*, but, of course, these would cost nothing. Instead, the largest 120 companies in France would be asked to take on these unpaid employees. There would also be some "testing" of hiring strategies (to see who was still rejecting perceived "non-BBRs") as a means of weeding out racial and religious prejudice aimed at *banlieusards*. The fight against drug trafficking would also be stepped up.

Macron was accused of another comms performance, suggesting a few cosmetic measures that in no way dealt with the real problem of the *cités*. The truth was that most of the internships were not being offered by multinationals, but by bakeries, sports shops, and pharmacies. Not only was funding not considered important, but the republic's refusal to recognize race and religion as factors used to discriminate against French citizens was not even mentioned. Fixing the *cités* requires an end to color-blind policies that do not officially quantify any problem with bigotry, let alone try to solve it.

French voters elected thirty-two deputies from ethnic minority backgrounds to the new National Assembly in the June 2022 elections—less than 6 percent. This compared to thirty-five ethnic minority deputies in the 2017 Parliament, so the figure was actually going down.[5] The far-right Rassemblement National—the party founded by Nazis and colonial nostalgists—meanwhile, won eighty-nine new seats, a record.

Just as significantly, the first day of the new Parliament in late June 2022 saw an opening speech praising the memory of French Algeria. According to the rules of the National Assembly, the oldest lawmaker chairs the first session, and thus José Gonzalez, seventy-nine years old and a newly elected Rassemblement National MP, took everybody back sixty years. Gonzalez, who was born to a *pied-noir* family in Oran, Algeria, described himself as a "child of a remote France torn from his native land and blown to the coasts of Provence by the winds of history in 1962. I left there a part of my France and many friends. I am a man who has seen his soul forever bruised."

After his speech, Gonzalez told journalists to "come with me to the Djebel region of Algeria, and I will find many Algerians who will tell you: When are you [the French] coming back?" Referring to the murderous terrorist group the Secret Army Organization, Gonzalez even said he was not in a position to judge "whether the OAS committed crimes or not."

That elected representatives still hark back to the colonial period, when segregation and murders were considered acceptable, tells us exactly how entrenched France's *cité* problem is. Sabrina Sebaihi, a Green MP and the daughter of Algerian immigrants to France, rebuked an unreconstructed nationalist who was "nostalgic for the OAS killers" and who "shamelessly and tearfully evokes the memory of French Algeria to a round of applause." Sebaihi said it was "an insult to our history and to our parents. A day of shame."[6]

The decrepit apartheid estates are symbols of the way France treats its perceived underclass, whose members can trace their roots directly back to former colonies. These housing projects are failed social experiments that have long needed replacing. This is not to say that the communities themselves are broken. On the contrary, there is dynamism and creativity among the people, but the potential of these huge communities must be fulfilled elsewhere.

Racism has existed in France for centuries. It still manifests itself everywhere, from social media feeds to the streets. There are microaggressions and there are murders, and everything in between. The language and behavior of street bigots have levitated up the social scale, even into the very heart of nominally left-wing governments. Manuel Valls, the Barcelona-born Socialist politician who pinpointed apartheid France, also insisted that Roma from Romania and Bulgaria should be deported because they "cannot integrate." Such views were similarly expressed by Sarkozy, who popularized slogans such as "France: Love It or Leave It" and organized hugely divisive national identity debates, which became a forum for race hate.

The spreading of collective guilt is routine in France. If drugged-up, white thugs from housing estates choose to become far-right terrorists rather than bank robbers or burglars, then they remain drugged-up, white thugs. If drugged-up, brown-skinned thugs from housing estates choose to become Islamist terrorists rather than bank robbers or burglars, then they are viewed as representatives of almost six million French Muslims.

George Floyd's death by asphyxiation at police hands in Minneapolis in 2020 was caught on camera, and it reminded the French of the case of Adama Traoré, a young Black man who died in similarly suspicious circumstances in a police station in a Paris suburb in 2016. Neighboring countries such as Britain are far more progressive in relation to investigating such race issues, and this is because they consider all available information. If you do not monitor a very serious problem using all obtainable data, then you have no hope of fixing it.

A scathing report by France's Human Rights Ombudsman in June 2020 conceded that racial discrimination was still a "systemic element" of society, and it called for an ambitious public policy response. "People with foreign origins, or perceived as having them, are disadvantaged in terms of access to jobs and housing," wrote Jacques Toubon, the government's *Défenseur des Droits*. "They are more exposed to joblessness, poverty, poor housing, police ID checks, poor health, and educational inequality." The report added, "Discrimination is not the result of individual responses, a few human resource directors who refuse to hire Blacks or Arabs. It's the entire system that is to blame."

Toubon also raised the alarm at a "crisis of public confidence in the security forces," saying there was a "war mentality" in law enforcement. At the same time, Human Rights Watch said French police had too much power "to conduct discriminatory and abusive checks on Black and Arab boys and men."

A way forward would be for a "Discrimination Observatory" to be set up, said Toubon. This would certainly help to identify the extent of the issue—Toubon suggested more spot checks on company recruitment policies to expose racial bias—but no firm solution was proposed.

Extremely unusually for a President of France, Macron used a TV address to the nation in June 2020 to acknowledge that someone's "address, name, skin color" could demolish their chances at succeeding in French society. He called for a fight to ensure that everyone can "find their place," regardless of ethnic origin or religion, but as Macron laid out the problem, he offered no valid routes to a resolution.

3

THE FAR-RIGHT

Back to Africa

Antagonism breeds extremism.

–ÉMILE ZOLA (1840–1902)

When we met for the first time in Paris, Marine Le Pen played gently on my appearance. Fixing me with a strained smile, showing off a small line of yellow teeth, she declared: "We could do with plenty more like you in the party—you're very welcome to join."

Le Pen, then the second most famous Front National politician in France after her father, Jean-Marie Le Pen, had the look of a conspiratorial club secretary in a smoky bar, the kind who seemingly becomes nicer with alcohol. The smell of tobacco on her breath wafted over me as she told me in a hoarse voice that she loved cats and karaoke sessions, with Dalida's "Paroles, Paroles" her favorite song. It is about a woman being gifted caramels and chocolates by a suitor, while describing his advances as just empty words.

The 2007 presidential election campaign was in full swing, so Le Pen was pitching for my vote as papa, the FN leader, was running for President. Her own "Paroles, Paroles" focused on my French identity card, which would in theory entitle me, under an FN President, to a priority choice of jobs, homes, and welfare provision over "newcomers"—in other words, immigrants.

She proposed a strict clampdown on those who wanted to enter France, meaning more resources for me and those close to me. It all sounded so easy—there is nothing complicated about *lepénisme*. Le Pen is an expert in shallow bonhomie. She hoped we might be on the same side, and she tried to sign me up, but—as in dingy bars in FN heartlands—there was a constant fear of sudden and extreme violence. This concern was intensified by the very large, unsmiling security guard wearing dark sunglasses and an earpiece who towered over us. He had a reputation for punching journalists and then dragging them along the ground by the arms while pretending he was looking for a police officer to report to.

Why should a Muslim from an Algerian background support Le Pen's overtly racist party, which places an "anti" before almost every policy statement, whether it's related to globalization, Europe, Islam, or anything else? I asked. "Because first and foremost we're all French. It's a question of loyalty," Le Pen replied, displaying her fondness for the banal sound bite. "And we're not racist," she added quickly.

Marine Le Pen comes across as the perfect daddy's girl. With her thickset features and meaty hands, she even looks like Jean-Marie Le Pen, the convicted racist and anti-Semite who founded the FN in 1972. This was around the same time that my parents arrived in Paris from Algeria, after my father was encouraged to seek construction work in a Republic still being rebuilt following the Second World War. The Algerian War had been over for a decade, but resentment still festered. Frenchmen such as Jean-Marie Le Pen had served as soldiers in Algeria and been linked with war crimes, including acts of torture.

It is often easy to forget that the Le Pens are the most consistently successful political dynasty in recent French history. I first met both father and daughter in 2007, but their ascendency had gone on for far longer. Their chilling story—and the way millions of French people support them wholeheartedly or else shrug their shoulders amorally about them—is a cause of macabre fascination. The popularity of the Le Pens—and that of even more extreme voices on the far-right who are viewed as perfectly mainstream—is an indictment of modern France, and the way it has normalized race and religious persecution. That a Le Pen continues to be the runner-up in presidential elections every five years certainly shames a Republic that is meant to be a bastion of human rights and equality.

A so-called Republican Front used to guarantee electoral failure for the *lepénistes*, but now an increasingly polarized nation, influenced by openly bigoted mainstream discourse, is becoming more xenophobic. On her third attempt to reach the Élysée Palace in 2022, Marine Le Pen added almost three million votes to her tally from five years earlier and was just 10 percent away from winning a majority.

A new intake of eighty-nine Rassemblement National MPs included one who would soon shout "Go back to Africa!" at a Black colleague during a National Assembly debate about climate change. The rotund Grégoire de Fournas, who had form for offensive comments, directed his poison at Carlos Martens Bilongo, who is of Congolese and Angolan descent. Fournas was suspended from Parliament, as France was left to consider how little the Rassemblement National had changed.

If just 6 percent of MPs in the new National Assembly intake were from an ethnic minority background, even less had dark-colored skin. The first day of the new Parliament saw RN veteran José Gonzalez, still apparently a proud *pied-noir* as he approached eighty, make a speech praising French Algeria and its colonial greatness. He wouldn't even say whether the outwardly patriotic OAS were criminals.

Such extremist nationalists had never been closer to ultimate power. A few more percentage points would have delivered a far-right elected monarch who could start enacting a discriminatory agenda by decree within days, and who would command a military force, her finger on the nuclear button. Colonial nostalgists—even ones with a sneaking admiration for the Third Reich—could join her in government. One might even be appointed Prime Minister. There would be no need for him or her to even be a politician, because the Fifth Republic created during the Algerian emergency does not require much democratic accountability. Power is all.

Using the traditional FN language of the street brawler, Marine Le Pen vowed to "keep up the fight" and to focus on "concrete solutions" to her country's problems. Could she ever be given the chance?

Does France Still Love Us?

The original Front National supporters were the *pieds-noirs*, the settler class in Algeria. The slang might have started out as a reference to the sailors who stocked the coal-fired engines of Mediterranean ships, and who blackened their bare feet while doing so. French officials often wore black boots with their white uniforms, too, or maybe it is a metaphorical, racist reference to ending up with black feet if you dip them into the African continent.

Whatever the case, the *pieds-noirs* were exported to the French territory, which became an integral part of the metropolitan state, over decades of colonization following France's conquest of Algeria in 1830. Many formed themselves into armed militias to fight tooth and nail to hang on to it during the War of Independence, which took place over nearly eight years until 1962. They were supported by military forces ultimately commanded from Paris, who used napalm and carpet-bombing to annihilate the indigenous Arab and Berber populations. Torture was routine, and the French also deployed primitive gas chambers to wipe out civilians. Algerians put their death toll during the war alone at 1.5 million. Some six thousand settlers and twenty-eight thousand French soldiers were killed, with sixty-five thousand wounded. The so-called Algerian *Harki* collaborators who fought alongside the Republic, in many cases as cannon fodder, also suffered mass casualties.

There were around a million *pieds-noirs* in Algeria by 1962, and most began to make emergency plans to get out that summer. "The suitcase or the coffin" was an Algerian nationalist slogan that played heavily on their minds. Dispossessed and traumatized, they swapped relatively glamorous colonial lifestyles—picturesque villas, beaches, and vineyards, status, and servants—for poky council blocks in the expanding *cités* of mainland France. All held full French citizenship, so they got limited state financial benefits, but they were immediately placed at the bottom of a society they knew very little about.

"Does France still love us?" was the headline on a *Paris Match* cover that showed a full-page picture of a young couple and their baby looking mournfully out to sea, toward the approaching coast of the French *Métropole*, from the deck of a passenger ship. *Non* was the answer in many cases. Some eight hundred thousand *pieds-noirs* who arrived in Marseille and other southern ports complained about crates containing all their possessions being dumped in the sea. Landlords refused to house them, and taxi drivers set extortionate rates for anyone who looked like one. "The *pieds-noirs* should go and settle elsewhere!" said Gaston Defferre, the Mayor of Marseille, bitterly.

Algeria was a lost paradise, and the perceived victims of a historic betrayal were determined to stamp their mark on France's political landscape as they tried to reassert their rights. Many *pieds-noirs* were drawn to the so-called Revolutionary Nationalism being preached by an aggressive fringe of young Frenchmen rallying under the Celtic Cross of the neo-fascist Ordre Nouveau (New Order) movement. It used street thuggery to express blistering resentment at the loss of Algeria and other former imperial strongholds. In 1972, Ordre Nouveau amalgamated with the Front National, the new party formed by Jean-Marie Le Pen, whose life to date had been characterized by near constant war.

The FN's early ideology was provided by Alain de Benoist, the ethno-nationalist writer who was born in France during the Nazi Occupation, and whose childhood was—like many of his generation—greatly influenced by the Algerian War. His Nouvelle Droite movement also went on to impact the alt-right in the United States, especially in the period leading up to and during Donald Trump's presidency. Its mission could be summarized as an attempt to protect traditional identities against the threats supposedly posed by immigrants, woke multiculturalism, and globalism, all the while championing those with white skin.

Benoist was an early supporter of the OAS terrorists, at a time when France's allegedly egalitarian values were being erased by the realities of colonial repression. More pertinently, as far as the Nouvelle Droite was concerned, survival depended on a nationalist revolution. Rather than fighting each other—as they had done in the Second World War—Western nations needed to unite in a "community of white people."[1] It was an expression of pure Nazism. Benoist wrote under a pseudonym in

1966, "Replace natural selection with a careful communitarian eugenics policy aiming to reduce the flawed elements and the flaws themselves."[2]

Le Pen Senior was typical of the bellicose white nationalists considered flawless by the fascists. He was from the Breton fishing village of La Trinité-sur-Mer, in the Morbihan department on the Atlantic coast. Go there now, and you can still see the quaint cottage by the Impasse des Farfadets where it all started for Le Pen in 1928. Inside, there is an open fire, rubber rings on the wall, oil lamps, crates of cider, and figurines of Joan of Arc.

The cottage sits above the port, with white-washed walls and an indigo gate leading to a stone path running through the front garden. Marine Le Pen later described the property as the "only place in the world where I am nobody except for Marine." A profile piece in *Le Monde* added the words of the elder Le Pen, who said, "Because I wanted my children to see cows, instead of Arabs." His claim was that North African immigrants were swarming around his home in the 15th Arrondissement of Paris, and his nautical idyll represented an escape.

La Trinité might have symbolized a comfortingly white France, but it was by no means a prosperous or peaceful one when young Jean-Marie was growing up. It was characterized by relative squalor. The house, which was shared by two families, had no electricity or running water, and the outside toilet was at the far end of the garden.

A short walk away from Le Pen's house is St. Joseph's Church and the village War Memorial, which includes the name of Jean Le Pen, father of Jean-Marie and a fishing skipper who was blown to pieces by a German sea mine. The explosive device became caught up in the nets of his trawler, *La Persévérance*, on August 22, 1942, when the fisherman was out trying to catch sole. Jean-Marie was given the status of Ward of the Nation after losing his father, meaning he was officially placed under the care of the French State.

Le Pen was an unruly schoolboy but thanked the Jesuits for instilling a sense of discipline in him, along with his rhetorical skills: his long speeches were always full of angry passion but also cutting quips. As a law student in Paris, Le Pen was continually involved in brawls with the *Cocos*, for Communists, and was keen to extend his muscular energy against those propagating the same ideology overseas. He signed up for the French Foreign Legion after his country's defeat to the Viet Minh at Dien Bien Phu, Vietnam, in 1954. Le Pen rolled into Suez two years later, right in time for the cease-fire that signaled victory for Egypt and Arab nationalism more generally.

Le Pen went to Algeria as a paratrooper and an intelligence officer in 1957, when a prominent slogan of the revolution there was "Arabic is my language, Islam is my religion, Algeria is my country." The message was just the kind of effective sound bite that the FN would tweak for French voters. Le Pen was already a Paris MP, but this did not stop him from getting caught up in war crimes allegations. The then twenty-eight-year-old Lieutenant described his role in Algeria as being "a mixture between being an SS officer and a Gestapo agent. That job, I've done it." In 1962, he told *Combat* newspaper, "I have nothing to hide. We tortured because it had to be done. When someone is brought to you who has planted twenty bombs that could explode at any moment and who will not talk, you use all the methods at your disposal to make him talk." Le Pen later took these words back, effectively saying that he had misspoken.[3]

Some of Le Pen's alleged victims even contributed to a book called *Tortured by Le Pen*, by the Algerian historian Hamid Bousselham, in which they said they were electrocuted, beaten, and subjected to water torture. When *Le Monde* published extracts Le Pen launched a libel claim, but it was unsuccessful. Evidence produced against him included a Hitler Youth dagger with "J.M. Le Pen" engraved on the sheath. It had been retained by Mohamed Moulay, who claimed his father, Ahmed Moulay, had been tortured by Le Pen using the weapon in March 1957.

For many years, Le Pen affected a black, pirate-style patch on his left eye, and one of the rumors was that it followed a wound sustained during active service in Algeria. Later on, he replaced it with a glass eye, and he still looked as tough and menacing, if less theatrically so.

After the Algerian War, Le Pen helped found a record label called Serp with the Nazi collaborator Léon Gaultier, who had served in the Waffen-SS against the Russians as an *Untersturmführer* (the equivalent of a Lieutenant). Gaultier was also a driving force behind the establishment of the *Milice*—the Second World War French paramilitary militia that was an integral part of the Vichy security state supporting the Nazis.

The French Resistance often feared the *Milice* more than the Gestapo or SS, because they were traitors with local knowledge, fluent French, informants everywhere, and a penchant for torture. Speeches by Marshal Pétain, the Vichy leader, were distributed by Serp, along with ones by Josef Goebbels and Hitler himself. Gaultier also worked as Information Secretary in the Pétain regime, broadcasting on Radio Vichy.[4]

When the National Front for French Unity was officially launched at the Horticulturalists Hall in Paris on October 5, 1972, Gaultier was a prominent founding member, along with its first Treasurer, Pierre Bousquet, another former soldier in the SS Charlemagne Division— the military unit that fought for Hitler right up until the end, including in the Berlin bunker where he ended his days. In 1986, recalling his time in the SS, Bousquet said: "Assuming—and I mean assuming— that there were gas chambers and torture, I condemn them."[5]

There were less than a hundred people in the Horticulturalists Hall, where former Nazi collaborators dominated the FN starting lineup, along with convicted OAS criminals such as Roger Holeindre. An early National Front General Secretary was Victor Barthélemy, who had spent time in prison for crimes including helping Paris police with the *Vél d'Hiv* roundup of July 1942, when 13,152 Jews, including 4,115 children, were arrested and sent to their deaths in German concentration camps. Eight years later, Barthélemy's successor as FN General Secretary was Pierre Gérard, a fierce anti-Semite who worked for Vichy's General Commission for Jewish Affairs and became director of "economic Aryanization" in May 1942. He was sentenced to life in prison but, like so many French collaborators, was released during an amnesty, allowing him to reinvent himself as an FN economics guru.[6]

Roland Goguillot, who used the alias Roland Gaucher, was another FN founding father who had worked directly with the Nazis, to the extent that he had fled to Germany when Allied armies advanced on Paris in 1944. Vichy records proved he had encouraged officials to "draw up lists of hostages" and speed up executions. This was the kind of collaborationist crime that saw him sentenced to five years in prison after the war. François Brigneau, the first FN Secretary General, had signed up with the *Milice* just before D-Day. He, too, was imprisoned after the Liberation of France. Both Brigneau and Gaucher had also

THE FAR-RIGHT: BACK TO AFRICA

been members of the Rassemblement National Populaire, the fascist party aligned with the Germans throughout the Occupation. Marine Le Pen later chose the same name—Rassemblement National—as an alternative to National Front. Little wonder that successive court judgments, in 2014 and 2015, ruled that it was perfectly permissible for Marine Le Pen to be referred to as a fascist.

Paul Malaguti was an FN founding member and former Nazi collaborator who in 1992 was exposed by the *Canard Enchaîné* as having helped with the massacre of eight Resistance fighters in Cannes in August 1944. Malaguti had acted as lookout outside Gestapo headquarters, the Villa Montfleury, during the slaughter. He was originally sentenced to death in absentia for collaboration with the enemy at the end of the war, but managed to get the conviction quashed. Malaguti spent time in the OAS, and then became a close friend and political ally of Jean-Marie Le Pen. He was FN Treasurer at one stage. When the Villa Montfleury scandal blew up in the media, Malaguti was standing as an FN candidate and—despite his proven Nazi links—was reelected as a regional councillor.[7]

Also among the FN founders was André *"Tonton Panzer"* Dufraisse—so nicknamed because of his time fighting alongside Third Reich forces on the Eastern Front as a French volunteer. Dufraisse spent time in prison in Paris for crimes associated with anti-Algerian violence, before becoming a member of the FN's political bureau in 1972. Another self-confessed former SS and OAS combatant who joined the FN in the early days was Gilbert Gilles, although some of his boasts about active service were placed in doubt by other veterans.[8]

Beyond the big-name FN founders who had embraced Nazism so enthusiastically, there were also plenty of extreme-right thugs and racists in the rank and file linked with Third Reich nostalgia, and this did not change as the years went by. In 2017, an FN regional councillor called Benoît Loeuillet was caught on camera selling revisionist Holocaust literature at his bookshop in Nice while telling an undercover journalist from the C8 channel: "I don't think there were as many deaths. There were not six million. . . . There weren't mass deaths as has been said." In the same year, a book titled *Marine Knows All About It . . .* by investigative reporters Mathias Destal and Marine Turchi alleged Le Pen had been friends with prominent neo-Nazis since her student days. In response, the FN removed Loeuillet from the party, while Le Pen denied having any associates with Nazi sympathies.

Marine Le Pen also evoked her party's dark affiliations and caused outrage in 2017 when she told broadcaster LCI: "I don't think France was responsible for the *Vél d'Hiv.*" She added: "I think that generally speaking, if there are people responsible, it's those who were in power at the time. It's not France." The remarks contradicted more than twenty years of state policy, which had already officially recognized that many French—including Paris policemen and collaborators who went on to found the FN—had willingly helped round up Holocaust victims.

Nazi antecedents had always attracted plenty of moderate enemies, but also ones who were every bit as violent and fanatical as many National Front members. In November 1976, a bomb blew up part of eight-year-old Marine's bedroom, along with an entire wall of their family home in the 15th Arrondissement of Paris. The perpetrators were trying to kill her father and were never caught. Marine Le Pen later wrote in her autobiography, *À Contre Flots* (Against the flow), "That night I went to sleep like all little girls my age. But when I woke up, I was no longer a little girl like the others." She also said, "It was then that I realized that there were people who had something against my father."

Security was stepped up at a time when admirers were showering Jean-Marie Le Pen with cash. The relative safety of the Villa Montretout, an easily guarded house at the center of a gated community in the western Paris suburb of Saint-Cloud, was bequeathed to Le Pen by Hubert Lambert—an heir to the Lambert cement fortune, and a monarchist, who died just before the bomb attack. Montretout was a Second Empire property built for Napoléon III's Chief of Staff. By the time the Le Pens moved in, heavies supported by Doberman dogs were already a normal part of family life.

Despite obvious fears, Marine remained loyal to her father. When *Libération* newspaper wrote about the elder Le Pen's record as a torturer in 1985, he told Marine to take the day off school, but she instead went to class to defend him. When she was sixteen, humiliation was added to the bouts of terror. Marine's parents went through a divorce that was played out in the national media as a soap opera. Le Pen had commissioned a writer to spend time at Montretout to produce his definitive biography. The author added a very lively chapter of his own to the book when he ran off with Pierrette Lalanne, Le Pen's first wife and the mother to his three daughters, including Marine. While the Le Pens were arguing about maintenance payments, Le Pen suggested his by now estranged spouse should get a job as a cleaner. Lalanne responded by posing for a nude photo shoot for *Playboy*, in which she appeared scrubbing floors. "It was brutal, it's true," Marine Le Pen commented on the divorce. "It marks you, and then it was public. That's what multiplies the suffering that we can feel."

The Le Pen name was certainly a traumatic burden. Marine and her two sisters were ostracized at school, where they heard teachers referring to them as "daughters of a fascist." This forged a siege mentality at Montretout, which was just a few miles from housing projects teeming with ethnic minority communities. Marine reacted by building her life inside the FN bubble. It provided her home, her job, her income, even her husbands. She formally joined the party when she was eighteen and then qualified as a lawyer, supporting her father through many of his five presidential election campaigns.

Revulsion against the FN multiplied in 1995 after four Le Pen supporters were arrested and subsequently convicted for the murder of a North African immigrant in one of the most beautiful parts of Paris. Marine certainly knew everything about the scandalous killing of Brahim Bouarram. She was already well into her career when—on May 1, 1995—Bouarram was tossed into the Seine from the quay by the Pont du Carrousel, which crosses the river from the Louvre and Tuileries Gardens to the Left Bank. Details of the death of the twenty-nine-year-old Moroccan father of two evoked memories of how Paris police officers had murdered Algerians in the 1960s.

On the day of the incident, both Le Pens were taking part in the FN's annual May Day march in honor of Joan of Arc. As usual, all those who looked as though they might come from a traditional French background, and who were preferably white and Christian, were invited to join in this show of devotion to the Catholic martyr. Muslims such

as Bouarram were, in contrast, viewed as targets. February 1995 had
seen a teenager, Ibrahim Ali, shot dead in the back by an FN supporter in Marseille. In a separate incident in March, Samuel Maréchal,
Jean-Marie Le Pen's son-in-law, had ended up with an eight-month
suspended sentence for attacking high school activists with a baton
in Auch, near Toulouse. Marine Le Pen was his defense lawyer. Just
before Bouarram's killing, neo-Nazis affiliated with the party and posing as policemen had assaulted a pregnant Algerian woman in the Paris
suburbs.

When Bouarram was spotted by the FN hordes, obscene insults
were shouted at him. He was accused of being a homosexual suffering
from AIDS, as well as an unwelcome foreigner. It was a sunny morning, and there were plenty of tourists around, but that did not save
Bouarram. One of his tormentors pushed him into the overflowing and
filthy water. A fierce current drove Bouarram away from the banks, and
his cries for help were ignored. Shaken by the fall, Bouarram began to
swallow large amounts of water and soon sank below the surface. The
attackers disappeared into the tail end of the FN demonstration, which
was unsupervised by police.

President François Mitterrand led tributes to Bouarram. The killing took place in the middle of the 1995 presidential election, and
campaigning was briefly forgotten. On May 3, between the two voting rounds, more than ten thousand people gathered on the Carrousel
bridge to drop flowers into the Seine.

There were criminal convictions three years later. The perpetrators, identified through a combination of tourist snaps and surveillance
camera recordings, had come to Paris from Reims, on a coach hired by
the FN. All said Bouarram had called them "skinhead sons of bitches,"
but no objective witnesses had heard this. One of the FN men was
imprisoned for murder, while three others were locked up for failing to
provide assistance to a person in danger.

The Le Pens remained unmoved. Jean-Marie Le Pen's most memorable comment on Bouarram's death was: "I regret that a poor man
died, but in an agglomeration of ten million inhabitants, this kind of
small news item can always happen, or it can even be created at will."
He accused the media of manipulating the Bouarram "accident" and

trying to provoke his party. Bouarram's killing showed exactly the sort of impact adverse publicity has on a Le Pen vote—it invariably goes up. Le Pen scored a then record 15 percent in the 1995 election.

Marine has tried to develop the myth that it was her alone who—despite outrages such as the killing of Brahim Bouarram—made the FN popular and brought it into the democratic process. This is absurd revisionism. Jean-Marie Le Pen was infamously runner-up in the French presidential election of 2002. Despite his antiestablishment bleating, he had always aspired to making his family party mainstream, and he succeeded. The country's political class pretended to be shocked and angry at what happened, but millions of ordinary people saw no reason why they should not embrace *lepénisme*.

Most had thought the crucial second round of the 2002 contest would be between the conservative candidate, Jacques Chirac, and his Socialist Prime Minister, Lionel Jospin. Le Pen got more votes than Jospin in the first round, however, leading to other politicians variously describing the result as "cataclysmic," "shameful," and "a disgrace to French democracy." Jospin said he would retire immediately, calling the result "a thunderbolt."

Chirac was more practical, saying, "I call on all French men and women to unite so as to defend human rights. Today, what is at stake is our national unity, the values of the Republic, the very idea that we have of mankind, its rights, and its dignity. It is the idea we have of France, of its role and its place in Europe and the world." Chirac won the second round with an 82 percent score and became France's new President, but he by no means saved his country from the ongoing assault by the far-right. The so-called Republican Front against an extremist ogre had just about held, but would it remain effective for much longer?

Such questions were a priority for me when I met Le Pen Senior at a rally in Marseille in March 2007. He came across as an aging boxer in a part of France full of FN-supporting veterans of colonial wars, unemployed dockers and laborers, and numerous others who were thoroughly disillusioned with how life was treating them. In contrast, Le Pen, who was almost eighty, claimed to be in fighting form. He told me he had installed a gym at Montretout and had improved his diet. Le Pen was also going through a cowboy phase—campaigning in Stetson hats and trying to act like an avuncular John Wayne. When I approached him for an impromptu interview after his long speech focused on kicking people just like me out of the country, he tried to turn on the charm.

Ignoring all the other journalists who were firing questions at him, Le Pen singled me out and said, "Come with me." His second wife, Jany Le Pen, then gently grabbed my hand and escorted me to her husband's hospitality lounge backstage as he led the way flanked by his bodyguards.

"I'll speak to you and answer any questions you like," Le Pen said, before turning everything I asked into another monologue about immigration. The idea was that his "France for the French" mantra would magic him into the Élysée Palace while allowing him to ignore any other vital subject, such as the economy. Particularly chilling expressions used by Le Pen included "hunting down fake tourists." It was almost as if he was back in Algeria in his paratrooper uniform and looking for enemies to torture.

Le Pen grabbed figures out of the air, in the manner of all barroom ranters. He claimed that ten million immigrants had arrived in France since 1977, "not forgetting a million illegal immigrants." When asked about the children of immigrants who were born in France—people like me, in other words—Le Pen said: "They will leave with their parents."

When a heckler had challenged Le Pen over such allegations inside the hall, he had been forcibly removed. At the end of my interview, Le Pen said to me, "You speak very good French!" When I told him that I was actually born and raised in France, he deliberately repeated the compliment.

Chip off the Old Block

There is a plane tree in the garden of the Le Pen cottage in La Trinité that was planted in 1968, to mark the day Marine Le Pen came into the world. She has admitted to hugging it and even talking to it. On August 5, 1987, a TV crew filmed her celebrating her nineteenth birthday next to it. It was all about showing off family roots and tying herself to her father's legacy. Jean-Marie Le Pen had been inviting journalists to the house for years, so as to present himself and his loving family as jovial Bretons from the real France.

Shortly after his daughter's birthday bash, Le Pen returned to Paris and told RTL radio: "I ask myself several questions. I'm not saying the gas chambers didn't exist. I haven't seen them myself. I haven't particularly studied the question. But I believe it's just a detail in the history of World War Two."

This kind of virulent anti-Semitism was typical of the senior Le Pen, as were numerous other racist comments. His daughter never threatened to admonish him for them, let alone resign from the FN during the years when he was at his most poisonous. On the contrary, Marine Le Pen's discourse could be just as divisive. At a presidential campaign rally held in Marseille in 2017, she blamed her rivals for letting "immigrants turn France into a gigantic squat." Marine spoke of "entire neighborhoods taken over by foreigners" and said that "a multi-cultural society is a multi-conflict society."

The FN rank and file loved such metaphors. One such member was Claude Sinké, another traditionally white and proud Frenchman who lived in a picturesque town and who blamed immigrants for all his country's problems. Sinké, a former French regional election candidate for the FN, particularly disliked Muslims, because they were such an easily identifiable enemy. Sinké did not just talk racism either. On a Saturday morning in October 2019, he arrived at a mosque in the southwest city of Bayonne armed with a gun, gas canisters, and a jerrican full of petrol. His intention was to burn the place of worship down, along with all those inside, including mothers with their children.

Before Sinké could start a fire, however, he was called out by two concerned pensioners. Sinké opened fire on both, hitting one in the arm and the other in the neck at point-blank range. He then poured fuel over a car belonging to one of his victims, while the severely wounded man was still sitting in the driver's seat, before setting it alight. It was only thanks to the swift intervention of other Muslim worshippers that the victims were rushed to hospital and survived.

Sinké was charged with two attempted murders, arson, and gun crimes. His compelling links to the FN were highlighted during remand hearings. The notoriously Islamophobic party had been happy for Sinké to represent them in his home village of Saint-Martin-de-Seignanx, six miles from Bayonne. He had won 17.4 percent of the local council poll in 2015—not enough to win a seat, but a clear indication that his views were not considered beyond the pale, even though there were plenty of clues to his radicalization online, where he regularly posted venom about Muslims and other minority groups.

Sinké told prosecutors that he attacked the Bayonne mosque to "take revenge" on Muslims for "starting" the devastating fire at Notre-Dame Cathedral in Paris in April 2019. The conspiracy theory about the blaze—which forensic investigators have proved started accidentally—was meat and drink to the kind of people traditionally drawn to the FN.

Marine Le Pen predictably tried to distance herself from the Bayonne terror attack, insisting that what happened was "absolutely contrary to the values of our movement." In fact, nothing could have been further from the truth. The Le Pen family record in public life was steeped in violence, especially against Muslims. At the time of the Sinké outrage, Le Pen was forced to admit that another one of her candidates, selected to run in municipal elections in Strasbourg, had spent eighteen months in prison for racist crimes against ethnic minorities. In separate incidents, Thibault Gond-Manteaux had assaulted two men of North African origin and also set fire to Turkish fast-food restaurants while carrying a gun and wearing a balaclava. Among numerous articles of Nazi memorabilia found by police in Gond-Manteaux's home was a copy of *Mein Kampf*, a swastika, and a watch engraved with SS insignia.

Despite her monumental effort to create distance between them, Marine Le Pen was undoubtedly a chip off the formidable old block of Jean-Marie. When she accepted the FN leadership from him at the party's annual conference in Tours in 2011, it was clear that the family resemblance was not solely physical. If there was anyone who could build on the emotional bigotry stirred up by founding father Le Pen, then it would be his daughter. There was certainly no question of her alienating the unreconstructed thugs who turned up at party rallies.

My interviews with both Le Pens have convinced me that there is no such thing as a Le Pen Lite. While Jean-Marie was a man of his time—a burly, ex-army bruiser who saw far-right "patriotism" and a return to colonialism as the answers to all socioeconomic problems— Marine could also do punchy prejudice. She had spent years canvassing in the smoky hotspots of high-immigration cities such as Marseille and could push and shove with the worst of them, mimicking her father's outraged face when necessary and then relaxing into back-slapping bonhomie to seal a vote. Beyond this—and in contrast to her father— Marine understood social media, focus groups, and all the other strategic essentials of twenty-first century electoral success. She has been particularly dynamic in building up her party's "inclusive" nature, pressing the flesh in suburban communities that have felt alienated from mainstream political life.

Marine Le Pen's election strategy was to move away from the jackboot racism and broaden the FN voter base. The senior Le Pen had deliberately wrecked such plans in 2015 by repeating the Holocaust denials that had landed him a series of convictions for hate speech and contesting crimes against humanity. Marine responded by ejecting him from the party. This was around the time that two of her father's Doberman dogs killed Marine's favorite cat, and she finally moved out of the Villa Montretout. It was claimed that father and daughter had stopped speaking. Two years later, after coming second in the 2017 presidential election, Marine Le Pen presided over the change of name from Front National to Rassemblement National.

Melodramatic feuds are integral to "fake news" politics, and few are more unconvincing than the supposed venom between the Le Pens. Their staged schism was crucial to propel the RN forward. Marine Le Pen was adamant that she had nothing to do with obscenities such as describing the Holocaust as a mere "detail" of history. This suited mainstream backers, including ones in Britain, who were desperate to promote her as an "antiestablishment" heroine to follow Brexit. A Le Pen triumph could trigger a Frexit—France pulling out of the

European project—and, potentially, the absolute collapse of the European Union.

A photo of Marine Le Pen shaking Vladimir Putin's hand in the Kremlin figured prominently in her presidential campaign posters for 2022. This was appropriate, because her party had accepted an $11.7 million loan from a Russian bank in 2014 to finance such electioneering. In an interview with the BBC that aired in early February 2022, Le Pen blamed the United States for the 150,000-plus Russian troops amassed along the Ukrainian border, saying the West was trying to push Ukraine into joining NATO. Referring to American President Joe Biden, Le Pen said, "So, he's doing what the leaders of the United States normally do when they feel politically fragile. Find an enemy, and if you don't have one, you can try and create one." The day after the invasion, Le Pen told French television viewers that she thought Putin was "rational and brutal" and she still found him "impressive."

Very little was said in 2017 about Marine admitting to borrowing the equivalent of some $6 million from her father to fund her presidential campaign. Aides to Le Pen confirmed that Cotelec, a company owned by her father, paid the cash, despite Jean-Marie Le Pen having been "excluded" from the FN two years earlier, while in fact quietly remaining the party's honorary president. The baggage associated with the Le Pen surname had already spurred Marion Maréchal-Le Pen, granddaughter of the FN founder and also an outspoken far-right politician, to drop the Le Pen name in favor of Marion Maréchal. Marine never considered such a move, despite her two marriages giving her the chance to do so. Yes, her election posters in 2017 simply read "Marine— Présidente," and she used a blue rose as her election badge instead of the FN's tricolor flame, but there was no question of getting rid of the world-famous moniker that had played such a big part in her political ascendency. The attempted deception was that voters should politely ignore her party's ugly antecedents and pretend that Marine was a fresh force for good who could appeal to all citizens, but the truth is that she was still as controversial as ever.

The FN traditionally wins most seats when trying to get elected to the European Parliament—a body that it professes to despise.

Jean-Marie Le Pen only gave up his seat there in 2019, long after his "rift" with Marine. He won seven straight European elections in all, compared to just two years spent in the National Assembly in Paris as an FN *député*. The senior Le Pen eventually left Brussels and Strasbourg—where the European Parliament meets—when examining judges were investigating him for fraud.

The deceit was that the all-new Rassemblement National had finally ditched such murky financial dealings, along with its racists and anti-Semites like the old Le Pen, but Marine's tactics in the EU Parliament were no different from her father's. Like extremist populists based in other European states including Italy, Austria, and Hungary, the RN remained focused on bigotry underpinned by economic illiteracy, not to say alleged criminal intent. Marine was charged alongside her father and other members of the European Parliament from her party over allegations that they illegally siphoned off millions of euros from Brussels and used them to bolster their domestic party fortunes back in France. This was part of a sizeable bundle of evidence that showed the Rassemblement National had by no means shed its past.

The RN's new blood was every bit as hateful and reactionary as the old timers too. Jordan Bardella, the Marine Le Pen prodigy who took over as party leader in 2022, certainly blamed new arrivals for failing to assimilate into his country, especially around Seine-Saint-Denis, the department north of Paris where he was born.

A few days after a gunman murdered fifty-one worshippers and wounded forty-nine others at mosques in Christchurch, New Zealand, Bardella went on national TV to pontificate positively on "Great Replacement," the theory embraced by the New Zealand terrorist that white people were slowly becoming outnumbered by immigrants, who should be treated as an enemy within. The killer had said he had been converted to the Nazi-style philosophy in France and acted on it back in New Zealand. Bardella was poor on facts and statistics but already an accomplished distorter who knew all about fearmongering. As a successor to Jean-Marie Le Pen—who had described his European Parliament colleagues as "blind, deaf, and dumb" and working inside an "illusion" posing as a Parliament—Bardella could not have been better qualified.

In November 2022, Bardella became the first leader in the party's fifty-year history not to be called Le Pen. However, it by no means meant an end to the dynasty. Marine Le Pen remained designated presidential candidate and in charge in the National Assembly. As elected party president, Bardella—just twenty-seven and a member of the European Parliament—would instead focus on finances and the party's deconstructive work in the EU legislature.

Bardella had come from a poor Italian family that emigrated to Drancy—the Paris suburb that was a holding center for French Jews before they were deported by train to Nazi gas chambers during the Second World War. He said, "I'm part of a generation that takes its destiny into its own hands, that wants to fight. I'm young, I grew up in the suburbs, I lived in the 93. My mother lives in a council block in Saint-Denis. I represent those of modest origin—the social fiber."[9] The subsidized social housing where Bardella's Italy-born mother lived in the Seine-Saint-Denis department was surrounded by ethnic minority communities, and this was clearly a cause of great bitterness to Bardella.

Bardella posted a tweet on August 25, 2021, reaffirming his belief in Great Replacement. Referring to National Institute of Statistics and Economics Studies (INSEE) figures that showed an increase in the population of France by 317,000—44 percent of them immigrants— Bardella wrote, "The INSEE data confirms what we have been saying for a long time: immigration is causing a change in population, unprecedented in our history by its speed and its magnitude. We have little time left to choose the face that France will have tomorrow." Bardella then retweeted his message under the words "Demography is destiny."

Asked during an appearance on BFM TV if his problem was with skin color, Bardella replied, "I'm talking about culture, religion, the establishment on our soil of a civilization with which we share nothing."[10]

Bardella's election by 85 percent of party members came during the week that MP Grégoire de Fournas was suspended from Parliament for his "Go back to Africa!" comment. A few weeks earlier, Bardella had claimed, "We are talking about a generation that has, beyond measure, nothing to do with the National Front and that is normal because the world is changing." He instead wanted a "return to the French pride in being French."[11]

Despite this, Bardella supported Fournas, saying his colleague was victim "of a witch hunt" carried out by political enemies. Calling for a drastic cutback in immigration numbers, Bardella added: "France shouldn't be the world's hotel."

The French Suicide

Speaking to the CNEWS TV channel just before the Bayonne attack carried out by Claude Sinké, Éric Zemmour, the "maverick polemicist" (as he is disingenuously referred to by many mainstream journalistic colleagues) said General Thomas Robert Bugeaud, the onetime Marshal of France and Governor-General of Algeria, "began massacring Muslims and some Jews" when he arrived in the North African country in 1836 during the early years of French colonization. Zemmour added nonchalantly, "Well, I'm on the side of General Bugeaud. That's being French."

This was in line with Zemmour's besotted support for controversial figures, including Vladimir Putin, as well as his undisguised sympathy for the Vichy collaborators. Unlike Jean-Marie Le Pen—who never once established a firm bolt-hole in the mainstream media—Zemmour was a favorite with CNEWS, which is owned by the billionaire industrialist Vincent Bolloré, the close friend of former French President Nicolas Sarkozy.

Zemmour's popularity skyrocketed during appearances on CNEWS. He was often one of a few guests on the early evening show *Face à l'Info*—best translated as Face the Press—where he was allowed to talk about whatever was on his mind. While complaints about Zemmour's extremism poured in, they did not damage the show's ratings. When he said the unsayable—a frequent occurrence—he was taken off-air for days at a time as alleged offenses were ostensibly investigated, but he always returned.

Bêtes noires discussed on CNEWS included so-called woke culture, Marxists, the #MeToo movement, and LGBT rights. Zemmour, another high-profile advocate of the Great Replacement theory, also bemoaned the demise of a strong and sure Christian France while constantly berating Islam. He seized every opportunity to ascribe collective guilt to France's entire Muslim population of nearly six million for the actions of radicalized criminals or overseas terrorist organizations.

Zemmour also wrote columns for *Le Figaro*, a nominally respectable conservative newspaper. He appeared regularly in pretty much every other French media outlet, along with plenty of foreign ones, when he ran to become President of France in November 2021. Zemmour by no means styled himself as a snarling outsider, as Jean-Marie Le Pen had done. On the contrary, Zemmour launched his candidacy with establishment nostalgia. He starred in his own online video, replicating General Charles de Gaulle's June 1940 call to arms. While the wartime leader of the Free French had been requesting resistance against Nazi occupiers, Zemmour said he wanted to "save France" from decades of immigration and liberalism. Like de Gaulle, he hunched over a microphone, as images of a mythical France—clean, beautiful, and full of Gallic icons from Joan of Arc to Édith Piaf—were juxtaposed with those of a decaying Republic plagued by violent disorder. De Gaulle infamously presided over France's defeat in Algeria in 1962, earning the eternal bitterness and hatred of the *pieds-noirs*, but such absurd contradictions are meant to be overlooked by those looking for a far-right savior in France.

Zemmour also felt he had something of the Donald Trump about him. The Frenchman encouraged this comparison to the former US President by producing a near direct copy photograph of the cover of *Great Again*, Trump's 2016 manifesto. Zemmour posed in front of his national flag and claimed that, despite decades of despondency, he could make his country "great again." His rallies had a glitzy, Trump-style feel to them.

When war was declared between Russia and Ukraine in February 2022, statements by Zemmour regarding Putin were highlighted. Zemmour, by now the leader of the so-called Reconquest movement, had, just two months before on the France 2 TV news channel, offered a "bet" that "Russia will not invade Ukraine." He defended the Russian regime, just as he had done for years.

In September 2018, Zemmour had told *L'Opinion* that he "dreamed of a French Putin." He had previously described the Russian leader as "the last resister of the politically correct hurricane, which, starting from America, destroys all the traditional structures, family, religion, fatherland." He had also told RTL radio station that "Ukraine does not exist," and that it was a "country of odds and ends" born in the "historic cradle of Russian civilization"—exactly Putin's justification for his invasion.

Pop polemicists thrive on such absurdly simplistic messages, and none more so than Zemmour. There was no mention in his candidacy video of his own alleged threat to public order. In November 2021, the same month as his broadcast, he went on trial for inciting racial hatred for saying that unaccompanied immigrant children in France were "thieves," adding, "They're murderers, they're rapists, that's all they are. We must send them back."

Zemmour had again made the comments on CNEWS, where he appeared as a full-time commentator on current affairs each weekday evening. Zemmour played the role of a professional depressive agonizing over the trajectory of the modern world, like a French Tucker Carlson. Through his media work and publications, he has tapped into the traditional French psychological condition of ennui—which, at its most extreme, extends to a near-suicidal disdain for life.

Spreading collective guilt was the cornerstone of Zemmour's discourse. By the time he was found guilty of incitement in January 2022 for his comments about immigrant children, Zemmour had already been convicted twice for inciting racial and religious hatred. He claimed France was being "submerged" by immigrants from Muslim countries, yet he traced his own heritage to a Berber family in what is now the Muslim-majority country of Algeria.

Zemmour identified as Jewish, yet arguably his most despicable deceit was his false theory that the Vichy regime did not collaborate with the Nazis to perpetrate the Holocaust. Instead, he portrayed Marshal Pétain as someone who had "protected French Jews." Zemmour was educated at a private Jewish school in the Paris suburb of Drancy. The remains of the Drancy internment camp for Jews are still there, making Zemmour's Vichy denialism even more shocking.

Zemmour's monstrous historical falsehoods—belying the fact that seventy-five thousand Jews were rounded up by French officials and sent to Nazi concentration camps—saw Zemmour taken to court in 2021 on charges of disputing a crime against humanity. However, on that occasion he used weasel words—"It's not my subject. I haven't studied it"—to avoid conviction.

Clément Beaune, France's then Europe Minister, nonetheless rounded on Zemmour, saying that his claims "do not stand up to historical analysis for a second" and were "vomit inducing." Beaune emphasized that "Éric Zemmour was one of the faces of what has a long tradition in our country—the hateful anti-Semitic French far-right."

Zemmour has described the mainstream media as a "propaganda machine that hates France" and "spits on the French people, whom they want to see disappear." Yet despite this professed hatred, he owed his entire career to appearances on popular radio and television programs. His best-known book, *The French Suicide*, is a study in cataclysmic negativity that frequently drifts into nihilism. It alleges that France has been in terminal decline since the 1960s and has failed to cope with waves of immigrants who cannot be integrated. *The French Suicide* also states that the country was damaged by student protests and contemporary social movements, including those for sexual liberation, feminism, and gay rights. Still, regardless of this supposed national demise, Zemmour was determined to run the country anyway.

Zemmour, a slight man of just five feet six, was physically attacked on arrival at the Villepinte arena in Paris for a campaign rally in December 2021. A member of the crowd briefly held him in a headlock before being pulled off by security guards. Zemmour suffered a badly injured wrist—a doctor advised him to take nine days off work—while the assailant was arrested and faced assault charges. It later turned out that the deranged attacker had previously supported Zemmour but apparently suddenly changed his mind. Further violence broke out in the Villepinte venue after anti-racism activists entered. Members of the SOS Racisme association, including a young woman, were repeatedly punched by Zemmour supporters after displaying "No to Racism" T-shirts.

Zemmour oozed defiance, despite the unrelenting onslaught on his character in the months leading up to the announcement of his candidacy. The Paris news outlet *Mediapart* presented testimony from eight women who accused him of sexual assault. Zemmour refused to discuss the accusations and insisted he had not been arrested or charged. Meanwhile, the married father of three was involved in a legal bid to prevent disclosure of his secret affair with his campaign manager.

There is no doubt that Zemmour got into such an extraordinary electoral position because of his media profile. At a time when France was massively divided, with public faith in its increasingly corrupt politicians and fragmented party system at rock bottom, he was leading the debates. Zemmour was well known for rehearsing the details of the culture wars, whether tackling *laïcité*, race, or identity. He did so with a poisonous intensity in front of an audience of millions on prime time TV. Hate sells, and an exploitative media was happy to champion him, with only marginal pushback.

A key aspect of Zemmour's appeal to the French Right was that, like the Front National, he was part of the *pieds-noirs* tradition. Among those who left Algeria in the 1950s were his parents, Roger Zemmour, an ambulance driver, and Lucette Zemmour, a housewife. Zemmour claims that they were not technically *pieds-noirs* themselves, instead tracing their Berber heritage back before the French Occupation that started in 1830, but he has conceded that they embraced the invader and wanted to stay under French rule.

The *pied-noir* mindset was based on unquestioning reverence to French overlords. Zemmour wants citizens of the modern France to express similar loyalty. This means renouncing Islam because of the challenge a strong cultural and religious identity allegedly poses to secular republicanism. He calls on Muslims to reject their faith and even wants a ban on names such as Mohammed and Ali.

Significantly, Jean-Marie Le Pen said he would vote for Zemmour if he thought he had a better chance of winning the presidency than his daughter. Marion Maréchal also said she would support Zemmour.

Mainstreaming Hate

Emmanuel Macron overcame far-right extremism in 2017 and 2022 to win two presidential elections. He positioned himself as a moderate centrist with more interest in fiscal policy than hate and division. Yet he also attempted to appease those who voted in such overwhelming numbers for Le Pen and Zemmour. Macron still tries to come across as a pragmatist who wants to reconcile opposing factions, but there is no doubt that he has moved further to the Right.

What is particularly alarming is the way racism is so underplayed across France. A relaxed acceptance of explicit bigotry sustains a legacy of insidious Gallic prejudice that shows no sign of ending. Something that astonished me very early on was how marches and rallies by the Front National and then the Rassemblement National passed off without counter-demonstrations. The tradition of protest in Britain is not what it once was, but you always got a sense of outrage when groups such as the English Defence League presented themselves to the public. I attended an address by the leader of the British National Party at the Oxford Union when I was teaching at the University, and the building was surrounded by opponents. Fighting and anti-democratic behavior is actually very common in France, but you barely got much more than a shrug of the shoulders at Le Pen rallies—even when skinhead thugs were throwing Arabs into the Seine.

In June 2022, two of the six Vice Presidents working in the Paris National Assembly (the role is the equivalent of Deputy Speaker in the British House of Commons) were Rassemblement National deputies. The parliamentary elections that month saw the RN win eighty-nine seats. It was still a relatively small proportion of the 577-seat National Assembly but nonetheless a historic breakthrough. Crucially, it meant a huge financial windfall. Public subsidies worth around €10 million a year would go straight into party coffers, helping to pay back their

Russian benefactors. It appeared that the RN Vice Presidents received 290 and 284 votes respectively because they had done a secret deal with Macron's centrist bloc. If the RN voted in favor of Macron legislation, their politicians would get key parliamentary positions.

Whatever the truth, the RN was certainly reshaping the political landscape. Zemmour got nowhere electorally—he failed to become President and was then rejected by voters as he tried to win a seat in Parliament—but his extremist views had still seeped into the mainstream thinking of both Right and Left.

June 2022 marked fifty years since the Front National was formed by postwar fascists, including those who had fought for the Nazis and against decolonization. Since taking over the reins of the FN in 2011, Marine Le Pen has played superficial games in moving away from such ideas and "detoxifying" it: expelling dad, renaming the party, talking about the price of peas, trying to recruit more women. At its heart, though, the project has remained the Benoist one, especially in its hostility to globalism, immigration, and Islam. There may have been less of an overt emphasis on white supremacy, but the motives for animosity against dark-skinned Muslims were clear. As far as ostracizing Jean-Marie Le Pen was concerned, Marine Le Pen made it clear that if she won the presidential race, her father would be warmly welcomed to the Élysée Palace to attend her inauguration ceremony. So much for the family schism.

Benoist's Nouvelle Droite has found mainstream support outside France too. British polemicist Douglas Murray authored *The Strange Death of Europe*, his 2017 book in which he wrote, "Europe is committing suicide. . . . By the end of the lifespans of most people currently alive, Europe will not be Europe and the peoples of Europe will have lost the only place in the world we had to call home." *The Spectator*, the London magazine that Murray helped edit, became a keen promoter of Marine Le Pen in the run-up to the 2022 presidential race and beyond. In America, too, conservatives from Fox News presenters to Republican congressmen have given legitimacy to far-right conspiracy theories.

In 2022, Le Pen won 41 percent of the vote in the second presidential round of voting. She celebrated her progress revealingly: "We were xenophobes, anti-Semites, racists, and national preference was a terrible shame. And all of a sudden, there is no more of that." No more xeno-phobia? Or no more rejection of xenophobia? It was hard to tell.

Nostalgia remains a very significant factor in the far-right vote. Marine Le Pen insists that the French Empire "brought a lot, especially to Algeria," for example. For extreme nationalists like the Le Pens, Algeria still represents lost French greatness—a period when the coun-try was not just another EU state or one of the Group of Eight industri-alized economies.

In fact, all the Le Pens and Zemmour have to offer France is decline. They are jumped-up propagandists, chancers who cobble together weak scripts full of malicious clichés and pseudo-academic theories. They get it wrong about everything and everyone, including Vladimir Putin.

All of the ogres will retain a significant constituency in a country where the far-right is indisputably on the rise, and where their televised tirades will continue to inflame and polarize the electorate. France is a case study in the advance of racist populism. Disillusionment with corrupt, useless politicians is long-standing. The Left–Right divide at the center is obsolete, and extremists have come in to fill the vacuum. Exercising power in a disenchanted society is hard enough at the best of times, but when a presidential election produces not one but two far-right candidates with a sizeable share of the vote, then the future looks very grim indeed.

Today the United States, Tomorrow France?

Political earthquakes in recent years have included the Brexit vote in Britain and the election of Donald Trump as US President. Many were desperate to portray the 2022 French presidential election as similarly dramatic. They said the center could not hold and that Marine Le Pen was on course to become head of state in a country associated with enlightened ideas of liberalism and human rights. According to the lepénistes, a coalition of true nationalists from across the political divide would get behind "Queen Marine" in the second round. This would ensure that the quasi-monarch in charge of the Fifth Republic would finally be a woman devoted to the values that made France great.

Such simplistic thinking was certainly well rehearsed in the United States and United Kingdom, where populist commentators longed to see a genuine extremist achieving real power in a highly influential European nation. Le Pen's dissent toward the European Union fitted in with the Brexit narrative, as did her antipathy toward ethnic and religious minorities that threatened the "true" nature of both Gallic and Anglo-American societies. An invigorating whirlwind was long overdue, and the dynamic Le Pen was the person to cause it, we were told.

Such myths are not supported by the facts. The reality is that Marine Le Pen was a serial loser who had spent decades struggling to make an impact. It was little known in America and Britain that she took four attempts to win a place in the French Parliament, and even then belonged to a minority party with just six seats out of 577 in the National Assembly, at the end of the 2017–2022 parliamentary period. This number went up to eighty-nine in 2022, but the figure was hardly an earthquake. It was the third time that Le Pen had run to get into the Élysée Palace, and the stark reality was that she had failed again.

Call Marine Le Pen's party what you like, but it is still deeply rooted in some of the vilest creeds known to humanity. Actual Waffen-SS veterans helped found it, and it was led for decades by a convicted Holocaust denier, anti-Semite, and racist. There is now little mention of the colonial, and indeed Third Reich, nostalgia that helped build the party, but it cannot be erased from history.

When Donald Trump won the US presidency in November 2016, Jean-Marie Le Pen tweeted: "Today the United States, tomorrow France!" I had appeared on the BBC's *Dateline London* program back in July 2016 and, based on interviews with contacts I made while living in America's Rust Belt, I predicted a Trump win because of his nationwide appeal. Marine Le Pen's power base was, in contrast, centered on small town and village councils. Like Hillary Clinton in the minds of the US voters, Le Pen appeared to have been knocking around for decades, owed much of her success to nepotism, and put her personal career fantasies before the good of her country.

That changed in 2022, when Le Pen spent a lot more time in depressed areas, suggesting "concrete solutions" to reduce the price of staples such as petrol, heating, and food. Low-earning blue-collar workers, and those without jobs, were impressed. Concerns about spending power and the cost of living were contrasted with an incumbent head of state described as a "President of the Rich." Jean-Marie was less visible than before, and—thanks to Zemmour—Marine was not the most obviously extreme candidate in the first round.

Zemmour had summed up yet another Le Pen failure to win the French presidency in April 2022 with the words, "This is the eighth time defeat strikes the Le Pen family name." Yet there was no doubt that Zemmour's incendiary extremism had helped Le Pen and the RN to come across as more respectable. If we were to add up first round votes that went to Zemmour, Le Pen, and Nicolas Dupont-Aignan, another extremist nationalist, then the far-right vote amassed 32.5 percent. The populist far-right had not only achieved its best ever score but had firmly moved into the political mainstream. First round cumulative votes for the extreme Right certainly outpolled Macron.

What can be done about this? A good start would be removing the constitutional possibility of a populist figurehead becoming head of state without a parliamentary majority. Macron came from nowhere to win the presidency in 2017. He had never won an election in his life before. His agenda was a moderate one—he offered Europhile, economically liberal policies—but he was still a disrupter who beat the system. Marine Le Pen is not too many percentage points away from doing the same thing, not least of all if she can unite the far-right— something that would not be too hard, given the simplicity of their messages.

Again, it is about time that statistics about the multicultural nature of French society were collected and used to solve problems of inequality and injustice. The US Civil Rights Movement exposed racism and widespread discrimination, and comprehensive data was crucial to tackling such issues. The 1964 Civil Rights Act led to the creation of the Equal Employment Opportunity Commission, for example. When you notice the lack of dark faces in key jobs in France, you can see how important it is to establish an equivalent for this country.

France needs to boost the status of its minority communities. Better representation in big business, politics, the media, and the arts is essential. When ethnic minority members do succeed in the restricted Paris establishment today, the old racist stereotypes are soon evoked. Christiane Taubira, a politician from the overseas department of French Guiana who served as Justice Minister for four years from 2012, was in 2013 portrayed as an ape by a former FN election candidate. Anne-Sophie Leclere posted a photomontage on Facebook that showed Taubira next to a baby chimpanzee. The caption underneath read: "At 18 months," and the one below Taubira's photograph read: "Now." Leclere was even allowed on TV, to say she would prefer to see Taubira "in a tree swinging from the branches rather than in government."

Leclere's discourse was by no means exceptional. The annual report by the French Interior Ministry into racist, xenophobic, and anti-religious offenses showed they had multiplied in 2021. Officials also said that racist crimes such as hurling abuse were "little reported." Despite the reluctance of the victims, who were identified to be mostly male African nationals, to approach police, the study said nearly 12,500 racist crimes were registered in 2021. Of these, 6,300 offenses were found to be in the high- or medium-level crime category. The total number of incidents jumped 16 percent compared to 2020.

Against the background of such mainstream hate—which is openly encouraged by the media—it is little wonder that the extreme Right does so well. France needs to stop normalizing it. People should instead attack and pillory men like Éric Zemmour when they appear on TV and not treat them like they are rational and moderate. Increased education about France's recent history of colonialism, and indeed of its collaboration with Nazism, would help a lot of people who might be drawn to supporting parties such as the RN and Zemmour's Reconquête. The genocidal hatred of recent decades had profound consequences for the French Republic, and there is every reason to fear that it might be repeated.

It was not just some of the RN's biggest names, including Jean-Marie Le Pen himself, who were impressed by Zemmour. Plenty of Républicain voters went over to him in 2022. I spoke to them at rallies in Paris and Lyon, when they said they admired someone who believed in the greatness of France. They did not call him a fascist, a racist, or an anti-Semite, as they might Jean-Marie Le Pen. Instead, they praised his lively speeches and the way supporters from all classes chanted his name while applauding rhythmically. Some of the messages were certainly mean-spirited, but they were stirring passions, especially when reviving chauvinism and xenophobia among the French.

Zemmour himself told me he aspired to be another great stand-alone power player. "I revere Napoléon and De Gaulle, and what they did for France," he said. "Macron represents a very different type of leader, but he will be the last in a long line who have failed France." The warning was an ominous one, and it spoke volumes about the direction in which France is heading.

4

PROTEST

Fight the Power

They were savages, yes; but the savages of civilization.

—VICTOR HUGO (1802–1885)

The sacking of the Arc de Triomphe is the kind of outrage that Paris protesters dream about. I was among the crowds that watched the historic monument being defiled by a mob on a Saturday afternoon in December 2018. Swarms of *Gilets Jaunes*—the "Yellow Vests," named after their trademark fluorescent road safety jackets—fought running battles with paramilitary police.

Officers just about held back from using lethal force, but they did rely on rubber bullets, tear gas, pepper spray, stun grenades, and a water cannon. Specialist firearms units and regular uniformed soldiers stood by with assault rifles and machine pistols, while blue armored cars were parked on most of the twelve straight avenues leading off the round-about that surrounds the Arc. These are the majestic thoroughfares originally designed by Baron Haussmann to be perfectly straight and wide, to make artillery fire and cavalry charges as effective as possible.

There were no heavy guns on this wintery afternoon at least, but the police resembled futuristic stormtroopers as they went out to take on their foes in their armor and helmets, and laden down with

equipment including bulletproof vests and plenty of ammunition. You
very seldom saw them running fast—at most, they would jog gently
toward the action. When the lumbering shock troops were isolated and
pulled to the ground, they looked like knights who had been tugged off
their horses and left to the mercy of snarling, lower-order foot soldiers
in a medieval battle. In turn, the scrunched-up faces of the rioters occasionally appeared from behind balaclavas and scarves they were using
to try and hide their identities.

Molotov cocktails flew through the cold air along with the debris
from smashed paving stones. Coins, cans, bottles, and anything else
hard and potentially painful that the protesters could get their hands
on were also used as projectiles. Police inflicted plenty of beatings in
return, bloodying men and women caught up in their regular charges.

Some of the vehicles that had been part of the constant stream of
traffic that usually circles the Arc were summarily set on fire by protesters, using matches dropped into fuel tanks. Top marque cars were
soon ablaze, and the windows of restaurants, cafés, and designer boutiques were smashed in. Other demonstrators focused on trying to get
into banks and cash machines around the Champs-Élysées. Smoke and
flames mixed with vast white clouds of noxious gas delivered by grenades, so reducing visibility to a few feet.

During a brief lull in the fighting, the forces of law and order abandoned their positions on the Arc roundabout, more commonly referred
to as *l'Étoile*, or the Star. This left the demonstrators free to spray the
sides of the Arc de Triomphe with slogans such as "The Yellow Vests
Will Triumph" and "Macron Resign!"

A particularly determined group wearing ski and gas masks bran-
dished hammers and metal poles as they got into the Arc de Triomphe
itself. There, they smashed up a bust of Marianne, the female symbol of
the revolutionary Republic. The figurine's facial features were hacked
off and splintered across the floor.

Displaying just as much ferocity against the legendary symbols of
France, another group moved on to the Tomb of the Unknown Soldier.
The Arc de Triomphe was originally commissioned by Napoléon Bonaparte to glorify the imperial victories of his armies, and it is revered
today because it commemorates the near one-and-a-half million troops

killed during the First World War. A granite slab reads: "Here rests a French soldier who died for his country, 1914–1918." An eternal flame is meant to burn above the tomb constantly, but the *Gilets Jaunes* briefly ended that tradition. They extinguished the blue and orange fire with their boots, while squads of police stared through their smeared visors at the *Étoile* roundabout. This was so much more than just another classic Paris riot. The protesters were attacking the very soul of France. What is the link between such organized violence and the Republic, and where does this tradition of anarchy come from? Does it achieve anything, and, if so, whom does it mostly benefit? What triggers it in the first place, and could it be prevented?

Infantry, Cavalry, Artillery

Violence in France has become institutionalized. Whether perpetrated by groups of dissenters or the authorities themselves, there is an acceptable level of savagery that belies the supposedly civilized nature of the Republic. Paris itself is one of the most celebrated protest cities in the world. It has been at the forefront of idealistic challenges to injustice and oppression throughout the centuries, and all involved insurrection. Years such as 1789, 1830, 1848, and 1871, when the doomed Paris Commune briefly gained power, are forever associated with uprisings. Civilian resistance contributed to the end of the Nazi Occupation in 1944, while the apparent watershed of May 1968—when a mass movement made up of Paris students and trade unionists shook Europe's old order—is still feted.

You do not have to agree with a protester's cause in France to concede that he or she has a right to take to the streets. Whether marching peacefully—as many do when permitted by the authorities—or fighting the police, tearing up the pavements, and setting fire to cars and property, demonstrating is a sacred right that frequently overrides basic laws concerned with keeping the peace.

The Paris-born eighteenth-century writer and civil rights champion François-Marie Arouet—or Voltaire as he is better known—is forever associated with the quote "I disapprove of what you say, but I will defend to the death your right to say it." He did not actually coin the phrase—his English biographer Evelyn Beatrice Hall did—but it sums up the sentiment of plenty of rioters.[1] Yes, there are all kinds of lies and distortions—and indeed misquotes by revered philosophers— used to underpin glorious legends, but the size and strength of the modern security state is testament to how seriously the troublemakers are viewed.

Germany was always considered the classic militaristic nation, and America was never far behind, but institutionalized force is also integral to France. The population has always been very proud of its armed forces, so much so that Karl Marx suggested that "Liberty, Equality, Fraternity" should be replaced by "Infantry, Cavalry, Artillery."[2]

The Fifth Republic itself was in many ways a military solution to the ungovernability of the Fourth Republic. Widespread disorder threatened to turn into full-blown revolution, and radical action was needed. De Gaulle, the very tall, lumbering, immensely brave soldier who preferred to be regarded as a General rather than a statesman, was at the center of it all. The system he molded to channel his statecraft was not far off the Napoleonic model. It combined France's monarchical and republican traditions, to include a highly sophisticated security state whose agents were always ready to do battle. France was so chaotic at the time that it was not just enemies of the State who were trying to murder De Gaulle but extremist patriots too. The terrorism they espoused remains the most extreme manifestation of dissent in the Republic, and is the subject of the next chapter.

The basic organization of the French nation intrinsically encourages violence. De Gaulle—a Roman Catholic traditionalist who considered himself to be superior to pretty much everybody else—championed the idea of an omnipotent ruler lording it up in his presidential fortress, the Élysée Palace, while surrounded by the Republican Guard and multiple paramilitary units. This supreme being would be far more important than a mere Paris Parliament, which was stripped of many of its Fourth Republic powers and left to rubber stamp the whims of the *Chef d'État*.[3]

That De Gaulle deserved his reputation as an uncompromising, lofty warlord is not in doubt. It is miraculous that he survived the First

World War at all, given his courage under fire and indeed his height, which would have made him a prime target for snipers. His first action as a Lieutenant in August 1914 was to charge toward German machine guns, and he was promptly wounded in the leg. Following a short period of convalescence, he returned to the front line to lead reconnaissance missions into no-man's-land.

In 1915, De Gaulle was shot in the left hand during the First Battle of Champagne. Opportunities for the Germans to kill the future President continued into the next year, when he joined the carnage at Verdun, the longest and bloodiest French engagement of the war. Bayoneted in the thigh, De Gaulle was captured and feared dead, while in fact he would spend just under three years as a prisoner of war. He devoted much of his time to learning German and working out tactics for the next world war.

De Gaulle became a tank commander who fought in vain to stop the German Blitzkrieg in 1940. He blamed his brother officers for not listening to his radical ideas about a new type of free-flowing warfare spearheaded by armored vehicles. They preferred to stagnate in useless defensive positions. Following France's capitulation to the Nazis, De Gaulle led his country from London, becoming the radio voice of the Free French.

After Paris was liberated in 1944, he claimed the victory was pretty much a personal one, that had allowed France to "free herself." He headed a victory parade down the Champs-Élysées, without paying much attention to the Americans and other Allies, including the British and Canadians, who had played such a crucial role in the victory. He was also careful to keep the Black and Arab colonial troops who had done so much of the fighting away from the celebrations.

De Gaulle's successors all inherited this arrogant, manipulative approach to public life. Despite being a hero of the nation, De Gaulle soon found people wanted to kill him. Most of his successors have also been targets of gunmen, including the current Jupiter, Emmanuel Macron. Plots to murder Macron followed his ascension to power. A would-be assassin was arrested in the Paris suburb of Argenteuil in connection with a planned shooting attack on Macron in 2017 on

Bastille Day, France's national celebration on July 14. A year later, police seized thirteen members of what they called a "far-right extremist cell" and charged them with plotting to kill the President.

In De Gaulle's case, it was his own security officials—army and police—who were usually conspiring to assassinate him, and they came very close to succeeding. There were multiple attempts on his life, and the most notorious was in connection with Algeria. A dozen would-be assassins fired some 150 bullets into De Gaulle's Citroën DS19 in the Paris suburb of Petit-Clamart as he traveled from the Élysée Palace toward Villacoublay military airport on August 22, 1962. The driver of *la Déesse* (the Goddess car) managed to speed away, despite two tires being blown out, so saving De Gaulle for the nation.[4]

The would-be killers were linked to a still mysterious group called *Vieil État-Major*. Other assassins had set up their own terrorist group, the Secret Army Organization, which was focused on retaining French Algeria. The OAS thought nothing of murdering civilians, as well as officials. British author Frederick Forsyth dramatized events like the Petit-Clamart assassination attempt in his best-selling novel *The Day of the Jackal*, which was later made into a blockbuster movie. Less glamorized was the OAS's horrific bombing of a Strasbourg-Paris high-speed train in 1961. It was an atrocity that claimed twenty-eight lives and wounded a hundred others during a period of turmoil when the very legitimacy of De Gaulle's new Republic was being questioned.

Military State

The soldiers and paramilitary troops who were out in force around the Arc de Triomphe during successive *Gilets Jaunes* riots were typical of those that De Gaulle envisaged playing such an important part in his new Republic. (You see them wearing battle fatigues and brandishing drawn weapons in all major cities, at all times of day.) The focal point of Bastille Day is a parade that involves a military machine that is revered by vast sections of society. Infantry and cavalry march with their bands down the Champs-Élysées into Place de la Concorde to salute their Commander-in-Chief.

L'Étoile —which was officially named Place Charles de Gaulle following *le Général*'s death in 1970—figures prominently. There is also an Air Force flyby, when blue, white, and red trails stream out of jets on one of the few days when aircraft are allowed in the sky directly above Paris. The Bastille Day parade—the largest of the Infantry, Cavalry, Artillery kind in Europe—has been held almost every summer since 1880, with a break during the Second World War, when it took place once in London in 1940 under De Gaulle (the Paris parade was also canceled in 2020 because of the COVID-19 pandemic).

Not only does France possess one of the most capable and well-equipped armies in the world, but the government continually promotes military service as a secure route to social cohesion. National service, including conscription for all healthy males, officially dates back to 1798, but recruitment spiraled in the years leading up to the First World War, and it continued after the Second World War, right up until 1997. Citizens aged between sixteen and twenty-five are still obliged to report for a Defense and Citizenship Day aimed at introducing young people to the military and fostering civic values. This special day is also used to check up on illiteracy rates.

Macron was the first President not to have done any military service at all, but he proposed a reintroduction of compulsory service for all—if not in the army then for a charity or other noble cause—while on the electoral campaign trail in 2017. Polls regularly showed a vast majority of the country favored it. One carried out by the French Institute of Public Opinion (IFOP) in January 2015 for the *Ouest-France* newspaper found that 81 percent of men and 78 percent of women supported a return to national service, agreeing that "France needs powerful tools to help promote integration, to mix young people of different social backgrounds and levels, and to instill Republican values and national cohesion."

Martial spirit extends to domestic policing in France like nowhere else in Europe. The *Gendarmerie* can safely be described as paramilitary, and those troops are supported by the Republican Security Companies (*Compagnies Républicaines de Sécurité*, or CRS) who in 1944 were set up by De Gaulle to replace the Vichy regime's domestic reserve forces at a time when the Nazis were still occupying part of France. The CRS soon built up a reputation of their own for extreme brutality. Unlike gendarmes, CRS officers are civilians specializing in anti-insurrection techniques. If you ever see a group of them massing in Paris—and you will, because they are everywhere—then don't ask them to deal with a theft or mugging. Their principal mission is riot control.

The CRS's first ever significant mission, in 1947, was to control millions of strikers across France. Many of the early CRS recruits were Communists who had fought in the French Resistance during the Second World War, and they were largely opposed to strike breaking. Some of the CRS companies were dissolved when they refused to go into action against comrade trade unionists. It was a time when military interventions in the affairs of state were to become commonplace, with attempted coups d'état in both 1958 and 1961.

The Algerian War was in full flow in 1958, when European settlers attacked the Governor-General's headquarters in Algiers and demanded a government that wanted to maintain French Algeria. *Le Général* was considered the only man capable of preventing the North African conflict from turning into a full-blown one in mainland France.

Far-right militants who marched down the Champs-Élysées from the Arc de Triomphe in support of the May 13, 1958, Putsch in Algeria included a young Jean-Marie Le Pen. Exceptional powers were needed to deal with such militants and, of course, the Algerian nationalists. At the time, the Fourth Republic—set up in 1946 after the ignominy of Nazi Occupation—was flimsy and very unpopular. The institutional framework of the new Fifth Republic was forged in line with an emergency government dealing with an escalating war. De Gaulle, the Second World War hero, thus started his career as a quasi-dictator, and ensured France would be run along similar lines right up until the present.

The role of armed force was central to most of De Gaulle's projects, and it would remain so. The military-industrial complex was expanded as *le Général* attempted to assert his country's grandeur over the superpower United States and other rivals, such as the United Kingdom. By 1961, French troops, and Foreign Légionnaires in particular, were outraged that De Gaulle was speaking about abandoning Algeria, especially because so many French Army officers had supported his installation as head of state in 1958.

In April 1961, the Generals' Putsch saw officers calling on their troops to ignore the government in Paris and to focus on saving France's most prestigious colony. De Gaulle ordered the soldiers to resist the coup "by all means" and then delivered a TV address in his Second World War uniform. He called on both troops and French citizens to back him. Strikes were held in support of De Gaulle, and airfields were occupied to prevent planes from Algeria landing in mainland France. By April 25, after four days of turbulence, the coup had failed. General Maurice Challe, its leader, told Hélie de Saint Marc, Commander of the Légionnaire parachute regiment that had supported him, "You are young, Saint Marc. We are going to pay a heavy price. I will certainly be shot. Let me surrender alone."

Both men were arrested the following morning and in fact got off lightly. Challe served only five years of a fifteen-year prison sentence before being pardoned by De Gaulle. Saint Marc got a decade in prison, but he, too, was pardoned. The paradox here was that De Gaulle had appealed to the French to resist a military coup while dressed as a soldier. The truth was that the Fifth Republic he had set up three years earlier was based on the militarization of society. De Gaulle had flooded the country with soldiers and paramilitary troops fearing threats from all quarters—from French Muslims from Algeria (as they were called) to Communists. The executive power invested in a single individual could not have been stronger, and it was all considered essential by De Gaulle and his lieutenants. The old-style parliamentary system that had collapsed along with the Fourth Republic was not deemed strong enough to deal with the increasing turbulence of the modern world.

Opponents accused *le Général* of using a permanent coup d'état to keep himself in power. They said it institutionalized a civil war that continues. Nowadays, France remains profoundly marked by this period of turmoil. A Jupiter is perfectly placed to crush ongoing dissent.

CRS detachments were set up in most overseas territories, including in Algeria during the War of Independence. Much of the over-policing of France with paramilitaries stems from this colonial period, when the French became experts at dealing with what was known as "revolutionary warfare." Their often barbaric techniques translated easily to domestic policing, to the extent that French law-and-order stormtroopers were compared to those of banana republics in South America and Africa.

This is why discourse about the minority communities alleged to be behind much of the trouble in French society is still so often carried out in colonial language. Dark-skinned suspects from immigrant or perceived "alien" backgrounds are clamped down upon, just as they were in the French colonies. Curfews and states of emergency—all regularly deployed against "troublesome" Algerians—are still used to keep those who are supposedly "foreign" in their place. "Enemy within" tropes are also continually propagated by those in power. Questions of identity and race retain maximum importance, despite the absurd claim that the Republic is color-blind.

These are the main reasons why France is one of the few countries in Europe to have dedicated units of riot control officers. The defenders of the state are on constant alert. In between training for the moments when trouble arises, they circulate in cities like Paris in convoys of vans. They put their flashing lights and sirens on randomly, simply to show that they are there and ready for combat.

Policing the Police

The development of police units runs in parallel with France's long history of insurrection. Their overall role is defined by Article 12 of the Declaration of the Rights of Man and of the Citizen, dated August 26, 1789. It states that "in order to guarantee the rights of men and of the citizen, a public force is necessary."

It is meant to act in the interests of all, and not solely to the advantage of those in government. To try to prevent abuses of power, three main forces were set up: the *Police Nationale*, *Gendarmerie Nationale*, and *Police Municipale*. The broad idea was that if one mutinied—as a whole regiment of Légionnaires did in Algeria—the others were there to fight back. The term *gendarmerie* derives from *les gens d'armes* (the people who bear arms) and was first established to bring police forces under the control of the revolutionary regime after 1789.

Interior Ministers in France are notoriously pugilistic and frequently set up new fighting units. Nicolas Sarkozy created the anti-riot Security and Intervention companies, focusing on civic disorder in suburban housing estates, for example. These ultra-tough intervention units travel around in motorbike gangs, like something out of *Easy Rider* or *Mad Max*. They carry truncheons, tear-gas sprayers, and firearms. When things get hot, they can whip out orange armbands to identify themselves, but often they find it easier to attack victims without identifying themselves at all. It is sometimes difficult to distinguish them from the delinquents they are meant to be arresting.

With all these aggressive gangs running around, it is little wonder that the business of policing has become so controversial. The route for marches is frequently agreed with local prefects, but unofficial demonstrations have become more prevalent. Even when there is cooperation between demonstrators and the authorities, groups break off and attack cars, cafés, or monuments such as the Arc de Triomphe. Radical outfits such as the anarchist *Black Blocs* often hijack a march, ignoring what it is protesting about to concentrate on destroying symbols of Western capitalism, such as Porsche and Mercedes cars or fast-food outlets.

What you soon notice is that the French police seldom, if ever, attempt de-escalation. This is mainly because they are trained and equipped to fight, not negotiate. There are no talks between demonstrators and senior officers. In countries such as Belgium, Holland, and Germany, bullhorns and digital screens are used to message protesters about police intentions. The French never show any interest in subduing anybody peacefully. They allow the violence to start—even trigger it at times—and then move in using extreme force.

Onlookers could certainly have got the impression of a nation at war with itself during the regular *Gilets Jaunes* riots between 2018 and 2019, when there were some 4,300 injuries to both police and protesters.[5] Most of the officers on duty were hiding their faces behind helmets and balaclavas, but in terms of profile—mainly burly

Caucasians—they were remarkably similar to the *Gilets Jaunes* themselves. Officers I spoke to informally expressed their support for the
movement, which had started online as a one-million-signature petition against rising fuel prices.

The *Gilets Jaunes* were particularly angry that Jupiter had introduced a new green tax to help reduce carbon emissions and combat
global warming. Rural workers who relied heavily on their cars were
massively involved. They saw the high cost of petrol and diesel as being
typical of the economic inequality and social injustice that dominated
France. Muscular demonstrations were organized on social media
sites such as Facebook. There were no official *Gilets Jaunes* leaders—
just determined protesters—and early targets for blockades included
roundabouts and crude oil refineries. There was widespread support
from nonrioters too. A BVA Group poll carried out during one weekend
of intense violence found 71 percent of the public backed the protesters. Commentators expressed sorrow for shopkeepers whose windows
were smashed, but many agreed it was worth it, because this was the
French way.

Confrontations with the police became more frequent, and there
were serious casualties. Blast balls fired by officers led to protesters losing eyes and limbs, and some *Gilets Jaunes* died as a result of tragic
traffic accidents. Saturdays became quasi-official riot days, and the
once-a-week disturbances were referred to in theatrical terms. The Arc
de Triomphe sacking came on December 1, 2018, and was known as
"Act III." In terms of mass protests in France, the *Gilets Jaunes* may
have been novel, but the violence was not.

Most significant of all, the *Gilets Jaunes* riots achieved quick
results. Three weeks of turmoil across France led Macron to announce
a U-turn in government policy in early December 2018. The President abandoned the fuel tax rise that had originally triggered the
trouble. He said there would be a six-month freeze on the eco-tax and
then promised that the measure would be dropped from the 2019
budget altogether. He had listened to the street, and the street had
won. Buoyed by their success, the *Gilets Jaunes* pledged to carry on
fighting—for pretty much anything and everything, including the
end of the Fifth Republic itself.

Government officials tried vainly to separate the rioters from the demonstrators, saying extreme elements who vandalized property—so-called *casseurs*—had infiltrated the *Gilets Jaunes* from both Left and Right movements. As Prime Minister Édouard Philippe put it after another intense day of trouble in March 2019, "Today's actions are not the work of protesters, but of looters, arsonists, and criminals. No cause justifies this violence."

President Macron himself returned from a skiing holiday at about the same time to say, "There are people today who try by all means to damage the Republic by breaking and destroying things, while running the risk of killing someone."

In fact, there was nothing momentary or unusual in any of it. The French capital has been associated with some of the worst riots in human history, and it is always a certain type who does very well out of them.

The Right Type of Rioters

Many of the rioters around the Arc de Triomphe were sons and daughters of *la France profonde*, the country's traditional provincial heartland. They were farmers, shopkeepers, truckers, and low-level civil servants. They appeared angry but elated. I recalled the lyrics of the Clash song "White Riot". It would certainly have been a fitting musical accompaniment to the *Gilets Jaunes* insurrection. During weeks of disturbances, there was barely a brown or Black face in sight. This absence was particularly notable in major cities such as Paris, where vast suburban communities habitually blamed for all social ills showed no interest in joining. It was the same in March 2023, when nights of violence erupted after Macron forced through a rise in the pension age from sixty-two to sixty-four without a parliamentary vote. Everybody, from the *casseurs* to thugs fighting the police, was overwhelmingly fair-skinned. Reactionary commentators and other bigots who like to dwell on a mythical "enemy within" were very disappointed by this.

When the Arc de Triomphe itself was ransacked, there was an outcry, especially when the statue of Marianne had her marble face smashed in and the Tomb of the Unknown Soldier was desecrated. It later emerged that the vandals included neo-Nazis obsessed with the Third Reich. The sense of an entire civilization being under attack was furthered week after week, with fires lit all over Paris, from just outside the postmodern Jeu de Paume art gallery to the medieval Saint-Germain Abbey. There were even skirmishes next to Les Invalides, where the tomb of Napoléon Bonaparte lies beneath a golden dome.

If the usual housing estate suspects had been involved in such acts of destruction, you could be sure that the establishment's "us against them" clamor would have gone into overdrive. Just imagine a group of Muslim or Black African men using a stolen forklift truck to bring down the main door of a government ministry, as the *Gilets Jaunes* did on one of their "day of rage" Saturdays. Or picture a well-organized gang of them attempting to assault the Élysée Palace itself or throwing a smoke grenade into a police van in order to steal an assault rifle, as happened in December 2018.

Words like "terrorist" and "radicalized" roll easily off the tongue when alleged lawbreakers fit a stereotype, but this was by no means the case when they are representing a movement from *la France profonde*. Banks, private homes, and cars were seriously damaged. Millions of euros worth of goods were looted, not least of all from luxury shops around the Champs-Élysées. Such scenes were replicated in most French cities and major towns. As propagandists struggled to link the chaos with those from immigrant backgrounds, white riot privilege allowed the Yellow Vest agitation to become routine.

Desperate to pacify the white rioters, Macron originally gave them some $10 billion worth of government concessions. Meanwhile, criminal courts were reluctant to hand down anything except for token punishments against those *Gilets Jaunes* rioters who were actually caught. This was despite their haphazard road blockades leading to horrifying accidents that claimed lives.

Contrast all this with 2005, the last time there were disturbances across France linked to ethnic minority communities living on housing estates. Then, the trouble was in fact triggered by police: the deaths of the teenage boys from electrocution while hiding from officers in an electricity substation in Clichy-sous-Bois, one of the most isolated of Paris's suburbs, were enough to mobilize hundreds of thousands. They rose up as their grievances ranged from anger at police brutality to discrimination in all walks of life.

The *banlieusards* involved were not allowed anywhere near central Paris, let alone the monuments of state, and were left to rampage through their own squalid housing warrens. They were given next to nothing in terms of government appeasement either. Instead, Sarkozy literally called them "scum." As a form of collective punishment, almost 6,000 were arrested, and nearly 1,500, including minors, received custodial sentences. Some suspects were threatened with deportation and having their French citizenship revoked.

Nowadays, the dismal prospects for social advancement for minorities, and the way they are treated by a ruthless establishment, remain unchanged. In many cases they are far worse. This was made abundantly clear when a police chief was caught on camera repeatedly punching an unarmed Black man during a *Gilets Jaunes* rally in the southern port city of Toulon in January 2019. The victim had his head banged against a wall. He was not even wearing a yellow vest.

Unsurprisingly, the Toulon prosecutor cleared the accused police commander of any wrongdoing within a day, saying he had used "appropriate force" after being knocked over by different protesters two hours earlier. This version of events was contradicted by videos showing that the bellicose officer had, in fact, been the first to administer blows after deploying a telescopic truncheon. Nevertheless, Commander Didier Andrieux had just been made a Légion d'Honneur. The fact that a career policeman associated with this type of horrendous conduct has been awarded France's highest medal for civilian and military merit says so much about how institutionalized the behavior is.

Gilets Jaunes, and those who opposed pension reform, were certainly being punched, beaten with truncheons, and smothered in chemical weapons on protest days. Projectiles called flash-balls, developed by a French firearms manufacturer, and ostensibly nonlethal grenades had been used to maim and otherwise hurt them, but these white rioters are not receiving anything like the state-condoned abuse that ethnic minorities still endure every day of the week.

Double Standards

Policing in France continues to be among the most violent in the world. The Macron administration has significantly bolstered the number of paramilitary troops, and indeed regular soldiers, on the streets. Before he came to power, the *Vigipirate* anti-terrorist plan was expanded to try to ensure safety around places of worship, schools, and hospitals. Up to seven thousand military personnel were deployed across the country. Armored cars became commonplace on street corners. Macron also introduced a law of "comprehensive security" that included French citizens being asked to engage in counterterrorism methods, looking out for fellow citizens acting suspiciously and reporting them.

A culture of paranoia did much to invigorate an increasingly sinister security state. It was further reinforced by the COVID-19 pandemic when lockdowns were accompanied by vast exercises in social surveillance. There were curfews and other security measures ostensibly aimed at keeping everybody fit and healthy. Police and gendarmes were dispatched to set up random checkpoints all around the country. This generated large amounts of money for the government and allowed them to tighten control over a rebellious population. If you could not produce a self-authorization form containing your identification details and your motives for leaving home, then you were liable to a fine of €135. When officers met resistance, they quickly invoked the emergency law and could stop and search. As usual, racial profiling was prominent.

Punishments of a one-year jail sentence plus a €45,000 fine were also threatened for anyone who shared a recording of a police officer— specifically, "disseminating by any means whatsoever and whatever the medium, with the aim of damaging his physical or mental integrity, the image of the face or any other element of identification of an official of the national police or of a soldier of the national gendarmerie when acting within the framework of a police operation."

The pandemic made matters worse, but the repression was nothing new. A classic example of the way the French authorities actively encourage confrontation, and indeed violence, is the way they try to ban major demonstrations. This happened in 2014, for example, when President François Hollande abandoned his "man of the people" liberal roots to throw his support behind a ban on Paris's vast pro-Palestine movement protesting against the attack on Gaza, in which one thousand Palestinian civilians, including hundreds of children, had been slaughtered by Israeli forces. Hollande said he did not want the Arab-Israeli conflict being "imported" to France.

Three days separated an entirely peaceful pro-Palestine march in Paris and one that turned violent. The first, on a Wednesday, was authorized by France's Socialist government; the second, on Saturday, was not. You do not need to be an expert in crowd control to draw a very simple conclusion from this: if you try to stop people from exercising their democratic right to demonstrate, then they are likely to exercise it anyway.

Amnesty International had said as much before the Saturday rally, which ended in seventy arrests and twenty-seven mainly young men being charged with a variety of minor public order offenses. In a strongly worded condemnation of Hollande's government, Amnesty said that it should not be allowed to suppress the "peaceful intentions" of the vast majority of demonstrators, who should enjoy the "fundamental right of peaceful assembly."

The banned demonstration coincided with the arrival in Paris of US Secretary of State John Kerry and numerous foreign ministers pushing for peace and, more specifically, an immediate cease-fire in Gaza.[6] The attempt by the Socialists to gag thousands of decent Parisians calling for exactly the same thing was shameful.

Many of Hollande's older Socialist Party colleagues were in fact *soixante-huitards* ('68ers): mainly bourgeois, white radicals who once thought that the way to bring about change was to organize riots in central Paris in May 1968. The difference was that the pro-Palestine demonstrations also involved thousands of Muslims from Arab and African backgrounds. The vast majority held the same values as those innocents being killed in Gaza.

I covered every one of the protests across Paris at the time, interviewing Jews, Christians, Muslims, and members of almost every other creed and no creed who wanted to express their support for the blighted people of Palestine. Everybody—including Hollande and his government colleagues—had every right to disagree with them, but the cynical campaign to get demonstrations outlawed was an outrage.

Pointless restrictions were also announced in June 2020, when the Paris police prefecture tried to ban shows of support for Adama Traoré, a Frenchman from a Malian background who had allegedly been killed while in custody on his twenty-fourth birthday four years previously.

Double standards are well reflected in "White Riot," a song about those who do not usually take to the streets being tempted to do exactly that. The *Gilets Jaunes* pushed their alleged oppressors to the very limit, because they knew white rioters would get away with a lot more than those who are far more reviled and whose problems are much more pressing.

The near constant use of cameras at French demonstrations by the *Gilets Jaunes* from November 2018 turned the issue of police violence into a subject for widespread debate. A stream of horror videos emerged including protesters losing eyes and hands to projectiles, while others showed crowds succumbing to noxious gas.

Chemical Weapons

An aspect of riot control that is seldom debated properly in France is the state's never-ending deployment of tear gas against its own citizens. No matter who is protesting—students, environmentalists, pro-Palestinians—the catalyst for much social disorder is almost always the use of gas. Astonishing as it may sound, French police are allowed to discharge substances designed to burn eyes, mouths, lungs, and skin against ordinary civilians, but, because of international treaties, soldiers up against genuine enemies are not. The 1899 Hague Declaration concerning asphyxiating gases made battlefield chemical and biological weapons illegal; it was followed by the 1925 Geneva Gas Protocol because it was actually the French who first implemented tear gas as a chemical weapon on the battlefield, hurling twenty-six-millimeter grenades full of lethal lacrimatory agents (ethyl bromoacetate) into German positions at the very start of the First World War in August 1914. By 1915, chlorine gas and worse was in artillery shells, causing the most horrifying massacres imaginable.

Although the International Committee of the Red Cross also banned chemical and biological weapons after the First World War, it still warns of a "slippery slope" that could see them reintroduced, particularly since the ban has inexplicably failed to apply to domestic riot control chemical agents such as tear gas. This raises the ongoing fear that the sort of compounds in Macron's armored cars could easily become stronger, to the point of causing fatalities.

France also set up primitive gas chambers during its conquest of Algeria in the nineteenth century—long before the Nazis. The extermination program was instigated by Thomas Robert Bugeaud, France's Governor-General of Algeria in the 1840s, who in a parliamentary address recommended scorched-earth policies to lethally subdue Algerians and "exterminate them to the last one," so as to place *pieds-noirs* anywhere "there is fresh water and fertile land . . . without concerning oneself to whom these lands belong." These policies included so-called *enfumades*, a killing technique that involved trapping entire indigenous tribes in caves and setting fire to the entrance, thus asphyxiating them with noxious fumes.[7]

The use of chemicals has a particularly horrific place in the history of crimes against humanity, yet its indiscriminate usage by France's security state on its own citizens has long been viewed as an acceptable part of life. While police forces in countries such as Britain will only resort to noxious substances very occasionally and in tiny measure, regular deployment in France has become institutionalized.

Those of us who were out on the streets of Paris on the second Saturday in December 2018 were covered in vast white clouds of tear gas, from Place de l'Opéra to the Champs-Élysées. It was "Act IV" of the *Gilets Jaunes* protests, and tear gas, designed to inflict harm on the human body, was once again seen as the best way of controlling the protesters. I saw plenty of distressed boys and girls coughing and wheezing as they struggled to breathe and their lungs and eyes burned. It was the same for others who also had absolutely nothing to do with the demonstrations—from asthmatic pensioners watching from balconies to terrified diners in the few restaurants that remained open during the disturbances.

What was particularly sinister about the freezing Paris streets on what should have been the penultimate shopping Saturday before Christmas was the presence of armored vehicles containing huge quantities of a highly concentrated chemical powder. The *Marianne* news outlet revealed that this largely undefined compound could be spread across some forty thousand square meters in ten seconds, "neutralizing" anybody in the vicinity, whether rioters or innocent bystanders. Richard Carminache, a gendarme colonel, said it was as powerful as two hundred grenades and would be a "last resort" if secure areas around the Élysée Palace and National Assembly were overrun.[8]

There were already eight thousand armed security personnel searching and herding everybody in Paris, meaning the *Gilets Jaunes* were outnumbered by at least four to one. In which case, what was the point in adding motorized military hardware and state-of-the-art chemical weapon dischargers to historic squares and boulevards? Veteran journalists who had worked in Eastern Europe during the Cold War suggested that the atmosphere was more like that found in unruly satellite states under Soviet dictatorship than the normally glamorous capital of France in 2018.

There is still much scientific debate about the deaths of more than 170 people by gassing during the Moscow theater crisis of 2002, when still-unidentified chemicals were distributed by Russian special forces to end a siege by Chechen terrorists. One of the principal reasons for outlawing all chemical weapons would be to prevent security states from developing ever more damaging products that are extremely difficult to analyze, let alone regulate.

Despite being a member of the Hague-based Organization for the Prohibition of Chemical Weapons, France displays little enthusiasm for this type of control. On the contrary, establishment figures see few problems with high-density substances they know nothing about.

When I discussed Paris's chemical powder–launching devices on Twitter, I was immediately reprimanded by a press officer at the French

Embassy in London, who said it was "inaccurate" to describe tear gas as a "chemical weapon" and even claimed this factual, literal, scientific, and legal definition was unethical. She was disturbingly wrong, as are all those who underplay the increasingly desperate measures that the Macron administration is taking to subdue dissenting French citizens, as well as those unlucky enough to be caught up in their protests.

Perhaps unsurprisingly, the worst gassing I have ever experienced was when the Algerian national football team—*les Fennecs*—won the Africa Cup of Nations in 2019. Hundreds of canisters rained down on thousands of men, women, and children who were celebrating on the Champs-Élysées. Among them were families with toddlers in strollers.

The crowd also included the kind of young men of North African appearance whom the French police, and especially those in Paris, tend to despise. I heard the screams of those caught in the worst *mêlées*, including the crying boys and girls who were vomiting and shaking with fear as the fumes spread. It was a balmy evening, and there were next to no hiding places on the Champs-Élysées itself. As the number of gas projectiles increased, many of the teenage fans ended up in side streets, where looting and vandalism took place. This is a classic pattern visible in numerous riots in Paris, not least of all those involving the *Gilets Jaunes*. The trouble is absolutely inexcusable, but the contribution of the gas toward already highly fraught situations is undeniable.

Despite all this, it was only the English-language media that reported on the gassing of children. Marine Le Pen, leader of the Rassemblement National, called for a ban on the Algeria football fans on the Champs-Élysées after actively encouraging the far more destructive and violent *Gilets Jaunes* to gather there.

The terrifying treatment of Liverpool football fans at the Champions League final in Paris in May 2022 did at least trigger international condemnation of the local police. Witnesses and videos testified to people scared for their lives, with children trembling with fear as officers fired tear gas into crowds outside the Stade de France. Tens of thousands of supporters were guided under a bridge near the stadium, with many left waiting for hours. Some were forced to clamber over barriers as queues began to swell behind them, and the kickoff was delayed by

thirty-six minutes after riot police moved in. It was further proof that
Paris police are capable of appalling abuses of power.

Street Fighting Man

A notable aspect of French mythmaking is the way the dramatic events
of May 1958 are nowadays woefully underplayed, while the compar-
atively far less effective protests of May 1968 are still commemorated
and indeed revered. The buildup to the '68 riots began in March of that
year on the University of Paris campus in the western suburb of Nanterre. It was a time when mainly white, Catholic, middle-class students
were rebelling against their parents, and indeed the teachers, priests,
and bosses whom—along with the police—they viewed as oppressors.

Vague demands of the young centered on an end to the Vietnam
War and to the excesses of capitalism. They also wanted more freedom
to sleep with one another in campus dormitories. The Summer of Love
had taken place a year before, when hippies converged on San Francisco
championing sexual freedom, hallucinogenic drugs, and the rejection
of consumerism. Serious politics took second place to a feel-good celebration of sensual pleasure, and that suited the French just fine.

When some of the students at Nanterre were arrested and the university temporarily closed, street fighting began on May 3. Factory
workers joined in, and by mid-May, some ten million people were
involved in the protest movement. The French economy ground to a
halt, along with transport systems. French TV and radio were mainly
controlled by the state at the time, leaving private and foreign broad-
casters to cover what was going on. Thousands were beaten by police,
mainly CRS units brandishing long batons and using tear gas. The rioters dug up Paris's cobblestone streets and hurled the debris at the forces
of law and order while starting fires and overturning cars. Symbols of
capitalism were attacked, and graffiti—much of it very poetic—was
painted everywhere.

By the time President De Gaulle left the country on May 29, it
seemed like a full-blown revolution might be in the offing. De Gaulle
arrived by helicopter at a French military base in Germany, allegedly to

see how many tanks he had available to fight back. He then returned to Paris to address the nation via a live TV broadcast, just as he had so often in the past. He would not resign, he said, but instead dissolve Parliament and hold new elections. The next day, May 30, hundreds of thousands marched along the Champs-Élysées in support of De Gaulle. His Finance Minister, Michel Debré, and Culture Minister, André Malraux, were among those pictured linking arms by the Tomb of the Unknown Soldier. De Gaulle had triumphed. In new elections held in June, his Gaullist party gained an outright parliamentary majority.

Despite the essential failure of France's most famous pseudo-revolution, those of us born and brought up in the Paris suburbs long after May '68 have never been able to ignore its legacy. The so-called *événements* remain a subject of endless discussion. The nostalgic focus is always on thousands of fresh-faced demonstrators battling riot police around the beauty of the Sorbonne. The medieval university was occupied and turned into a symbol of antiestablishment protest. That is why the legions of misty-eyed chroniclers reminisce about a period of exuberant volatility that could have changed French society for the better.

In fact, it did nothing of the sort. There was no brave new world, and those of us whose futures were effectively ignored by the movement's instigators and the ineffectual reformers who came after them are the ones with the most to complain about. Millions of ethnic minority French citizens are as alienated from society as they were more than half a century ago, and that is a cause for national shame.

Let's start with the real birthplace of May '68. It was not ancient Paris at all, but the capital's troubled outer districts, where France was struggling to accommodate its former colonial subjects. More specifically, an American-style extension to the Sorbonne was being built in the town of Nanterre. Its campus model was meant to represent inclusion, a chance to open up higher education. Poignantly, the glittering new buildings were taking shape next to the then largest immigrant shantytown in France. It contained ten thousand Algerians who were without a permanent home but who were desperate to find low-paid manual work. A 1964 law had officially banned the *bidonvilles*, but their population was growing.[9]

Revisionists have claimed that the March 22 student movement that occupied Nanterre's main administrative center in 1968 was concerned with the plight of the poor and disenfranchised, but there is scant evidence to support this. Examine the photographs and films of those who took to the streets, and you will see that they were overwhelmingly white. The leaders were predominantly middle-class, too, as were those who produced the music, poetry, and other literature that sealed the 1968 myth. "Street Fighting Man," by the Rolling Stones, became the anthem of the period.

Yes, workers from minority communities participated in the strikes that accompanied the rioting, but a lack of identity papers often excluded them from the trade unions that joined the students. As today, many from immigrant backgrounds stayed away from officialdom because of the constant menace of deportation.

People from minority communities were particularly fearful of the police. Contrary to the misinformation, the brutal reputation of the armed and baton-wielding CRS was not earned in 1968 but during the Algerian War. Remember that after one peaceful pro-independence demonstration in Paris on October 17, 1961, up to three hundred Algerians were murdered by the police. Many were thrown into the Seine and drowned close to the Sorbonne. Thousands more were rounded up, beaten, even tortured.

In comparison, '68 was far less bloody. There were no fatalities, and those arrested were generally well treated. Despite dramatic images of burning cars and smashed pavements, the riots were more of an early media spectacle than a genuine display of grievance.

The French economy was doing very well at the time, as the *Trente Glorieuses*—thirty boom years starting in 1945—kept the traditional bourgeoisie replete with disposable cash and consumer goods. None had any real stomach for a fight. Some claim Charles de Gaulle's administration was threatened at one point, but a simple call for new parliamentary elections in June 1968 was enough to end all the trouble.

Paris is a city of illusion, and those who watched the *événements* fizzle out as quickly as they started soon began to fantasize, awarding the protests a significance that was not warranted. Now *bidonvilles* like the ones in Nanterre have been turned into Sensitive Urban Zones— state jargon for areas of decrepit housing, high unemployment, and rampant discrimination. Unlike countries like Britain, where integration and social mobility have been given a far higher priority, France's "territorial, social, and ethnic apartheid" persists, in the words of former Socialist Prime Minister Manuel Valls. There is a national amnesia.

Pledges are made to pour millions of euros into improving estates, but this really misses the point. What is required is for *banlieues* residents to be permitted to move into mainstream society and to be guaranteed equal opportunities there. They need to be treated like the *soixante-huitards*, most of whom are now enjoying comfortable retirements as their children and grandchildren prosper in their France, a country of exceptionally high living standards for those from the right backgrounds.

In terms of protest, the Fifth Republic started with government-organized violence being used to fight dissent. It was a time of terrorism carried out by agents of the state, officially and unofficially. There were assassination attempts, bombings, murderous repression, and torture. It was not a period of democracy or a welcome new start but a time of lethal cynicism, with a new regime held together by myths and brutal paramilitary troops.

Getting rid of the paramilitary police and replacing them with community officers would go a long way toward demilitarizing France and making protest a less antagonistic business. Officers would get to know fellow citizens and try to work with them, rather than against them. Everybody should be allowed to film what they like in public, especially police activities. Clear communication between protesters and those maintaining law and order would also help. Why not remove the need for dedicated riot squads altogether? Other European countries get by fine without them, even if regular police sometimes have to don body armor and full-face helmets.

Ditching measures that hark back to colonialism, such as curfews and states of emergency, would ensure that members of ethnic minorities do not end up feeling like their forebears when they take to the streets. Trying to ban legitimate protest, and failing abysmally, is another tactic that the French authorities should review with some urgency. Ending the highly provocative but routine use of gas would help turn protesters into members of a nation that believes in legitimate protest, rather than an autocratic one that smothers it using chemical weapons.

5

TERRORISM

Exemplary Vengeance

Terror is nothing else than justice, prompt, severe, inflexible.

—MAXIMILIEN DE ROBESPIERRE (1758–1794)

There were unwitting cheers when the first suicide bomber in France's history blew himself and a bystander up outside the Stade de France. To begin with, hardly anybody knew what the explosion really signified: most assumed it was a supersized firecracker ignited by a rowdy football supporter during a friendly between Les Bleus and Germany at the national stadium. The France defender on the ball looked mildly concerned as he played a clumsy back pass in the opposite direction to where he was looking, but otherwise the match went on.

It was 9:20 p.m. on November 13, 2015, an unseasonably warm Friday night. President François Hollande was among the eighty thousand people packed into one of the great symbols of modern France. It was here, in 1998, that a team of Frenchmen from numerous ethnic backgrounds had won the World Cup, uniting an unofficially multicultural nation in glory. The arena, in the northern Paris suburb of Saint-Denis, became a resplendent distraction from the kind of social problems that plagued the troubled *cités* surrounding it. *Le Stade* represented nationalistic pride and passion, a place of sporting greatness showing off the very best of a united Republic.

None of that mattered to the foreign-born terrorist who set off his explosives belt outside Gate D, on the Rue Rimet. The killer—a recent immigrant from Iraq or Syria whose identity has never been firmly established—had been seen in the toilets of a fast-food outlet a few minutes before, wiping sweat off his face and shaking visibly as he stared into a mirror. Then came the blast and accompanying low thud.

At pretty much the same time, the rattle of assault rifles broke through the conversation and laughter outside a bar less than ten miles away. It was called Le Carillon, a word that means "chime" in English. Many of those drinking and smoking on the packed terrace near the Canal Saint-Martin also thought firecrackers were going off. Again, there were one or two cheers at the loud noise, especially from those who had been drinking since arriving from work. Some of those sitting on wooden chairs or springless sofas inside jumped up, peering through the windows in the mauve-painted wood façade, beyond the blackboards offering pints of beer for €3 and free Wi-Fi. Their faces were young and inquisitive. All stayed put, refusing to believe that unusual bangs could upset their night out.

Then blood began to spurt on to the pavement on Rue Bichat. It mixed with the spilled drinks and cigarette butts. There were screams of agony and panic. Gunmen wearing suicide belts packed with explosives could be seen picking off targets at will. The bars and restaurants were in the 10th Arrondissement of Paris, and just a stroll from the offices of *Charlie Hebdo*, the magazine that had lost cartoonists and other staff in a gun attack in January of that year. Police commandoes and army units had flooded historic boulevards and squares in the hunt for the *Charlie Hebdo* attackers before they, too, were eliminated. Two days later, another terrorist had laid siege to a kosher supermarket and killed four Jewish shoppers before he himself was killed by police.

By November, France had raised security to its highest level, deploying troops in all major cities. The government had pledged a crackdown on radicals and the ease with which they had acquired weapons, but it would make no difference. The Friday, November 13 killers moved around Paris as if they owned the place, maiming at will. During a single night of horror, they succeeded in killing 130 people and wounding more than 400. Worst hit was the Bataclan music venue, on the Boulevard Voltaire. Almost 1,500 people were packed in to watch the American band Eagles of Death Metal when three fanatics stormed in with assault rifles. The song "Kiss the Devil" was being performed when the shooting started. At first, some thought the noise was part of a pyrotechnic display linked to the act, but then the victims began to pile on top of each other in the dark, confined space. There were ninety deaths and hundreds more wounded.

ISIS, the self-styled Islamic State of Iraq and Syria, claimed responsibility for the November Paris attacks. It said they were in retaliation for French air strikes on their fiefdom straddling Iraq and Syria. Two of the attackers—both blown up at the Stade de France—were from ISIS's self-proclaimed caliphate, while the seven other so-called commandoes were born in France and Belgium. At the time, ISIS saw itself as a transnational power, one that claimed authority over anyone linked to Islam. They had overcome their former partners, Al-Qaeda, to become the leading jihadist group in the world. The ISIS black flag was easily recognizable, even though it failed to convey the extent of their nihilistic cruelty, which could be traced back to the abject chaos caused by the Iraq War when an American-led alliance invaded the country in 2003. The ISIS caliphate was meant to be the successor to past Islamic empires, including the Ottomans.

This illusion did not stop ISIS operatives from killing and maiming Muslims indiscriminately, including plenty in Paris. They had every opportunity to engage with soldiers and police but preferred to target unarmed civilians who had no hope of defending themselves. ISIS had learned how to turn vile acts into global propaganda, using burgeoning social media platforms, along with compliant mainstream broadcast outlets and bellicose politicians, to spread their evil. President Hollande validated the ISIS myths when he declared a full-scale conflict, saying his country was "at war with terrorism."

Hollande prepared his considerable military forces for battle with an enemy that, domestically, was all but invisible right up until they executed their cowardly acts.

What French authority figures failed to recognize was that one of the country's industrial giants had been directly financing ISIS in the months leading up to November 13. Lafarge—the largest cement producer in the world and a flagship of Gallic commerce ever since its establishment in the nineteenth century—paid millions to the terrorist group to keep the company's operation in Syria open.[1] Lafarge's Director of Security at the time was not only indicted over this financing but a fervent supporter of Marine Le Pen and indeed a candidate for her far-right party. There were even compelling accusations that the French government knew exactly what was going on between Lafarge and ISIS and, at best, turned a blind eye to the corruption.

Shock at the Paris atrocities was qualified by the city's less publicized reputation as the cradle of terrorism. The very word comes from the French *terrorisme*, which originally referred to the mass killings that followed the monumental political and social upheavals of 1789. Thousands of "enemies of the Revolution" were put to death throughout France's *Terreur* of 1793 to 1794, when Maximilien Robespierre used his august position on the inappropriately named Committee of Public Safety to murder and maim. Robespierre, a radical Jacobin who now has a station named after him on line 9 of the Paris Métro, argued that lethal force was the only way to maintain security in post-monarchical France. All citizens of the new Republic were liable to be summarily executed on suspicion of "crimes against liberty," and tens of thousands were.

Before the Reign of Terror had even started, foreign enemies of the Revolution had threatened "exemplary vengeance" against Paris— namely, the "total destruction" of the city and its civilians—if France's royal family was harmed in any way. The Revolutionaries responded with similarly gruesome pledges. It was a time when the Paris writer Louis-Sébastien Mercier described his fellow citizens as "a fighting race," who "lacked all power to control their cruel violence."[2] When the Bastille prison fell in the first major flash point of the 1789 Revolution, rioters proudly placed the head of its commander on a spike, showing off a sadistic streak that would characterize French history for centuries to come.

Numerous other justifications have been offered for terrorism in France since 1789, ranging from the advancement of animal rights to libertarian Communism. The most persistent perpetrators of terrorist violence have been separatist groups in regions such as Brittany, the French Basque Country, and the Mediterranean island of Corsica.

Ilich Ramírez Sánchez, the Venezuelan hit man better known as Carlos the Jackal, helped seal his gruesome legend with a range of grenade and gun attacks in Paris throughout the 1970s and '80s, and in his case, the liberation of Palestine was the preferred cause. The Jackal remains incarcerated in one of the city's most secure prisons, but those of us who attended one of his most recent trials in 2011 came face-to-face with the master criminal. He used Robespierre-style submissions to tell the court that he was by no means a base killer but "a professional revolutionary." In good health almost three decades after his last known atrocity, the Jackal relished the chance to recount and explain his record as a Paris terrorist. The conditions that allowed him to glide through the French capital, killing and maiming with impunity, had clearly not changed much by November 2015. Like the Jackal before him, the only surviving member of the ISIS suicide gang escaped easily and went on the run for months.

Terror not only played a crucial part in bringing modern France into being but was essential to the founding and development of the current Fifth Republic. The French nation is a militarized one that responds swiftly to lethal attacks, but often in a way that exacerbates the problem. The state works with terrorists, and it is not unusual for authority figures, including senior military officers and police, to become terrorists themselves.

Wolves in the City

Retaliation from the forces of law and order for the November 13 and *Charlie Hebdo* attacks was quick and massive. Most of the terrorists ended up riddled with bullets or blown to pieces, just like their victims. In an age of twenty-four-hour news channels and social media dedicated to instant half-facts and analysis, reportage and commentary on the drama were also brutally contemporaneous. They offered everything from racist diatribes to morbid soul-searching about the state of modern Europe and its alleged underclass. This cacophony highlighted a plethora of acute problems, including the legacy of a bloody colonial history, the rise of global terrorist organizations, and the extremism that grows out of downtrodden communities dumped on the edges of major cities.

In fact, the focus on Islamist terror, and the tiny minority of radicalized thugs from western European countries such as France who are drawn to it, needs widening. Without going too far back in history, we can see how murderous violence forged the identity of the Fifth Republic, at a time when groups such as Al-Qaeda and ISIS had never been heard of. Instead, it was mainly white Christians who followed the violent tradition of the original French Revolution—one of the most barbaric periods in the history of Western civilization.

Typical were those who repeatedly conspired to murder Charles de Gaulle. These would-be assassins also thought nothing of indiscriminately massacring men, women, and children as a means of achieving their political aims at the beginning of the Fifth Republic, turning cities like Paris into their killing fields. The attempted assassination of De Gaulle in the suburb of Petit-Clamart in August 1962 was just one of many outrages carried out by extremist nationalists desperate to keep Algeria part of France.

Up until the November 13 attacks in 2015, the deadliest terrorist attack in modern French history was the Secret Army Organization bombing of the number 12 express train from Strasbourg to Paris, killing twenty-eight civilians and wounding more than a hundred. OAS attacks mainly happened on weekends, when the soldiers and police officers recruited to carry them out were off duty. The train derailed on Sunday, June 18, 1961, while traveling at high speed past the town of Vitry-le-François, in the Marne department of northeast France.

The next day, investigators found the remains of an explosive device in the wreckage. It also emerged that the stationmaster at Vitry-le-François had earlier received an anonymous threatening letter from the OAS saying, "We will blow up the track shortly." He gave it to local police, but there was no follow-up. The note was not made public until two decades later, despite containing a warning that "sabotage actions were to be carried out along the railway lines, in accordance with the orders of insurrectional leaders in Algiers." Jacques Duclos, a French Communist Party member, brought up the possibility of OAS involvement in a parliamentary debate in late 1961, but few were interested. Duclos attacked "the official statements made after the disaster to rule out the possibility of sabotage."

Le Monde reported three years later on February 2, 1964, that "the derailment of Vitry-le-François was caused by an attack." The explosive charge had been placed near a signal, at the exact spot where two express trains had been due to cross, so the death toll could have been far higher. But, to this day, details about the Vitry-le-François carnage remain sparse. Jacques Delarue, who headed an Interior Ministry counterterrorism unit targeting the OAS at the time, later wrote that the plastic explosives were intended to "kill the greatest number of people possible." Despite this, excessive speed, a broken axle, and subsidence on the line were just some of the possible reasons for the disaster preferred by the authorities. The criminal inquiry ended in late 1963, when the State Security Court dismissed it. Documents relating to the attack remained confidential and were hidden away in France's National Archives.

It was only after November 2015 that there were brief references to "this attack which never happened," according to the investigative journalist Pierre Abramovici. He further described it as "the railways attack that remained a state secret." Why? Because Vitry-le-François and all the other major crimes carried out by the OAS were textbook examples of how French establishment figures backed terrorism as an effective political tool.

Jean-Marie Bastien-Thiry, the French Air Force Lieutenant Colonel and weapons engineer who was brought to justice for the Petit-Clamart attempted assassination of De Gaulle, was typical of those involved. He was from a Catholic military family and had three daughters. His wife, Geneviève Lamirand, was herself the daughter of an official who had served in the wartime Vichy government (the rest of her family were Free French). Bastien-Thiry's father, Pierre Bastien-Thiry, was a Lieutenant Colonel who had met De Gaulle professionally during the 1930s. In terms of class and status, the two men were very alike.

De Gaulle pardoned the gunmen who had fired the shots at his car at Petit-Clamart, but—despite a personal appeal from Pierre Bastien-Thiry—refused to let the organizer of the plot go. Calling the younger Bastien-Thiry "an idiot," De Gaulle said he might "get off with twenty years in prison and then I'll free him."[3] De Gaulle was outraged that his wife, an innocent woman, could have been killed, along with other civilians caught up in the shooting, which Bastien-Thiry had directed from afar while acting as a lookout. De Gaulle thought this was all extremely cowardly.

A massive security operation was organized to take Bastien-Thiry to his place of execution on March 11, 1963, when he was thirty-five. Some two thousand police and gendarmes were posted around Fort d'Ivry—part of the fortifications built around Paris in the nineteenth century. There were intelligence reports about a plot to free Bastien-Thiry, who clutched a rosary as he was killed by gunfire.

"The French need martyrs. . . . They must choose them carefully," De Gaulle said afterward. "I gave them Bastien-Thiry. They'll be able to make a martyr of him. He deserves it."[4] In *The Day of the Jackal*, the movie based on these events, Bastien-Thiry was played by the French actor Jean Sorel.

Rigid discipline and obedience to the state came naturally to men like Jean-Marie Bastien-Thiry, yet this did not stop them from being radicalized. In his case, the war against the FLN, Algeria's National Liberation Front, took precedence over anything else, including his loyalty to his President. In their rhetoric, OAS members favored the kind of anti-Muslim fearmongering prevalent among the French Right today. They portrayed Islam as an inherently violent religion focused on world domination, while ignoring the fact that it was actually the

French who invaded Muslim-majority countries and turned their indigenous populations into, at best, a servant class, while also annihilating many of them.

In the words of a former OAS operative who used the pen name Edmond Fraysse, "The way I saw it, the attitude adopted by French authorities left civilians with no choice but to take control of their own destiny. The government's inability to take urgent action against terrorists triggered our activism, at a time when numerous signs indicated that a new outbreak of violence was on the horizon. . . . What motivated me and countless others was failure to act, which we interpreted as cowardice."[5]

By "activism," Fraysse of course meant "terrorism." Describing the assassination of an FLN suspect in the then French-Algerian city of Constantine, Fraysse recounted how he put a balaclava on his head and entered the man's greengrocery with a gun stuffed into his trousers. "While we parked our car on a side street, I kept going over the plan in my head. Once my balaclava was properly on, I was the first to enter the store. I lifted my shirt to grab my gun. The target turned around, registering that his life was in danger, but it was already too late. The first bullet went through his temple, his face contorting grotesquely in response. Until then, everything had gone according to plan, but it turned out that he wasn't alone. Another man, stunned and momentarily paralysed by the bloody scene, tried to hurry away to safety. Making a split-second decision, I took him out, knowing that he, as a witness, could cause us serious trouble during a police investigation later on."

Knives were just as likely to be used by OAS operatives as pistols. Pierre Popie, a devout Catholic and barrister devoted to uniting communities in Algiers through a number of Christian movements, became one of the group's first targets. The organization's Commando Delta attacked his office in Rue de l'Abreuvoir on January 25, 1961, after he went on TV and said, "French Algeria is dead."

As a left-leaning Gaullist, Popie was a member of the Popular Republican Movement, but his commitment to democracy meant nothing to the increasingly reactionary authorities. In May 1958, he had received an expulsion order from the French military, who wanted him out of Algeria, but he had ignored it. During the attack in 1961, Popie, who was thirty at the time, was stabbed at least fourteen times in the head and body.

OAS barbarism was as varied as it was widespread. Its founders were former military officers Pierre Lagaillarde and Raoul Salan, both of whom had served in Algeria. General Salan took part in the Algiers Putsch in 1961. Their operation on the French mainland was called *OAS-Métro* (for Metropolitan), where a campaign of blood and *plasti-quage* caused terror. Plastic explosives were easy to hide in briefcases, elevators, and window boxes. Civilians ranging from cleaning ladies to Education Ministry inspectors were among the two thousand people killed by the organization in the year up to April 1962, in metropolitan France and Algeria itself. Many more were wounded. Paris department stores, nightclubs, boutiques, and private apartments were all hit.

The writer Paul Henissart described the OAS as *Wolves in the City*, the title of his 1970 book about the organization. He recounts how French officers who had suffered a decisive defeat in Indochina against the Communist Viet Minh in 1954 had "come upon Mao Tse-tung's precept on guerrilla war and subversion. It is curious that to the rigidly logical French mind, the proposition of adopting Communist techniques to battle Communism did not seem paradoxical."[6]

Describing the atmosphere in Paris at the height of the OAS bombing campaigns, Henissart wrote, "The three talismanic letters OAS dripped black on school walls. Night fell swiftly, and Parisians learned to recognise the dull whoosh of plastique blasts after dark. One night, a black OAS flag was surreptitiously hoisted atop one of Notre Dame's bell towers, and created a scandal the next morning since it flew in full view of the neighbouring police prefecture."[7]

In their battle against Algerian nationalists and their less determined one against the OAS, the French security services sunk to extremely low depths. They were involved in clandestine sabotage and targeted assassinations. Raymond Muelle, a French commando at the time, said: "The *homo* [homicide] operations were directed by Matignon, the seat of the Prime Minister, which relayed instructions to the External Documentation and Counterespionage Service. But it was Jacques Foccart [a key lieutenant to De Gaulle who was France's Secretary General for African and Malagasy Affairs from 1960 to 1974] over at the Élysée Palace who was calling the shots."[8]

The Battle of Algiers

The dirty war was not limited to the OAS and agents of the French State, of course. There was plenty of barbarism perpetrated by the Algerian National Liberation Front. Muslims who served France—the so-called *Harkis*—were seen as legitimate targets by the FLN, along with the *pieds-noirs* European settler class. Internal power struggles led to frequent FLN purges. As in all civil wars, plenty of Algerians were killed by their own people.

The difference was that members of the FLN were feted as freedom fighters. They earned a heroic image by portraying themselves as insurgents who lacked the backing of a government or a military-industrial complex to keep them in hardware. Deprived of fighter jets and napalm, or even tanks and artillery, Algerian guerrilla combatants had to rely on low-impact attacks, including ambushes and sabotage, that struck terror into the hearts of their enemies.

The FLN campaign featured in the 1966 film *The Battle of Algiers*, which still has the feel of a documentary. Director Gillo Pontecorvo used mainly amateur actors who had survived the conflict. Ali La Pointe, the real-life revolutionary fighter, is a lead character and is pictured engaging with French paratroopers in Algiers. The battle in the capital of Algeria started with the *pieds-noirs* bombing of the Algiers *Casbah* in 1956. A *plastiquage* blast at an apartment block in Rue de Thèbes by vigilantes, including a policeman, claimed seventy Muslim lives. It led to the FLN launching coordinated attacks on September 30, a Sunday. The fighters included Djamila Bouhired and Zohra Drif, two female FLN operatives who bombed the Milk-Bar ice cream parlor and a café. The women wore European clothes and makeup to avoid police detection.

Pontecorvo captured the full horror and hypocrisy of the country that produced the Declaration of the Rights of Man and of the Citizen in 1789. The French authorities moved to quell civil liberties in response to the bombings. France was losing its democratic identity, as well as its ability to maintain order on what it considered French soil. Collusion in violence against Algerian Muslims spread to the mainland, along with discriminatory curfews and similarly repressive methods. *The Battle of Algiers* still provides lessons about terrorism, and how it brutalizes society while also bringing about political change.

The Battle of Algiers was first briefly shown at a single Paris cinema in 1971, but extreme French nationalists vandalized the auditorium and started fights at screenings. This led to the film being censored for three decades until 2004, partly because it portrayed the Algerians who fought and won their liberation war as heroes. Despite this, *The Battle of Algiers* was nominated three times for an Oscar, and it won the Golden Lion at Venice in 1966. The insurgency methods highlighted in the film were studied by the George W. Bush administration in 2003 during the Iraq War, when Gillo Pontecorvo's work was regularly shown at the Pentagon. The examination of torture methods used by the French, America's oldest allies, caused a lot of soul-searching, but the film itself was widely acclaimed by American audiences.

The FLN was not a regular army, so it had to use irregular methods to achieve its aims. It offered hope to liberation movements around the world, especially when France decided to abandon its imperialist cruelty. The cost of terrorism to morale and social cohesion, as well as the economy, proved too much. On March 18, 1962, peace treaties were signed. The Évian Accords brought the war to a halt, and Algeria became an independent nation. France's reputation as a global power was severely diminished as its empire fell apart. Algeria's *pieds-noirs* community was disowned as an anachronism. They represented violent repression and a constant state of conflict. French intellectuals such as the power couple Jean-Paul Sartre and Simone de Beauvoir were among those who decried the colonialism that had created them.

Industrialization and a leading role in a community of European nations—the Common Market—was what De Gaulle envisaged for the new France. American-style consumerism, peace, and prosperity beckoned. There needed to be a better way than the conflict with Germany, and within far-flung overseas territories, that had gone on for centuries. But the kind of violence that had created the Fifth Republic did not simply disappear.

Up to one hundred thousand *Harkis* fled to mainland France after the war, because they rightly feared reprisals for their cooperation with the colonial master. They were forced into desultory holding centers and then even more primitive camps. France's negligence toward them continued indefinitely. Hundreds of thousands of other Algerians, including many who had fought with the nationalists, were also imported to France to help rebuild a country devastated by a long period of warfare.

Officially, *jus soli*—birthright citizenship that allows anyone born in France to French nationality—was the cornerstone of France's immigration policy, but Algerian Muslims were infamously denied the full benefits of being members of the French State. *L'Algérie française* had always quashed such rights for indigenous Algerians, whose land and property were instead handed over to the *pieds-noirs*. It was impossible for most Algerians to gain French citizenship if they remained Muslims.

Under colonialism, "French Muslims" became a euphemism for nationalist terrorists. Thus, the FLN advanced Islam as a pillar of the emerging Algerian identity. In return, Algerian immigrants to France suffered from presumed guilt. A decree in October 1961 read, "It is advisable in the most urgent way for Algerian Muslim workers to refrain from circulating at night in the streets of Paris and its suburbs, more particularly from 8:30 p.m. to 5:30 a.m."

The Algerian crisis exposed a French nation that was neither moral nor just. It was one in which throat slitting and *plastiquage* became commonplace, and which had taken part in *ratonnades*: "rat chase" pogroms against Algerian civilians who were demeaned as *bicots*, the racist slur still aimed at dark-skinned North Africans to this day. The historic myth had always been that Moors defiled and tortured, but— just a few years after the most cataclysmic war in human history— the French proved themselves masters in such practices. The brutal

reaction of the French authorities to the FLN had included extrajudicial killings, multiple acts of torture, and media censorship. All diminished France's reputation as a civilized nation. When Beauvoir argued
as much in a passionate column in *Le Monde*, the French government
tried to seize and destroy all copies of the newspaper. "When the government of a country allows crimes to be committed in its name, every
citizen thereby becomes a member of a collectively criminal nation,"
she wrote.[9]

The most murderous episode in the postwar history of Paris came
in October 1961, when up to three hundred peaceful French-Algerian
protesters were slaughtered in cold blood around iconic national
monuments, including the Eiffel Tower and Notre-Dame Cathedral.
The police responsible cracked down on a demonstration by thirty
thousand people calling for an end to the Algerian War and immediate independence from France. The march had been organized
by the FLN, in breach of the colonial curfew legislation. The most
memorable—and vicious—atrocities saw policemen herding pan-
icking crowds onto Paris's bridges, where many demonstrators were
tossed into the Seine.

Normally a romantic symbol of the most popular tourist city in the
world, the river became a watery morgue for scores of victims, whose
lifeless bodies washed up for weeks afterward. Others were shot or
beaten to a bloody pulp in police stations, where their mutilated bodies testified to truncheon and rifle-butt injuries. Some ten thousand
more were rounded up inside the city's sports stadiums and attacked
and interrogated. Torture methods included captives being forced to
drink bleach.

My father told me about compatriots his age who were hanged
from trees by police in the thick Vincennes woods, on the eastern
edge of Paris. It was the site of the concentration camp for dissident
Algerians, just near the Château de Vincennes where King Henry V
of England died. One of the hangings made a small item in the *Manchester Guardian* in early 1962 under the headline "Strange Fruit in the
Trees," which was taken from the lyrics of the song most famously performed by Billie Holiday about lynchings of African-Americans.

TERRORISM: EXEMPLARY VENGEANCE   139

More incongruous still, the gruesome event was covered in a column entitled "La Vie Parisienne," which usually focused on artists honing their talent in the City of Light. So it was that the bloodbath, which amounted to state terrorism, was relegated to quirky corners of the press. By contrast, historians Jim House and Neil MacMaster described the massacre as the "bloodiest act of state repression of street protest in western Europe in modern history."

Maurice Papon, the Paris police chief who instigated the October 1961 killings, died in 2007, and some of his unrepentant and unpunished henchmen still remain at large, albeit unidentified. Like Papon, many of the killers had been Nazi collaborators who learned their crowd control methods from the Gestapo. They were experts at disinformation too: the official death toll after Papon's self-proclaimed "Battle of Paris" was initially said to be three, then revised to a vague "several dozen" almost forty years later. No judicial inquiry ever took place, with many French still blaming Algerian infighting and terrorist attacks for the deaths. Papon was finally brought to justice for crimes against humanity—but only for those he committed during the Second World War. President Charles de Gaulle, and then successive governments, ensured he was never indicted for what he did to the French-Algerians of Paris. There was no trial, or any kind of public inquiry, let alone an apology or reparations.

There has never been a "Holocaust moment" for the victims of the police brutality of October 1961. It was in 1995—more than fifty years after some seventy-five thousand Jews were rounded up by the French authorities and sent to the Nazi gas chambers—that President Jacques Chirac finally confessed and pinned responsibility firmly on "the folly of the French State." "France, the homeland of the Enlightenment, and of the Rights of Man, a land of welcome and asylum . . . committed the irreparable," said Chirac. "Breaking its word, it handed those who were under its protection over to their executioners." Yet in 1961, the French did not hand their Algerian Muslim victims over to anyone. On the contrary, they did the killing themselves.

Few would argue that the tribal murders committed by Paris police more than sixty years ago are likely to be repeated today, but nor would anyone pretend that the discriminatory policies that gave rise to such horrors have left modern France. A sense of "otherness" for millions of Muslim citizens helped define the Fifth Republic, and the colonial tradition has by no means disappeared. It can be measured by the amount of draconian policing and indeed in the widespread discrimination suffered by Algerian communities in France, alongside other Muslims from the Maghreb and the rest of the African continent. Yes, France moved away from imperialism and attempted to guarantee its material wealth and security through the far more enlightened European project, but the brutality developed over decades of terrorism still lingers.

A Historic Monument to Terrorism

France has undoubtedly tried to erase what we might call "white terrorism," such as the Vitry-le-François train bombing, from the public consciousness, along with all the other crimes associated with Algeria. Countries routinely open public inquiries into relatively recent events: for example, allegedly unlawful killings involving the British state during the Troubles in Northern Ireland, or historic allegations of criminality by public figures. Prosecutions of old men said to have acted illegally many decades ago are common in the United Kingdom, but there is never any appetite for similar accountability in France. Despite this, the Republic did want to turn the November 2015 barbarity into national history.

The mammoth trial centered on the surviving perpetrators of Friday the thirteenth terror attacks would turn into the longest in French legal history. More than that, the process—which involved examining acts that had "sent France into mourning," according to submissions by Paris prosecutors—was videoed in its entirety and the film placed in the National Archives.

It would be half a century before the footage could be made public, but this would not stop every other aspect of the ten-month trial from being publicized contemporaneously. The proceedings were unprecedented in scale and complexity. A dedicated wooden court was built inside the ancient Palais de Justice, on the Île de la Cité. The island on the Seine from which Paris had grown was partially locked down by police throughout the trial. The new court seated six hundred people, and there was a bulletproof dock for defendants. French Justice Minister Éric Dupond-Moretti was more excited by the case than most. "It's the trial of all superlatives—the longest trial in our history," he gushed as he admired his new courthouse, which would be destroyed at the end of the process.

Pretrial inquiries by judicial police directed by magistrates took six years. Their findings stretched to 174 feet (53 meters) of written notes. The early weeks of the trial were taken up by around 450 plaintiffs—many of them wounded or bereaved—rehearsing stories of horror and survival. Many were still leading shattered lives. Testimonies included those from the former President of France François Hollande and the failed suicide bomber, Salah Abdeslam, who largely relished his time in court—something that made the entire process feel particularly unseemly. In his black T-shirt and a face mask worn to protect him against coronavirus, Abdeslam knew he should have been dead, or at the very least locked away forever, but he was instead being given a public platform. When asked what he did for a living, the bar owner and convicted burglar said nonchalantly, "I abandoned all profession to become a fighter for the Islamic State."

Abdeslam was one of twenty suspects tried over the November 2015 Paris attacks. The coordinated assaults were carried out by nine men. Aside from Abdeslam, all the other on-the-ground perpetrators, including his brother, Brahim Abdeslam, were dead. The pair had run Les Béguines, a Brussels bar, together, while also dealing dope. Five of the other dead defendants were tried in absentia, having disappeared during Western air strikes in Iraq and Syria.

"I am of Moroccan origin, but I only have French nationality," Abdeslam told the court. "My parents came to France first, and that's why they have French nationality. Then they left for Belgium. My childhood was very ordinary. I was a calm, kind person. There was a good atmosphere at home, there was always a good atmosphere with everyone."

Abdeslam did relatively well at school, passing the equivalent of the baccalaureate in Belgium and then becoming an apprentice mechanic.

Then he turned to crime and spent his first stint in prison following an attempted break-in. Fellow inmates had included Abdelhamid Abaaoud, the acknowledged ringleader of the Paris attacks, who was killed during a firefight with police in Saint-Denis afterward.

Abdeslam described himself as "yo-yoing" between jobs, unemployment, and crime, saying that many of his previous convictions related to fast cars because "I like speed." Discussing his brother—one of two siblings—who ended his life blowing up a bar called the Comptoir Voltaire in Paris, Abdeslam said, "He's the brother I liked best. I love them all, but he was my favorite brother. I can't explain why. Love has no logic. He took care of me more so when I was young, perhaps."

Explaining why he dumped his explosive vest—which was faulty anyway—Abdeslam said: "I go into the café. I order a drink. I look at the people around me, and I say to myself, 'No, I'm not going to do it.' I changed my mind out of humanity, not out of fear." Beyond such mawkish nonsense, a picture emerged of a small-town gangster who was more interested in cannabis, nightclubs, and gambling than world politics or religion. He condemned Western values as "libertine" because people lived "without worrying about God," but his prison radicalization—which is said to have started during his first spell inside in 2014—evidently did not prevent him from indulging in a libertine lifestyle of his own.

Perhaps the most satisfying moment for the victims of the attacks came when Abdeslam was asked to talk about his new life in the Fleury-Mérogis prison. Asked to describe his cell in the high-security unit in the Paris suburbs, Abdeslam said: "It's nine square meters. There are two surveillance cameras. I can't do anything. I have no activities. I can just go out in the morning for a walk, or to play sports for an hour. It's the same in the afternoon. Even animals aren't treated like this."

The Paris trial was a charade. Rather than serve as an exercise in justice by a defiled state, it gave Abdeslam a stage he could never have dreamed of in his humdrum, crime-ridden, cannabis-riddled life. People were yearning for answers but instead got Abdeslam grandstanding and lying. Reviewing an early claim that he would say nothing, Abdeslam sounded like a public official when he said, "I'm going to explain myself because it's the last time that I'll have the opportunity to do so.

All these people in here need my answers. I can't promise anything, but I'll do my best."

In a concluding speech, Abdeslam, who had already been convicted to twenty years in prison in Belgium for the attempted murder of Brussels police officers while on the run, said, "Who can make an insincere apology for so much suffering? I'm not a murderer. I'm not a killer." Three of the other accused accomplices—Osama Krayem (a Swedish national of Syrian origin), Sofian Ayari (a Tunisian national), and Mohamed Bakkali (a Belgian national of Moroccan origin)—abruptly stopped answering questions altogether, as was their legal right.

Where were the six assault rifles—code name "Clios," according to phone interceptions—used in the attacks sourced from? Nobody was saying. Was an attack on Charles de Gaulle Airport also being planned? Nobody was saying. An alleged plot to stage a simultaneous attack at Amsterdam's Schiphol Airport also remained a mystery. Perhaps most crucially of all, how on earth did just three terrorists manage to murder ninety people inside the Bataclan concert venue?

The first officer to arrive at the Bataclan was a local patrolman who ignored protocol that should have prevented him from taking offensive action. He shot one attacker dead, exploding his suicide vest. The officer was then ordered to withdraw and wait for specialists. It was a full thirty minutes before they arrived. The surviving terrorists had plenty of time to carry on shooting before assembling hostages and barricading themselves in an upstairs room. Had friendly fire from the police contributed to the slaughter? Nobody was saying.

War on Our Soil

The abiding message related to the period of terrorist attacks that started in 2015 came from François Hollande as he tried to place the perpetrators at the center of a full-scale war. His portrayal of these butchers as elite soldiers was by no means supported by the evidence. On the contrary, all of them had the profile of drugged-up delinquents, pathetic individuals drawn to a life of crime. Shooting unarmed civilians at point-blank range, or blowing them up, was the height of their contemptible combat skills.

Survivors of the Paris attacks described members of the Friday the thirteenth "commando" as being in a zombielike trance when they carried out the carnage. They appeared serene and without a care in the world, suggesting that they were high on Captagon, a synthetic amphetamine-based pill that helps to mask pain, fear, and hunger. It was designed to treat depression and keeps users up for long stretches, even those contemplating suicide. ISIS operatives are well known for using it, so much so that it is dubbed the "jihadists' drug." Production and consumption soared in Syria following the start of the country's civil war in 2011.

When police raided the rooms in the southeast suburb of Alfort-ville where many of the Paris terrorists had stayed, they found a stash of syringes, needles, and plastic tubing. Salah Abdeslam had rented two rooms in the Appart'City hotel in the lead-up to the attacks, and video footage showed a pile of used drug paraphernalia scattered on a coffee table. The men had clearly used it before heading off on their murder spree. Abdeslam had admitted to being a regular user of cannabis and cocaine, while jihadis were also known to steel themselves with heroin.

The attempt to portray men like Abdeslam as trained warriors was not in the least bit convincing. Those who had been to the ISIS caliphate spent very little time handling firearms or learning combat tactics. Attacks that came after the Friday the thirteenth outrages were all carried out by lone-wolf delinquents, most with a history of drug abuse and psychiatric problems, rather than anybody with anything approaching military competence.

When a cargo truck weighing nineteen tons was deliberately driven into a crowd celebrating Bastille Day on the promenade in Nice on July 14, 2016, the driver turned out to be a Tunisian living illegally in France. Mohamed Lahouaiej-Bouhlel killed 86 people and wounded 458 others. Fifteen of the dead were children and, according to local Islamic groups, a third were Muslims.

ISIS claimed responsibility, despite having had next to no contact with Lahouaiej-Bouhlel, a thirty-one-year-old with severe psychiatric issues. He had convictions for domestic abuse against his estranged wife and three children, as well as for theft. François Molins, the Paris pros-ecutor who led the inquiry into the Nice attack, said Lahouaiej-Bouhlel was "a young man completely uninvolved in religious issues and not a practicing Muslim, who ate pork, drank alcohol, took drugs, and had an unbridled sex life."

No evidence of direct contact with ISIS emerged. He had certainly not honed his fighting skills on battlefields in Iraq and Syria. Instead, Lahouaiej-Bouhlel stored photos of the group's macabre propaganda videos on his computer, including images of beheadings. He also had photos of Osama bin Laden and the black ISIS flag.

Lahouaiej-Bouhlel had carried out Google searches using expressions such as "terrible fatal accidents." One yielded a newspaper photo of a car crashing into a packed café terrace. Rumors circulated by some sections of the media that Lahouaiej-Bouhlel was heard shouting "Allahu Akbar" at some stage of the attack turned out to be fake. He had spent the entire time in the driver's cabin of a Renault Midlum truck, which reached speeds of more than fifty miles per hour, before he was shot and killed by officers. It was inconceivable that anybody could have heard him shouting anything.

Despite the circumstances of such attacks, the trigger response by the French authorities was to clamp down on Muslims at home, and indeed to demonize them. At the same time, the French military engaged in conflicts against Muslims across Africa and the Middle East.

President Hollande—who had completed his compulsory period of national service as a military officer in 1977—said he wanted to pull the nation together after the bloodbath. He used the language of a chief warlord to call for more air strikes. At home, he said there would be more paramilitary police and soldiers on the street and—more notably still—a change in the Constitution to extend states of emergency, which were then limited to twelve days without a parliamentary vote. He also implied that men like Lahouaiej-Bouhlel and the Bataclan attackers should be viewed as warriors. "In the face of acts of war on our soil, we must be merciless," Hollande said.

Anybody trying to gauge the public mood at the time needed to be in Place de la République—the great Paris protest square—on the Sunday night after the Friday the thirteenth attacks. Thousands gathered to remember the victims, ignoring government warnings to stay at home. Wreaths were laid, candles were lit, flags were waved, and there were spontaneous renditions of "La Marseillaise."

The idea was that a proud capital was united against the barbarians who had created carnage just two days before. Liberty and democracy—both represented by the statue of Marianne, the national symbol of France that dominates République—would prevail. The country was under attack, but it would never be beaten.

Then a few firecrackers went off. Within seconds, members of a panicked crowd were stampeding for their lives. People were screaming, convinced that the gun-wielding murderers were back. Restaurants and bars emptied. Others crouched on the pavement, crying uncontrollably. Even the police looked terrified.

In fact, the way to defeat the terrorists responsible for the urban savagery was to view them as what they were, not as soldiers in an army. Those who blew themselves to pieces were easily expendable losers from damaged, criminal backgrounds—men who spent their daylight hours getting high on drugs and surfing online.

Not only had some spent time in prison but many had been placed under surveillance. Yet, incredibly, all of these killers ended up being pretty much ignored by the security services as they built up their arsenal of illegal weapons. Samy Amimour, a twenty-eight-year-old Frenchman who was part of the Paris cell, had freely traveled to Syria two years before. He was charged with terrorist offenses but was left to his own devices while nominally under judicial supervision.

Members of the gang who perpetrated the attack on *Charlie Hebdo* staff were treated similarly. Two were monitored by the intelligence agencies, including having their phones tapped, but all of these measures were dropped just before the attacks. Chérif Kouachi, one of the brothers involved, simply took no notice of the terms of his bail. Amimour, too, failed to turn up at his local police station for appointments and was in touch with fellow suicide bombers as well as ISIS operatives based abroad. They all used telephone encryption technology that clearly baffled the French.

Salah Abdeslam went on the run for a full four months after the Paris attacks, as did others involved in the planning of November 13, 2015. All lived in Belgium. On the morning of March 22, 2016, three coordinated bombs went off around Brussels: two at Zaventem Airport and one at a metro station in the city. Thirty-two innocent civilians and three suicide bombers were killed, while more than three hundred were wounded. The killers, having already taken one chance to carry out a spectacular atrocity in Europe, had been left free to have another go.

State of Emergency

The last time a state of emergency had been imposed in France before 2015 was exactly a decade earlier, when mainly teenagers and young men rioted on the estates, causing millions of dollars' worth of damage. Since then, a handful of troubled men had gravitated to forming highly effective death squads. Under such circumstances, agenda-led commentators and politicians failed to see the difference between hateful terrorists and the millions of ordinary Muslims in France who wanted nothing more than equal opportunities as the key to a peaceful, secure, happy life.

Meanwhile, the perception among Muslims who would never think of taking up arms was that the French State was involved in an onslaught against societies just like their own. In 2011, French President Nicolas Sarkozy and British Prime Minister David Cameron had been the main proponents of the NATO military intervention in Libya that overthrew Colonel Muammar Gaddafi. It got rid of a dictator—bringing about a controversial, not to say unlawful, regime change—but it also caused a power vacuum that allowed groups such as the Islamic State and Al-Qaeda to expand their bases in an African country just across the Mediterranean from Europe.

France had also intervened against Islamist insurgents in Mali, its former colony and another Muslim-majority nation, in 2013. French air strikes on Syria started in September 2015 and intensified after the Paris attacks in November. Such concentrated interference in the Muslim world played into the narrative that the West wanted to attack anything to do with Islam at all costs.

France's tradition of secularism did little to appease Muslims living in the country either. While antipathy toward religion was traditionally directed against Catholics and Jews—often lethally—Islam was increasingly being viewed as a culture that did not adapt. Measures such as the 2010 ban on wearing full veils in public—the so-called burka ban—angered many.

Emmanuel Macron himself used the *Financial Times* to spread fake news about his country's more than five million Muslims by conjuring up a picture of lawless council estates where Muslim parents poisoned the minds of little girls while covering their bodies under burkas. Without a shred of evidence, he wrote in November 2018, "Visit the districts where small girls aged three or four are wearing a full veil, separated from boys, and, from a very young age, separated from the rest of society, raised in hatred of France's values."

Macron also stated that such children spent their time in hellhole communities surrounded by "hundreds of radicalised individuals, who we fear may, at any moment, take a knife and kill people." Introducing disturbing biological references into his narrative, Macron even said these areas were "breeding grounds for terrorists in France."

If the purpose of Macron's sulfurous prose had been to spread collective guilt, it certainly had the desired effect. An actual President had confirmed what venal propagandists had been saying for years: that France had been overrun by alien hordes and that murderous, cradle-to-grave radicalism was widespread. Everyone from anonymous social media trolls with swastika avatars to the kind of racist pop philosophers who dominated French political thinking suddenly had the President's—and by implication the State's—backing.

The burka (or niqab)—a full-veil garment that covers a woman's body, including her face, apart from the eyes—was banned in France, and anyone would face a possible prison sentence if they forced a child to wear one. There was not a single recorded incident of a child in a burka, let alone any prosecutions or convictions. The urban myth that Muslims hid their offspring away while teaching them to hate was similarly obscene. It simply played into macabre legends.

Prosecutors and Interior Ministry sources I spoke to were all baffled by Macron's sensational and reckless fantasies, which would have instantly made front-page news if they were true. In an era when cameras are everywhere, there were no images to back up Macron's fabrications about these infants with sociopath parents. Additionally, the terms "Islam" and "Islamist" were regularly interchanged in the media, as Muslims were portrayed as a dangerous underclass largely made up of savage misfits prone to suicidal barbarism.

The most high-profile lone-wolf terrorist knife attacks of 2020 were carried out by a Russian Chechen, a Tunisian, and a Pakistani, rather than by homegrown French nationals. Yet Macron's implication was that the "breeding ground" estates on the edges of major cities, such as Paris and Marseille, produced all the knifemen.

What was clear was that Macron was coveting far-right votes. Using weasel words to evoke the thought of entire communities of French Muslims being involved in terrorism was very important to this objective. This was obvious from the passage through Parliament of Macron's draft measures seeking to tackle radicalism. Macron originally called it a bill to combat "Islamist separatism"—a concept that fitted in neatly with the kind of Muslim estates depicted in his *Financial Times* letter—but then he altered it to legislation "bolstering the respect of the principles of the Republic."

Such rhetorical tweaks did not stop the Macron administration from proposing much stricter controls on Muslims, however. Closer monitoring of the perceived enemy within ranged from tougher rules on the funding of religious organizations to banning homeschooling for Muslim children (even in the middle of a global pandemic, when such classes were being encouraged for all others).

The emphasis was on increased security and the usual crackdowns on those who display their religious affiliation via their choice of clothing, for example. Thus, another spectacular inaccuracy in Macron's *FT* letter was his claim that the French State "never intervenes in religious affairs."

Perhaps the most disingenuous, however, was Macron's allegation that "I will not allow anybody to claim that France, or its government, is fostering racism against Muslims." As with so much of the President's doublespeak, this was not worth the pink paper it was written on, despite its promotion by certain sections of France's media.

Grenade, gun, and arson attacks on French mosques and physical assaults against Muslims increased by some 500 percent after the *Charlie Hebdo* attacks. Islamophobia was, meanwhile, turned into a major vote winner by parties such as the Rassemblement National, Les Républicains, and, of course, Macron's own electoral movement.

The state of emergency allowed investigators to raid homes and take suspects into custody without judicial approval. French law-and-order officials, including magistrates and judicial police, spent years trying to prove that isolated attacks had in fact all been coordinated as part of an ingenious plot by legions of like-minded Muslims who wanted to take over Europe. In fact, the vast majority of those pulled in for questioning were exposed for what they were: innocent, or else small-town criminals who acted as useful idiots as they got hold of stolen cars or weapons from eastern Europe.

The National Antiterrorism Prosecutor's office tried to build up grand plot charges based on conjecture and guesswork, but they were in fact dealing with maladjusted young men who had chosen to die. Most were untrained and had never met any commanders. They made their own plans and trained themselves, using whatever information they could find on Google. Ritual sacrifice suited them; it did not matter whom they killed or wounded, as long as they had attacked someone before their own suicides.

Officers conducted hundreds of warrantless searches, almost all of them on Muslim homes. It all added up to a country that was as divided as it was scared—deeply shocked by horrendous terrorist incidents and fearful that there could be many more to come. Sending jets to bomb foreign countries and flooding the streets with soldiers and paramilitary police did not provide a fix, either short or long term. Instead, such measures made towns and cities such as Paris feel even more vulnerable to attack.

Unconditional Surrender

The marathon Paris terrorism trial provided cathartic moments for survivors and relatives of the dead, but there were no surprises in the sentencing. Salah Abdeslam was condemned to life in prison, with instructions that he would never be released. It was confirmed that his explosive vest had malfunctioned, allowing judges to dismiss claims that he had experienced a pang of conscience before pulling out of the attack.

Mohamed Abrini, a Belgian-Moroccan who admitted to driving some of the attackers to Paris, got a minimum term of twenty-two years. He was also later found guilty in Belgium of multiple terrorist murders in connection with the Brussels bombings. Swedish national Osama Krayem, who had been identified in a notorious ISIS propaganda video showing a Jordanian pilot being burned alive, was sentenced to thirty years. Mohamed Bakkali, a Belgian-Moroccan, and Sofian Ayari, a Tunisian, were given life sentences for their "fundamental role" in preparing the Paris attacks. These were by no means all regular French Muslim men from the *cités*, as many had hoped.

One defendant got off, which was incredible considering the work that had gone into the trial. Many of those convicted had already spent years in pretrial detention, and the handful of defendants whose sentences were relatively short would not return to prison.

Salah Abdeslam was not turned into a martyr. There was no question of him getting the chance to clutch a religious icon to his chest, as attempted De Gaulle assassin Jean-Marie Bastien-Thiry had done before his death by firing squad. Abdeslam was simply escorted back to his isolated cell in a suburban prison containing alienated, angry, pitiful young men just like him. Everybody had known that he would spend the rest of his life there anyway. Camille Hennetier, one of the Paris prosecutors, said the verdicts "will not heal the wounds, visible or invisible, will not bring the dead back to life, but at least will be able to guarantee them that justice and law have the last word here."

The judgments came at a time when enthusiasm for the Global War on Terror was waning significantly. A crucial part of it had ended in relative defeat for Western forces when the Americans pulled out of Afghanistan after two decades. US President Joe Biden explicitly conceded that an all-out military solution to terrorism was a pipe dream. The longest war in his country's history had ended with the victory of their stated enemies on August 15, 2021. President Ashraf Ghani fled Kabul, the capital, by helicopter to Uzbekistan. An offensive by the Taliban—the Islamist group the Americans had pledged to destroy—succeeded in recapturing the whole country almost at once. The war had cost billions and claimed at least 175,000 lives, including more than 45,000 civilians.

A year later, President Macron would welcome Saudi Arabia's Crown Prince Mohammed bin Salman to the Élysée Palace with a long, warm handshake and dinner, amid outrage from human rights groups. MBS, as he styled himself, had become a pariah following the gruesome murder of journalist Jamal Khashoggi in the Saudi consulate in Istanbul in October 2018. Saudi agents had used a bone saw to dismember Khashoggi's body.

MBS, the de facto ruler of one of the world's biggest oil suppliers, was also prosecuting a war in Yemen, where a diseased, starving civilian population was suffering every bit as much as the Afghans as they were massacred and maimed. France was supplying weapons worth as much as $1 billion a year to the Saudis. While in Paris, MBS stayed in the $300-million new-build mansion the Château Louis XIV at Louveciennes—a house that mimicked the extravagant luxury of the nearby Palace of Versailles.

July 2022 then saw Macron welcoming Abdel Fattah el-Sisi to the Élysée Palace. Two years earlier, Macron had awarded Sisi the *Grand-Croix* of the Légion d'Honneur. This was despite the Egyptian dictator having presided over the killing of almost one thousand unarmed civilians in Rabaa Square, and locking up some sixty thousand political prisoners without trial, following his military coup in the summer of 2013.

A subject Macron remained distinctly quiet about was Lafarge's financing of ISIS before the 2015 attacks on Paris. The largest cement manufacturer in the world could not have been closer to the Paris establishment. It grew out of a limestone quarry in the southern Ardèche department and by 1864 was delivering materials to Egypt to build the Suez Canal. Its management collaborated with the Nazis during the Second World War, helping with the building of Hitler's Atlantic Wall. While the company was rightly castigated for this, the fact that it had remained active during the conflict meant Lafarge was best placed to undertake the postwar reconstruction of France. Keeping it in operation thus became a governmental priority.

Lafarge's close governmental links certainly helped during the Syrian civil war, when the fighting threatened its plant in the Jalabiya region of northern Syria. Rather than pulling out, Lafarge paid ISIS and the Al-Nusra Front, another terrorist group, at least $6 million in protection money. In 2022, Lafarge pleaded guilty to this in a US court and had to pay $778 million as part of a plea agreement. The cash had been handed over to ISIS while it was kidnapping and killing Westerners, and just a year before 130 people were murdered on a single night in the French capital.

US Attorney Breon Peace said in a statement, "In the midst of a civil war, Lafarge made the unthinkable choice to put money into the hands of ISIS, one of the world's most barbaric terrorist organizations, so that it could continue selling cement. Never before has a corporation been charged with providing material support and resources to foreign terrorist organizations." Lafarge—which became part of the Swiss company Holcim in 2015—also faced charges of complicity in crimes against humanity in Paris.

Crucially, there were allegations that the French government was fully aware of Lafarge's collaboration with ISIS at the time it was happening. Turkish President Recep Tayyip Erdogan claimed to have warned Macron. "When I explained how the cement giant Lafarge supported terrorist organizations in northern Syria, the French did not understand," said Erdogan, who specified that he spoke to Macron directly.

The head of Lafarge's security in Syria was Jean-Claude Veillard, a former French Navy commander and former far-right candidate for municipal elections in Paris who was a firm supporter of Marine Le Pen. Veillard admitted to taking part in secret negotiations with ISIS. Emails and other correspondence highlighting the close relationship between the terrorists and Lafarge were obtained by *Mediapart*.[10] Following a criminal complaint by the Sherpa anti-corruption group and the European Center for Constitutional and Human Rights based in Berlin, French magistrates opened an inquiry into multiple charges, including "funding of a terrorist enterprise" and "complicity in war crimes and crimes against humanity."

It was around the time when he was negotiating with ISIS, in 2014, that Veillard stood as a candidate for the Rassemblement Bleu Marine

(Marine Blue Rally)—a right-wing coalition created by Marine Le Pen. The Directorate-General for External Security, France's overseas intelligence agency, had been aware of the Lafarge payments to ISIS. Yet a parliamentary fact-finding mission led by MP Jean-Frédéric Poisson, who would later go on to back Éric Zemmour, categorically cleared Lafarge of any wrongdoing in 2016. Welcoming the Lafarge conviction in the United States and calling for judicial investigations into the company to continue in France, the parliamentary group of the left-wing party La France Insoumise (France Unbowed) said in a statement that they blamed the French government for "cautiousness, complacency, even complicity."[11]

Dark deeds are often overlooked if they can be justified in the interests of realpolitik, but such benevolent pragmatism does not extend to cultural expressions that allegedly challenge tradition. Fierce anti-clericalism in France now manifests itself not so much against the Catholic Church—a cornerstone of the monarchical Ancien Régime— but against a religion that is considered alien in every respect: Islam. This "war" against one of the three great monotheistic faiths is one that France prosecutes to its shame while demonizing millions of its own citizens and radicalizing a tiny minority of delinquents toward further acts of nihilistic violence.

6

EDUCATION
The Kindling of a Flame

The more I read, the more I acquire, the more certain I am
that I know nothing.
  —VOLTAIRE (1694–1778)

O n my first Monday morning at Oxford University, in what they
call Michaelmas term—named after the Feast Day of Saint
Michael and All Angels—I stood amid the bustle of incoming students
at the front gate of Jesus College, which was founded by Elizabeth I in
1571. I was taking up a post teaching French and would be pursuing
my own advanced studies, but of course I was by no means an obvious
inhabitant of honey-colored quads, timbered halls, and manicured croquet lawns. Oxford is a place where mannered English airs and graces
flourish, along with flamboyant eccentricity. A sense of assured elitism
dominates.

Being used to the Gallic system, I presented a folder to the official
who greeted me. France—the most bureaucratic country in Europe—
loves its paperwork. Nothing means anything to the administrative
regime until it is neatly stored in a dossier. You need one for pretty
much everything. Ideally there will be duplicates of all documents
inside too, and it's best if everything is stamped with an ornate seal.

I offered all my available papers, including exam certificates, Algerian and EU passports, French Republic identity card, second identity card (slightly out-of-date but with a nicer picture), and provisional driving license.

In fact, the official showed no interest in anything that might justify my arrival at the oldest university in the English-speaking world. Directing me away from the Porter's Lodge and toward my ancient quarters, he grinned and asked amiably, "Have you come far?"

Well, yes, I had come very far indeed. In a manner that would be unheard of at an elite French seat of learning, Oxford had accepted me on the strength of a short application and an even briefer interview. My status as an obvious Arab Muslim certainly didn't preclude me from an institution named after the central earthly figure of Christianity. Oxford academics were impressed by my potential and gave me carte blanche to start mixing with those who would soon be running Britain. The small collection of colleges that I was to spend most of my time in have by now produced the last five British Prime Ministers: Rishi Sunak was at Lincoln, Liz Truss at Merton, Boris Johnson at Balliol, Theresa May at St. Hugh's, and David Cameron at Brasenose. The alumni at Jesus include Harold Wilson, the late Labour Prime Minister.

At Oxford, I had no sense of being part of a visible minority (*minorité visible*), the politically correct term used in France for those who are discriminated against because of features that are easily noticed. Nor did I feel like a non-BBR, the poisonous administrative jargon meaning that a nominally French person is not truly representative of the blue, white, and red of the French tricolor. Non-BBRs in France do not tend to get into top colleges, as either students or teachers.

The extraordinarily centralized nature of the French education system, with its militaristic emphasis on strict regulation and hierarchy, shares all the characteristics of French society as a whole. It includes a national curriculum and obsession with *laïcité*. Finding Jesus—as I did on that early October morning at Oxford—is certainly not allowed, whether in classrooms or lecture halls. What kind of citizens does the

French education system produce, and does this system reflect France's universal values?

Socrates likened education to the kindling of a flame, which would expand and grow more intense over time. In the case of French republicanism, the fire of inquisitiveness has been crucial to the development of the State. Hence the rationalism of the Enlightenment triggering the 1789 Revolution. Intellectuals such as Montesquieu encouraged independent thinking in ordinary people.

Jean-Jacques Rousseau's treatise *Emile, or On Education* helped inspire Republican education. "Everything is good as it leaves the hands of the Author of things; everything degenerates in the hands of man" is the rather bleak opening line. *Emile* goes on to suggest that teaching is the means by which humans elevate themselves within a society that would otherwise be left open to corruption.

As the new Republic developed, so did the role of the highly educated thinker. France likes to think it invented the engaged intellectual: Rousseau attempted to define freedom within a rigidly organized society, Voltaire denounced religious extremism, Victor Hugo railed against Napoleonic revivalism, Simone de Beauvoir championed liberation for women. The best global debates about philosophical theories such as rationalism, republicanism, socialism, and positivism were all instigated in France. The classic *intellectuel engagé* was Jean-Paul Sartre, who sat in cafés and restaurants on Paris's Left Bank questioning orthodoxies. Sartre supported anti-colonial revolution in Algeria while challenging the conventions of bourgeois life at home. His utopianism, sense of style, and power as a communicator made him famous around the world.

Who today is thinking constructively about contentious issues and coming up with real-world solutions? There is no doubt that so-called intellectuals get plenty of airtime. They are all over radio stations such as France Culture, get numerous TV slots, and write newspaper columns and books, but are they any good? Socrates cautioned against viewing education as the mere "filling of a vessel": overloading people with facts without teaching them to use them properly. Rote learning is not enough. Flair and original thinking are required for a dynamic nation. An advanced, civilized, ambitious society needs educators that inspire all citizens. Does modern France have any?

Parlez-vous Newspeak?

The private colleges at Oxford are full of undergraduate students bursting with ambition, but academic prowess is not essential to their chances of future success. If they get a Bachelor of Arts first degree, they can upgrade to a Masters by simply applying for one, and then roll up at a fancy degree ceremony involving gowns and mortarboards. Some renowned Oxford students didn't even bother sitting for their first degree, let alone later ones. They "go down"—to use the vernacular—with no formal qualifications at all and can still boast for life that they were once "up at Oxford." This follows in the British tradition of prioritizing common-sense pragmatism over intellectualism. The Anglo-Saxons are suspicious of those who consider themselves to be formally clever, seeing them as pompous and lacking in real-world skills.

This record of anti-intellectualism is prevalent in the United States too. Software geniuses such as Bill Gates, Steve Jobs, and Mark Zuckerberg were all university dropouts, and this made no difference at all to their careers as billionaire entrepreneurs who have had a profound, worldwide influence.

It is inconceivable that such a dismissive approach to formal education could work in France because employers and officials demand stamped documents, including exam certificates, all the time. Bureaucratic papers affirm status and open otherwise rigorously guarded front doors. The French have a "right way" of doing things, and if you beg to differ, then you won't get very far.

As a French-Algerian originally from an insalubrious Paris suburb, I can say that none of this has much to do with creating a meritocracy. While my CV in "color-blind" France was regularly scrutinized for an undesirable postcode and possible links to radical groups, I barely had to provide one during my time in Britain or America. Interviewers instead concentrated on what I could offer.

Almost everything in France is tightly controlled from the capital, and this includes the national curriculum that is central to the education system. There is a civil servant corps of teachers and inspectors, all of them agents of the state ultimately employed to mold the right kind of citizens. The chain of command includes rectors, who are appointed as heads of regional academies. The Ministry of National Education liaises with them to control teaching programs and budgets. Adequate funding is always a high priority. In 2019, national education spending was €160.5 billion, accounting for 6.6 percent of France's GDP. Average spending per student was €8,920.[1]

As far as classroom work is concerned, the emphasis is on instruction—conveying hard facts—rather than encouraging individuality and creativity. Teachers turn up for their classes, but there is no expectation that they will stay in school for anything else, least of all socializing or simply getting to know their pupils. Employees known as *surveillants* deal with discipline in common areas, such as hallways, recreation yards, and canteens. The teachers have little, if any, interest in this side of the job. There is hardly any effort made by anybody to bond through sports teams, for example, as is the case in Britain and America.

Instead, the focus is on sharp-elbowed individualism. Students compete constantly. Their rankings are formalized by exams, and results are made available to everybody in a manner that can be extremely humiliating (if you are bottom of the class, your name will be read out last). Mathematics is revered, along with all other subjects that have a clinical structure to them. Fun is not considered desirable. French students who do well—and who have the diplomas to prove it—tend to be as dour and calculating as the kind of inspectors who regulated them throughout their schooling.

The proportion of students leaving the French education system early—that is to say aged fifteen with only a basic attendance certificate—was 6.9 percent for men and 4.8 percent for women in 2020. In contrast, up to 95.7 percent end up with a *baccalauréat*, the certificate that testifies that you've had a solid secondary education, including completing courses at a *lycée*. The *bac* dates back to 1808,

when it was implemented by Napoléon Bonaparte, but medieval educational packages were not dissimilar, albeit with more emphasis on
Latin. Nowadays, students take a general, technical, or professional
bac. The highest success rate is in the main general one, with passes
reaching 98.4 percent in 2020.[2]

The outstanding *bac* pass rate owes much to social engineering.
Around 70 percent of French people left school without a *bac* in 1985,
and the Socialist administration at the time was determined to see a
change. Jean-Pierre Chevènement, the Education Minister, said a common base of knowledge was essential in the fight against inequality.
People needed a degree to become valued, employable members of
society.[3]

The conforming process starts far earlier than preparation for the
bac, with handwriting. Little French boys and girls are taught one style,
swirly and very arch. Its consistency is monitored ruthlessly. This is the
reason that almost all school notebooks, *cahiers*, use blue grids in place
of straight lines. The idea is that neatly joined-up writing will represent
an ordered mind—one that stays inside the little blue grid boxes and
does not wander off at tangents.

Writing style is crucial in France too. There are very different but
precise ways of discussing facts and ideas, including a simple *explica-
tion de texte* (explanation of a text) to the more stylish *essai littéraire*
or *dissertation* (literary essay). Students are instructed to create a plan
before anything else. This *plan détaillé* is often more important than
the finished product. Emmanuel Macron would undoubtedly produce
a perfect one: there needs to be a "pro" (*thèse*) and "against" (*anti-thèse*)
argument, followed by an all-in-one *synthèse* covering both sides of
the argument and everything in between. This is very similar to
Macron's "at the same time" (*en même temps*) weasel words.

This sense of waffly rigor extends to the spoken language in France.
There are official bodies that try to prevent sloppy words and phrases
from becoming commonplace. The Académie Française, set in an
Oxford-style gold stoned building on the River Seine in Paris, was
founded in 1635 by Cardinal Richelieu, King Louis XIII's Chief Minister. The Académie is committed to averting the pernicious spread of
unwelcome language. It particularly despises English terms and has

also campaigned against regional French dialects being given official recognition.

The Académie has forty members who hold office for life. The fact that they like to be known as the Immortals (*les immortels*) gives the best idea of how seriously they take themselves and indeed the Académie's fantastical nature. Interestingly, the Académie has occasionally tried to modernize French handwriting and punctuation, but it is overwhelmingly a conservative institution.[4]

There is also a French Language Enrichment Commission—a name that evokes George Orwell's "Newspeak" in *1984* and indeed Stalin- or Mao-style "engineers of the human soul." It reports directly to the Prime Minister, and its mission statement is to "create new terms and expressions in order to fill the gaps in our vocabulary and to designate in French the concepts and realities that appear under foreign names." If that sounds like jargon, enjoy some of the terms that the enrichers have come up with in recent years. Millennials—a convenient reference to those born in the 1980s and '90s, who came of age around the year 2000—became *les enfants du numérique*, which translates clumsily into "children of the digital age." Skateboard became *planche à roulettes* (plank on wheels).

This kind of *anti-anglicismes* crusade is reinforced by government legislation relating to the media, including radio and television programs and advertisements. The public is meant to be informed, entertained, and educated in the French language only, meaning that any English phrase has to be translated into French. Thus, "prime time" becomes *heure de grande écoute* or *première partie de soirée*, for example.

France's Ministry of Education regularly rules on correct language usage. The premise of its work is that there is only one official language, and it should be promoted across the country, as well as globally through the European Union and La Francophonie (the international organization made up of countries where French is widely used).

Gold Standard Conformity

Those progressing through France's education system first attend *l'école maternelle* (nursery school) and then the primary system from six to eleven. By the time they are eight, they are already being taught about word structures and similar technical concepts. Secondary education starts at a *collège* from age eleven to fifteen, followed by a *lycée*—a general or technical high school that prepares students for the *bac*. In class, as in later life, gold standard conformity is always expected. Those who fail to write or speak properly (and written French is by no means a simple expression of spoken French) are not just considered to be academic failures; they are treated as if they have major character flaws.

This contempt extends to those who do not read the classical works of French literature, such as Gustave Flaubert's *Madame Bovary*, Jules Verne's *Le Tour du Monde en 80 Jours* (*Around the World in Eighty Days*), and Honoré de Balzac's *La Peau de Chagrin* (*The Wild Ass's Skin*). Myths are drilled in very early on too. The first major work higher-echelon pupils are taught is the epic poem *La Chanson de Roland* (*The Song of Roland*). It is all about romanticizing the account of Roland's killing by the Basques in Iberia at the eighth-century Battle of Roncevaux Pass. Despite a crushing defeat, Roland was later glorified by a medieval Norman poet called Turold, who depicted him as Charlemagne's nephew and elevated him to the status of a chivalrous Christian martyr who bravely fought "one hundred thousand" Saracens—thus disingenuously evoking a struggle between Christianity and Islam.

There is no doubt that those who read great books and who master the French language—and all its rhetorical flourishes—as if it was some kind of science get ahead. Macron is a classic example of this. His early ambition was to become a Flaubert or a Balzac. Initial personal projects included "an epistolary novel about the Aztecs, a love story, and one about a pianist that plays with time," he said.[5] "I have always written novels and poems—all largely for my drawers," the President continued. "Then as a minister, a candidate, a president, I wrote speeches, policy statements, and a book. Writing is essential to me. It means confronting oneself with something greater than oneself, so as to seek clarity and emotion."

The young Macron also tried to become a Turold, planning a "big picaresque novel," full of heroic poetry, presumably about himself. Macron's first encounter with his future wife, Brigitte, came when he was just fifteen and she was his drama teacher at La Providence school

in Amiens, where they were both born and brought up. The then Brigitte Auzière, a thirty-nine-year-old married mother of three, gave her
Turold-style pupil the lead in Milan Kundera's *Jacques and His Master*.

Macron, the son of two medics, was one of the roughly 20 percent
of French children who are sent to private school, in his case a Catholic
one. La Providence, which was founded by Jesuit priests in 1850, was
just a short walk from the redbrick villa where Macron grew up. Almost
all private schools sign a state contract—*contrat d'état*—with the Education Ministry to ensure that their curriculum is identical to the state
one. The private schools receive generous subsidies in exchange. La
Providence was bombed by the Allies during the Second World War, so
moved away from the center of Amiens to the outer ring road. It is now
made up of a sprawling set of unremarkable buildings surrounded by
security fences and gatehouses.

"He was ideally suited to benefit from the system," Gérard Banc,
Macron's onetime natural science teacher, told me.[6] "He always stood
out as a proper thinker, and he had the determination to apply himself
to problems. He of course came from a home where learning was valued and seen as the key to success in life."

Macron's advancement certainly had much to do with his status as a settled member of the bourgeoisie. Henriville, the district of
Amiens that was his first home, was always full of the rich and privileged, including Jules Verne, who was obsessed by a bright future for
the world built on new technology. In a novelette published in 1875, he
described Amiens as *An Ideal City*.

There is less idealism on the council estates of northern Amiens,
however. Food poverty action plans are regularly introduced for those
living in the high-rises there. When I visited the city during the presidential campaign in 2022, Amiens Nord had the official status of a
Priority Security Zone, which allowed the authorities to flood the area
with riot police when there was any sign of a disturbance. There were
also Priority Educational Establishments, where social difficulties were
most pronounced. Nationally, these schools and colleges are attended
by around a fifth of primary- and secondary-age pupils, according to
government figures. Such priority schools have the highest propor-
tions of pupils from disadvantaged backgrounds. Three-quarters have

unemployed or working-class parents, compared to just four in ten in public secondary schools outside the educational priority networks.

As government researchers reported in 2020: "Across the board, secondary schools are marked by wide disparities in social composition, and private secondary schools have a more privileged social composition than public schools—a trend which has been on the rise since the 2000s."[7]

The report continues, "From the time children enter primary school, disparities in social composition (as well as academic levels) between different schools are extremely pronounced, which accounts in large part for the varying performance levels between schools. Academic performance levels are strongly linked to students' social background; this is the case for example in written comprehension, but also in less well-known areas such as the grasp of Information Technology skills. Academic performance is more strongly linked to social background in France than in any other OECD [Organization for Economic Cooperation and Development] country."

Despite the republican motto, inequality prevails. The report reads, "In high school, children from more privileged backgrounds are therefore over-represented in the groups that are more likely to gain access to higher education. As such, disparities persist in terms of access to qualifications depending on students' social background. These are particularly pronounced at the higher levels of education—67% of upper-class parents' children will obtain a higher education degree, compared to 16% of working-class children."

Even if they manage to make it to university, students from underprivileged backgrounds—like their bourgeois classmates—have by no means reached the top of the educational tree. Success cannot be achieved at undergraduate institutions alone, not even at the most famous one in the country. The original Sorbonne College was founded in Paris in 1257, at a time when the French capital was considered a great seat of learning. One of the reasons Oxford developed so quickly as a university was because King Henry II did not want bright young Englishmen (women were not expected to go anywhere) heading to France for their education. Nowadays, the Sorbonne University processes some fifty-five thousand students a year, and many of those who enroll have only very basic qualifications. All public universities in France are obliged to accept an applicant if they have a *bac* or equivalent.

With so many students to deal with, teachers have little time for individuals. The professors have huge classes and are largely disconnected from each student's progress. All they have to do is teach and then organize examinations and other evaluations twice per academic year. Reading lists are handed out at the start of term, and there is not much emphasis on turning up for formal lessons.

Thus, public universities are a bit like super social engineering farms: the fittest survive and end up with a pretty unimpressive degree. The basic one is the *licence*, which is comparable to the British and American bachelor's degree. Rigorous competitive exams are held for special teaching qualifications called the CAPES and *Agrégation* (to teach at the high school and university level, respectively), and there are also specialist technical and business certificates.

Higher education in France is overcrowded and—despite the billions involved—still underfunded considering the number of students enrolled. French universities do poorly on the Global Shanghai Ranking. Harvard was at the top in 2022, Cambridge was fourth, and Oxford seventh. The highest-placed French university was Paris-Saclay at number sixteen. It catered to thirty thousand students at the time.

This is why anybody who wants to get anywhere has to get into a *grande école*—the specialist graduate schools that make up the top tier of France's education system. They are rigorously focused on fields including public policy and administration. Unlike Oxford, you would not be able to breeze in on the strength of your potential and personality. Instead, there are highly competitive entrance examinations called *concours*, all of them set and regulated by the French government. There are rankings based on the results of these exams. If you do badly, then your failure will be published nationally, rather than simply being read out in class.

The *grandes écoles* have an undisputed monopoly on all systems of power. They cover every field of national life, from architecture to the military, and produce France's Presidents, Prime Ministers, senior civil servants, and captains of industry. One of the most famous is the École Polytechnique, founded in 1794 to train technocrats to run a modern army. Now in the southern suburbs of Paris, its alumni include three heads of state. The focus is on science, engineering, and problem-solving, rather than on turning out well-rounded generalists who will dazzle at dinner parties or on the croquet lawn.

Is this a good thing? The English philosopher John Stuart Mill, who started studying Greek at the age of three and had read the whole of Herodotus by the age of eight, went to University College London and espoused the distinctly British notion of producing civilized individuals over churning out narrow-minded technocrats. His favored form of education was discussing interesting matters, ideally on a long walk with a mentor through beautiful surroundings. Mill summed up what educational institutions should *not* be doing with the words: "A general State education is a mere contrivance for moulding people to be exactly like one another; and as the mould in which it casts them is that which pleases the dominant power in the government, whether this be a monarch, an aristocracy, or a majority of the existing generation; in proportion as it is efficient and successful, it establishes a despotism over the mind, leading by a natural tendency to one over the body."[8]

"Moulding people to be exactly like one another" are the key words here, because that is exactly what the French education system does, but there are distinct gradations of conformity. Despite France offering free public (meaning state) schools and a broadly similar education to all children, quality is not standardized. On the contrary, there is a growing crisis within the system, reflected in the gap between the performance of children from different social backgrounds. Many feel excluded from the entire system from a very early age and have no chance whatsoever of reaching its higher echelons—the levels that lead to the positions of power and authority, as well as to the best salaries. The French system is meant to ensure *Égalité* for all, but in fact it favors a minority who gets to the top because they are from the right *Français de souche*—French from the roots—families. Teachers are far more interested in motivated, ambitious types than those from poor backgrounds. Pastoral care, to ensure the pupils' general well-being, is limited, as the priority is on rigorous instruction, rather than John Stuart Mill–style educating.

Coming from a social class supported by large amounts of money is, of course, a huge advantage everywhere. Those who traditionally do best at Oxford are from an impossibly privileged elite. Rishi Sunak is a Wykehamist—meaning he went to the very exclusive Winchester College, an academic hothouse going back to medieval England that has produced alpha males in every field for centuries (Winchester only started accepting a few girls to its Sixth Form in 2022). Beyond being Prime Minister, Sunak is one of the richest men in Britain. Both David Cameron and Boris Johnson are Old Etonians, former pupils at the all-male Eton, the most socially prestigious private school in England, which I visited in March 2014 to speak about British and French foreign policy in the Middle East. The sense of polished elitism was hugely impressive but not surprising considering that annual fees at both Eton and Winchester at the time were upward of $50,000.

Cameron's maternal grandfather was Sir William Mount, the 2nd Baronet, while Johnson—full name Alexander Boris de Pfeffel Johnson—studied Classics at Balliol after spending a gap year teaching Latin and English in Australia. While up at Oxford, the future Tory leaders both joined the Bullingdon, the upper-class Oxford dining club known for its alcohol-inspired rituals, including smashing up restaurants and "pleb-bashing"—slang for beating up commoners.

A picture taken in the mid-1980s shows Cameron and Johnson in their bespoke, tailored navy tailcoats with matching velvet collars and brass monogrammed buttons, along with mustard waistcoats and sky-blue bow ties. This uniform cost the equivalent of some $4,500 at Ede & Ravenscroft, "purveyors to the British Royal Family" and the oldest tailors in London. Bullingdon members were also expected to spend thousands more on champagne and cordon bleu food. They naturally had their own cricket team too.

You never hear about groups like the Bullingdon at French universities, or indeed tales of any kind of affluent excess. You would think the *jeunesse dorée* would be in its high-spirited element in cities such as Paris but—apart from periodic rioting—most university careers are startlingly restrained. Again, this fits in with the dour nature of a French education, but there is no doubt that elitism flourishes. It's just a lot more subtle, and in many ways more intimidating because of it.

At least toffs like Boris Johnson show themselves and don't try to hide their boorishness. You can see them coming, whereas in France the elites are low-key. They manage to keep people out of their circles by remaining out of sight.

Top of the Tree

Given the mediocre standard of much undergraduate study in France, getting into a graduate school is essential for any highflier. Theoretically, anyone can take the entrance exam to a *grande école*, but only a very select few get in. There are huge numbers of French youngsters who barely even know such schools exist.

So-called *conseillers d'orientation* (orientation counselors) are meant to guide bright students to the best colleges, but at schools and colleges around the *cités* they are commonly referred to as disorientation counselors. They are far more likely to direct deprived youths into vocational training or, more likely still, a job in a bakery or sports shop.

Preparatory classes—the *classes préparatoires*—are thus left to the elite. The idea is to perpetuate the leader class of a highly conservative republic. Those who become power players within the French system shamelessly hand top jobs to people just like them.

I contributed to this process after passing the *Agrégation*, the highly competitive exam that made me a *professeure agrégée* who was well qualified to teach agonized students trying to get into the *grandes écoles*. I used to meet them in a classroom near the Tuileries Garden in central Paris, and we would burrow through every English language text available. Those attending these *classes préparatoires* were known as moles, because when they turned up they looked like squinty-eyed, subterranean mammals who had not seen daylight for months. Teaching was for nine hours a day, with an hour off for lunch, and assessments took place constantly, either with four-hour exams on a Saturday or fiendishly difficult home exercises.

My students were hoping to gain entry to the hugely selective École Normale Supérieure, or l'ENS, to use the acronym. The ENS system, which produces *normaliens*, originated during the French Revolution to bring together bright citizens from all backgrounds and social classes and so set up the intellectual foundations of the new Republic. The elitism of the ENS nowadays belies its initial egalitarian aspiration, however.

At this stage of my career, my students were as delightful as you would expect of highly motivated young people from good homes, but there was very little fun or civilized banter, as there would be at Oxford. Everybody in Paris was pushed far too hard. Plenty dropped out because of the pressure.

I went through a very similar experience with my own study for the English *Agrégation*. The work was intense, because I knew that 3,000 people would be competing to pass, but only 150 positions as an *agrégé* in English—someone with the certificate to teach at both high school and university—would be available at the end of my academic year.

I first learned about the *Agrégation* through British and American academics who lived in Paris. I had never considered trying for a *grande école* because—like so many others—I had no idea they existed. Many of my *classe préparatoire* students were convinced that I was an upmarket type too. They speculated about me being the daughter of a Gulf oil baron or minor royalty from the Middle East. It seemed inconceivable to them that I might have grown up in a council flat in nearby suburbs and managed to end up teaching them. Statistically, it was indeed practically impossible.

The institution at the top of the French education system was the École Nationale d'Administration, or ENA. Oxbridge has always had a huge amount of establishment clout, but the power wielded in France by the select band of men and women known as *énarques* was immense.

General Charles de Gaulle founded ENA in 1945 to prepare French leaders. He said all would be "called by your vocation and your abilities to exercise the most important and noble function that exists in the temporal sphere—that is to say, the service of the State." Entrance to ENA involved a fiendish written exam that could include questions about seventeenth-century literature as well as contemporary political problems, and then an even harder oral one.

A candidate like Macron was, of course, perfectly placed to handle it, thanks to the elocutionary skills developed at La Providence. Madame Brigitte Auzière had embarked on an affair with the young

Macron, and he was sent to the Lycée Henry-IV in Paris, because his parents wanted him to stay away from his amorous teacher. Macron was like Frédéric in Flaubert's *Sentimental Education*. Lovestruck and confused, he failed the exam for the École Normale Supérieure, the *grande école* once attended by Simone de Beauvoir and Jean-Paul Sartre. It was only then that Macron switched career strategies and ended up at ENA. Thus, he became a civil servant, banker, and then politician, rather than a literary great or philosopher.

The *grand oral* at ENA was a lengthy ordeal in front of a jury, members of which were allowed to pose all kinds of tricky questions. Candidates from rich, confident backgrounds had the social and educational skills necessary to show up those from modest homes. Aloofness and dogmatism were encouraged, and a sense of superiority persisted into professional life and beyond.

The test of success on finishing the eighteen-month ENA course was said to be the ability to come up with a convincing case for either side of an argument using the same set of data, just as Emmanuel *"en même temps"* Macron would do. High theory, rather than grubby British pragmatism or a no-nonsense American approach, was viewed as the be-all and end-all. Almost all ENA graduates perpetuated the remote and elitist image of De Gaulle.

Macron's romantic, artistic streak is immediately obvious to all who meet him up close, but it has been ruthlessly suppressed. He retains the air of an actor, but he knows more than anybody that this side of his character is largely irrelevant to being a French public servant in the twenty-first century. Instead, he fits into a long technocratic tradition focused on creating rational systems to deal with prevailing problems.

Only around one hundred new students a year win entry to ENA, which was originally in Paris before moving to Strasbourg in 1991. It was seen as an incestuous club for the ruling class. Socialist politicians who met there included future President François Hollande and Ségolène Royal, who became one of his ministers. They ended up having four children together before Hollande embarked on his true vocation of Élysée Palace Romeo.

Before its dissolution by the first Macron administration in December 2021, ENA had produced four Presidents and nine Prime Ministers. The principal objection to it was that—like the rest of the French education system—it was too stuck in its ways. More than that, it had the same elitist image as Oxbridge or the Ivy League universities in the United States, albeit with none of the glamor.

Under fire from the *Gilets Jaunes* and an increasingly populist opposition, Macron knew he had to turn on the culture that had led to him being dubbed Jupiter, and this is why he decided to shut ENA down. There were calls for public officials to come up through the ranks, rather than relying on privileged bourgeois backgrounds to prosper. The *hauts fonctionnaires* class of the Fifth Republic is often highly efficient and supremely dedicated, with employees numbering some 2.5 million in government departments alone, along with a further two million in local authorities and one million in public health care.

The legitimacy of all French public services derives from such staff being servants of the State. They are meant to guard the public good while promoting fairness in everything. The public service is ultimately supervised by the Council of State, the country's highest administrative court.

In typical French style, ENA was replaced by INSP, the National Institute of the Public Service. It is too early to assess how similar it will be to ENA, but judging by the dreary name alone, it is unlikely to be very different. Excellent private education is a fact of life in countries such as Britain and the United States, but France's republican ideology is meant to be all about equality. Unlike Oxford or Harvard, ENA was a public institution, one mostly funded by the state. In such circumstances, its overwhelming bias in educating students from privileged backgrounds, such as Emmanuel Macron, was considered a blatant contradiction.

Black Hussars

France's concept of national education dates back to the 1789 Revolution, when the victorious republicans wanted the State to be responsible for teaching, in the hope that all sections of society would benefit. As the revolutionary wars progressed and the empire expanded, it was clear that sturdy, well-educated officials were needed to run France's growing global infrastructure.

It was Prime Minister Jules Ferry who promoted both colonial expansion and *laïcité*—the very distinct form of secularism that is enshrined in France's Constitution—and who made free primary education compulsory in the early 1880s. Ferry envisaged a modern, prosperous, forward-thinking country that rejected the religious dogma of the Ancien Régime.

This meant republican schools were needed, and not ones run by clerics. Ferry's so-called Black Hussars (*Hussards noirs*) were the cloaked teachers of the Third Republic. They acted very much like soldiers, and especially like the cavalry officers who slaughtered enemies with their sabers. There were frequent tensions as the Hussars tried to teach classrooms full of largely illiterate Catholic children without reference to God. Local priests were naturally infuriated, as were plenty of parents. Catholicism was still an important part of life for a great many people. They trusted what was written in the Holy Bible far more than they did public officials known for their strict discipline.

Another of the Hussars' tasks was to enforce a sense of militarism in their classes as France enlarged its colonial empire. The legacy of the Hussars can be found in the soldierly sense of duty with which many French teachers approach their work today. They are not simply educators but agents of the state instilling secular republicanism in all their students. The idea is that all members of the nation embrace common values and goals.

To this end, the Ministry of National Education was formed in 1932. The preamble to the French Constitution of October 27, 1946, reads: "The Nation guarantees equal access for children and adults to instruction, vocational training, and culture. The provision of free, public, and secular education at all levels is a duty of the State."

According to the Black Hussars' tradition, and indeed the one that started with the 1789 Revolution, education is the best tool the French government has to prop up the country's citizenship values. Curiosity about a fast-developing world and a global media that spreads new principles do not fit easily into this rigid system, however. Trying to teach love and respect for a Republic does not sit well with a history of colonialism, including genocide and slavery.

Thus, there is always the potential for US-style culture wars, but setting the national curriculum gives the government control. At no point in my education was I taught about the horror caused by France's colonial acquisitions, let alone in regards to Algeria—a subject that would naturally have been of huge interest to me and many of my classmates. It was not until my history lessons in high school that the national curriculum magically jumped straight to decolonization.

Philosopher Nation

Philosophy is an essential component of a French public education because it was so important in the development of the Republic. Hence the Panthéon—the secular Paris mausoleum full of feted Frenchmen (with a few recent exceptions, almost all are men)—is dominated by philosophers. René Descartes was the founder of modern philosophy, while postmodernism, existentialism, and numerous other schools of thought are all considered French creations. Theories developed in France also include rationalism, eclecticism, positivism, structuralism, and, of course, republicanism.

Macron himself is a certified deep thinker. He studied philosophy at Paris Nanterre University, where he wrote a dissertation on Hegel. "Philosophy's intellectual refuge, its chance to represent the world, to give it meaning via a different filter, is important," he said.

All *lycée* students are required to take a course in philosophy, which leads up to a four-hour *bac* paper. Lessons cover themes such as consciousness, art, duty, and happiness. The latter belies the rather joyless nature of French learning and its focus on homegrown philosophers, but John Stuart Mill's "greatest happiness" Utilitarianism is still considered important.

The *bac philo* exam is made up of questions such as, "Is it absurd to desire the impossible?" and "Is working less, living better?" There are also set texts that have to be analyzed. The exam is considered a rite of passage that should technically set examinees off on a lifetime of philosophizing—except that many students actually hate it. They consider it too abstract and unnecessarily confusing.

Opposition to the *bac* "philosophizing" exam was widely expressed in 2022 when a piece written by Sorbonne philosophy graduate Sylvie Germain was on the exam paper. It was from *Jours de Colère* (Days of anger), her 1989 rural fantasy full of rich, imaginative language that was extremely hard to understand. Infuriated *lycée* students filled social media with insults directed at Germain, and there were even death threats.

The *Frankfurter Allgemeine* wrote, "Because French high school graduates found the exam topic too difficult, they hated the author Sylvie Germain on the Internet."[9] The newspaper suggested that the *bac* was an illusion, and that the entire French educational model was bankrupt. There were references to Socialists François Mitterrand and Jean-Pierre Chevènement opening up a *bac* utopia in the 1980s—one in which at least 80 percent of candidates were expected to pass, despite hundreds of thousands being left baffled by subjects such as philosophy.

Germain added support to such arguments. In an interview hitting back at the students' criticism, she said she did not feel personally insulted (living philosophers are challenged as much as dead ones) but added, "I'm rather worried by the symptom that this reveals. It is serious that students who are nearing the end of their schooling can show so much immaturity, and hatred of language, of the effort of reflection as much as imagination, and also so little curiosity, so little open-mindedness. They want diplomas without any effort, proclaim themselves victims for a yes or for a no and designate as persecutors the very people they insult and threaten. What adults will they become? All of this is as absurd as it is distressing."[10]

The development of a kind of nationalized philosophy—which is taught as part of the standard curriculum and the whole country is meant to be interested in—is an odd characteristic of modern France. As the nineteenth-century statesman and writer Alphonse de Lamartine put it: "La France est une nation qui s'ennuie." He was ostensibly stating that France is a bored nation, while actually instigating a debate on the subject. The country's shortcomings may well manifest themselves in ennui, the abstract feeling of despair that overwhelms when people do not think they are achieving very much. It's certainly an interesting philosophical question even if, as ever, nobody has a clear answer.

T'es nul—you're worthless—is an often-heard claim that plays on the minds of many, but there is no tangible evidence that this is linked to exam frustration. What is certain, however, is that advanced philosophy is now an elitist discipline, rather than the mass one that the system of public education tries to create.

Questioning Voltaire

Voltaire, the eighteenth-century Paris scholar, is a cornerstone of French national education and indeed the entire Republic. If you go through the school system, you hear about him all the time, and this carries on into university and beyond. There was even a "Voltaire" class at the elite ENA graduate school when future President François Hollande was studying there. None of us are left unmoved by the philosopher's prodigious talent and his contribution to liberal thought. Voltaire's place in the Panthéon as an establishment intellectual was always guaranteed.

Voltaire's satirical novel *Candide, ou l'Optimisme*—better known in English as *Candide: or, All for the Best*—is a prime example. It is the story of a naive (*candide* means "ingenuous" in French, not "blunt," as it does in English), privileged young man who is ejected from a comfortable castle home somewhere in Westphalia to experience physical hardship and all-round disillusionment as he travels around the world with his friends. The story is based on true events (as Hollywood would put it), including the Seven Years War of the mid-eighteenth century and the Lisbon earthquake of 1755.

Candide is full of black humor, and it ridicules everything from religion and politics to the military. My favorite part comes at the end when Candide reaches Constantinople (in modern-day Turkey) and meets a wise old Muslim man sitting under a tree. Rather than getting involved in complicated discussions about international diplomacy and the ills of the world, the old man confesses that his stability in every field comes from his smallholding. He is able to cultivate fruit, which he sells at market, and thus ensures a happy life. The key adage is: "We must cultivate our garden," or "Il faut cultiver notre jardin," as Voltaire wrote it.

I loved this idea of seeking out simple pleasures and not being too worried about the wider world when I first read it as a teenager. I imagine a lot of *France profonde* thinking is based on this saying too. If you can sort out your own little plot, you'll be fine. Gardens certainly say a lot about the French. The Tuileries in central Paris—near where I taught my preparatory classes for the *grandes écoles*—are beautiful and inspiring in parts but also highly controlled, just like the country's national education system. Everything is in straight lines, you get fined for walking on the grass, and if trees or bushes start to look even a little bit unruly, they are immediately cut down. Water features including fountains, and statues reinforce a sense of symmetry. Jules Ferry— father of the modern Republican school—also held the office of *Ministre de l'Instruction Publique et des Beaux-Arts* in the 1880s. This title conveyed the state's mission to impart knowledge and to promote fine arts through strict *instruction*, rather than a more relaxed, Oxford-style *education*. Thus, we can pinpoint two models of schooling, and two types of society—each reflected in the shape of their gardens.

Indeed, early French Kings saw their landscaped gardens as expressions of high ideals centered on spiritual order deriving from God. Beyond the Tuileries, the most famous classic gardens in France remain those at Versailles. They were designed by architect André Le Nôtre in the seventeenth century, and they illustrate perfectly how nature could be conquered and manipulated, in line with the wishes of the most privileged conformists imaginable.

Divine right of Kings' gardens such as the Tuileries and the ones at Versailles survived the Enlightenment. They still stand in contrast with the haphazard gardens in England, where random tree planting, serpentine borders, and oddly shaped lakes and ponds are commonplace, reflecting the more disruptive nature of the British. French Enlightenment rationality, and especially its emphasis on science and mathematics, turns out citizens who are as straitlaced as their long lines of plane trees. Queen Marie Antoinette had a modest English garden built for her at Versailles, but look what happened to her.

My reading of *Candide* can be considered a limited triumph of a French education, but it will not stop me questioning the Voltaire myth—on the contrary. Self-styled moderates of all political persuasions believe he should be untouchable, but this kind of reverence should not be the case. The French establishment should stop putting Voltaire on a pedestal while glossing over darker facts about his legacy.

Voltaire—who was eighty-three when he died in 1778—defined himself as a "merchant philosopher"; he was indisputably involved with the colonial slave trade. He funded the French East India Company in the 1740s, when its armed frigates were focused on triangular trade voyages to Africa. Voltaire also put his money into slave transportation adventures by ships such as *Le Saint-Georges*, which left Cádiz, Spain, in December 1751 bound for Guinea.

The European slave trade has ended, and we can perhaps forgive Voltaire his links with it, apologists would say, just as we can forgive Thomas Jefferson's involvement in chattel slavery. Jefferson, the third President of the United States, owned hundreds of slaves thanks to inheriting plantations in Virginia from his father. Emancipation became important to Jefferson in later life, but—like Voltaire—financial considerations often took precedence over common decency: he kept hold of some of his human assets.

Both Voltaire and Jefferson were men of their time who never claimed to be perfect, their unyielding defenders argue. Although Jefferson drafted the Declaration of Independence, paving the way for the Revolution against British rule, he was a hardheaded politician first, and a philosopher a rather distant second.

In contrast, Voltaire's elevation of science and reason above the superstition and obscurantism of religion and royalty did not stop him from promoting some of the vilest creeds in human history. His virulent hatred of religious groups was enough to incite violence against them, while his biological racism maintained that there were gradations of life forms, with Black people coming somewhere near the bottom, just up from "monkeys." In *Les Lettres d'Amabed* (1769), Voltaire portrayed Africans as "animals" with a "flat black nose with little or no intelligence."

Voltaire was also an obsessive anti-Semite who placed Jews well outside the great civilizations of ancient Greece and Rome that he admired. Writing about Jews in his *Letter of Memmius to Cicero* in 1771, Voltaire opined, "They are, all of them, born with raging fanaticism in their hearts, just as the Bretons and the Germans are born with blond hair." In an essay the following year, Voltaire's judgment on the Jews was blunt: "You deserve to be punished, for this is your destiny."

Unlike the usual motivations for anti-Semitism—irrational fear combined with ignorance—Voltaire based his prejudice on quasi-scientific reasoning. This was typical of Enlightenment philosophers who provided disturbing "justifications" for their hate. In "Of National Characters," David Hume wrote, "I am apt to suspect the negroes to be naturally inferior to the whites." Immanuel Kant called Jews a "nation of cheaters."

Such philosophical racism had a real-world objective: it offered pernicious excuses to imperialists who wanted to conquer and oppress supposedly lesser races. Enlightenment wickedness was widely read across Europe, including by Voltaire's great friend, King Frederick II of Prussia. Voltaire joined the monarch's court at Potsdam in 1750 as his live-in mentor, when he was ostensibly promoting the ideas behind such works as his woefully ill-named 1763 *Treatise on Tolerance*. At the same time, Frederick II was issuing anti-Jewish decrees while promoting militaristic nationalism.

As he formulated his plan for the Third Reich, Adolf Hitler is said to have studied discussions between Frederick the Great and Voltaire, whose advocacy of biological racism and white supremacy still gives succor to extremists, including Nazi sympathizers. The latter are traditionally linked to parties such as the Rassemblement National, as well as terrorists who target synagogues and mosques.

With national role models such as Voltaire, it is little wonder that millions in France still vote for a party founded by Jean-Marie Le Pen, a convicted anti-Semite and Holocaust denier. In which case, it is about time that France stopped revering Enlightenment racists as if they were secular saints.

The Intellectual Is So Often a Fool . . .
Until He Proves Otherwise

Philosophical writing is hugely complex, and often highly idiosyncratic. A lot of the time it is unintelligible. What might be considered important to many, however, is the effect it has on real life, and it does not always have to be as negative as Voltaire's racism. As the Paris writer Georges Bernanos put it, "The intellectual is so often a fool that we should always think of him as such, until he proves otherwise."

The tradition of the public intellectual influencing policy is long and proud in France. We might consider Émile Zola's "J'accuse" to be a classic example of serious thought affecting public policy. It exposed anti-Semitism at the heart of the French State during the Dreyfus scandal. Zola personified the national conscience when his accusatory letter to President Félix Faure was published in *L'Aurore* newspaper in January 1898. It blamed the military for falsely accusing Alfred Dreyfus, a Jewish officer, of treason and then trying to cover up the lies. Thanks to the letter, Dreyfus was pardoned by the President and later cleared on all charges.

When Louis-Napoléon Bonaparte staged a coup and overthrew the Second Republic in 1851, republican thinker Victor Hugo escaped to Belgium and became a dissident. Hugo, who is best known for his classic novels such as *The Hunchback of Notre Dame* and *Les Misérables*, continually attacked the new Napoleonic regime. His political pamphlet *Napoléon le Petit* (Napoléon the little) was smuggled into France via bales of hay and in sardine tins. It ridiculed the new Empire of Napoléon III, whom Hugo described as a criminal and a thief. Louis-Napoléon was portrayed as a grotesque figure in comparison to his uncle, Napoléon Bonaparte. The onslaught was so powerful that Hugo had to flee Belgium—where he could easily be targeted by the French—and go to the British Channel Islands.

One of the finest intellectual devices used by Hugo in *Napoléon le Petit* was the 2 + 2 = 5 adage that illustrates how despotic governments come up with patently fake statements to try to "justify" their irrational excesses. George Orwell later made it famous in his dystopian novel *1984*, along with the dogma "war is peace."

Hugo remained in exile for almost twenty years, constantly promoting his belief in the French Republic until it was reestablished in 1870. His politically charged work helped shape the course of French history, and ultimately contributed to the fall of another Napoleonic Empire.

Simone de Beauvoir was one of the most recent French philosophers to have a seismic impact on society. *The Second Sex*, her 1949 book, was a radical challenge to traditional female role models. Beauvoir argued that women were scandalously treated as an "other," and she became a leading advocate for women's liberation. In 1971, she authored the "Manifesto of the 343," in which women admitted to having had illegal abortions. It led to the Veil law of 1975, named after Health Minister Simone Veil, which repealed legislation criminalizing termination of a pregnancy before ten weeks. As a secondary school teacher, Beauvoir was never afraid to attack France's plodding education system. She was repeatedly fired, normally because her feminist ideas were considered a corrupting influence on bourgeois students who were invariably Catholics. One of Beauvoir's more controversial views was that society forced women to take on subservient roles.

Beauvoir's most prominent associate in Paris was Jean-Paul Sartre. The pair were editors of the left-wing *Les Temps Modernes* (*Modern Times*) and regularly pressed for revolutionary political change around the world. Sartre popularized existentialism, the humanistic idea that "existence precedes essence."

"Man simply is," Sartre argued. "Not that he is simply what he conceives himself to be, but that he is what he wills, and as he conceives himself after already existing—as he wills to be after that leap towards existence. Man is nothing else but that which he makes himself. That is the first principle of existentialism."[11] Sartre's most quoted line, from the play *No Exit*, is "L'enfer, c'est les autres." It is most satisfyingly translated as "Hell is other people," but the exact meaning is, fittingly, up for a long discussion, preferably on a Left Bank café terrace.

Beyond the kind of imponderable questions that go over the heads of many, Sartre was engaged with the problems of the underdog everywhere. Not only did he attack colonial oppression carried out by his own countrymen in Algeria, but he also vehemently criticized the French university system. Sartre called himself a "traitor" but an all the better philosopher because of it. Being an effective *intellectuel engagé* meant challenging the status quo and not simply relaxing into a comfortable lifestyle.

Who are today's *intellectuels engagés*? The sad truth is that they tend to be right-wing TV pundits who have more in common with half-educated rabble-rousers than the *philosophes* they pretend to be. These populist reactionaries stoke racism, intolerance, and—in particular—hatred of Islam. The populists who are allowed to drone on endlessly in the media focus on decline without conceding that they are one of the primary reasons for it. The *pseudo-philosophes* and their ultra negative theses helped *déclinisme* enter France's *Larousse* dictionary in 2017.

Few French public intellectuals are known outside France, except perhaps as parody figures. Bernard-Henri Lévy, a perma-tanned media celebrity known for showing off his chest hair by unbuttoning his pristine white shirts as low as he can, advocates for universal human rights, but on Western terms. The flamboyant BHL—as he likes to be known—infamously met up with Libyan rebel leaders and persuaded Nicolas Sarkozy to support them militarily in 2011.

In typically self-promoting fashion, BHL turned his adventure into a 2012 TV documentary called *The Oath of Tobruk*, in which he starred. As a tribute to the vanity of BHL, the film works as well as the rest of his output, but it does little to address the cataclysmic problems caused by Western forces once more bombing a Muslim-majority country into regime change. In fact, French fighter jets were already bombing Gaddafi's compound before the United Nations resolution had even been voted on and passed.

The French and their allies facilitated the murder of Libyan dictator Muammar Gaddafi in a manner that had not been authorized by the international community. UN Security Council Resolution 1973 had permitted the protection of civilians in Libya but not the change of leadership that men like BHL and Sarkozy—who was said to have accepted millions in illegal cash from Gaddafi—clearly wanted.

The military intervention caused a power vacuum in Libya, which was easily exploited by terror groups such as Al-Qaeda and ISIS. It also reinforced the belief that the West was primarily interested in the country because of its oil wealth and other commercial opportunities. As an exercise in intellectual dynamism bringing about change that would benefit humanity, BHL's efforts fell very short.

Check out the bookshops on the Left Bank nowadays (hurry up! Many are being converted into fashion boutiques or fast-food outlets!) and you'll find skimpy publications that often read like hastily written propaganda for the Rassemblement National or Éric Zemmour's Reconquête movement. Talk of decline and extinction dominates such books.

The economics essayist Nicolas Baverez was responsible for *Chronicles of French Denial* and *La France Qui Tombe* (France in free fall). In these books, there are nonstop quotes by past leaders such as De Gaulle and Napoléon Bonaparte and references to great technological achievements, such as the TGV high-speed trains and the Airbus project. Subsequent Presidents of both Left and Right are accused of "turning France into a loser" during a long period of deindustrialization. The end of the *Trente Glorieuses*, which came with the 1970s oil crisis, is one of the key economic events that led to wider feelings of pessimism, Baverez argued, although he at least believed his country's problems could be reversed.

Michel Onfray, who has produced around a hundred books, many of them about philosophy, wrote *Décadence: Vie et Mort du Judéo-Christianisme* (Decadence: The life and death of the Judeo-Christian tradition). In it, he described a country that was no longer strong enough to defend itself from perceived enemies (non-Judeo-Christian ones, naturally).

Gilles Kepel, a Sciences Po professor, wrote *Terror in France: The Rise of Jihad in the West*— an alarmist caricature of how radicalized

French Muslims in the suburbs are allegedly tearing their whole country apart. Éric Zemmour blames pretty much everyone and everything for the decline of France, from feminism to "wokeism," but immigration remains the biggest villain in *The French Suicide*. Like far-right politician Philippe de Villiers's *Le Moment Est Venu de Dire Ce Que J'ai Vu* (The time has come to tell you what I have seen)—a 2015 study in decline and decay—it was a bestseller.

Alain Finkielkraut's 2013 *L'Identité Malheureuse* (The unhappy identity) says pretty much all you need to know about what he thinks about modern France in the title. Finkielkraut, a retired professor of history of ideas at the École Polytechnique—one of the most prestigious *grandes écoles* in the country—and an Académie Française Immortal, was a leading member of the group of "prominent intellectuals." He warned against multiculturalism and mass immigration. Just like Jean-Marie Le Pen, Finkielkraut—although a self-proclaimed left-wing intellectual rather than the leader of the far-right National Front—has particular views about the France football team. In an interview with the Israeli newspaper *Haaretz* in 2005, he commented that the team was "black, black, black, which causes sneers all over Europe"—thus vilifying the celebrated "Black, White, Arab" (*black, blanc, beur*) diversity of the squad, which had won the World Cup in 1998. To Finkielkraut, the France players in general were nothing more than "a gang of billionaire thugs" and "a mafia" that represents a "scum generation." Finkielkraut extended this racist sentiment to African-Americans, too, as he railed against the "islamisation of the Blacks" both in France and the United States.[12]

When, in 2015, Les Républicains politician Nadine Morano described the true France as a "white race country," Finkielkraut defended her. As the son of a Polish Jew who had survived Auschwitz, Finkielkraut in turn accused the anti-racism lobby of conducting a witch hunt against him. The negative and the nasty sell across the media.

The appointment of historian Pap Ndiaye, who is of French and Senegalese descent, as France's Education Minister in May 2022 caused particular anger among the ideologues who oppose globalism and liberalism, and especially "woke theories" imported from the United States along with more fast-food chains. As an academic, Ndiaye specialized in racial discrimination in France and America and the shared suffering of minorities in both countries. Ndiaye wanted safe spaces for people with dark skin and supported positive discrimination to fight "structural racism." Ndiaye was said to be typical of those threatening France's universalist tradition, which was technically oblivious to people's ethnicity or religion.

Wokeism—the term that generally means an overbidding aware-ness of prejudice and discrimination in the United States—was anathema to the Republic, critics argued. Yet Ndiaye had replaced Jean-Michel Blanquer, an arch secular reactionary when he was Edu-cation Secretary. Blanquer had set up the Laboratory of the Republic, a think tank furthering the ideals of *laïcité*. This group had concluded that "the veil itself is not desirable in French society" and confirmed *le wokisme* as an unwanted American import.

Marine Le Pen accused Ndiaye of planning "the deconstruction of our country, its values and its future." She added, "I don't give a damn about the color of his skin, but if this is the ideology we are going to impose on our children, it is a catastrophe." Le Pen's reaction to the appointment of Ndiaye was shared by those *pseudo-philosophes* or pop philosophers dominating prime-time media discussion panels and writing newspaper and magazine columns and best-selling pamphlets. All were challenging what they thought of as political correctness and defending "ethnic French" people threatened by perceived foreigners, including those born in France with overseas backgrounds.

For his part, Éric Zemmour's "suicidal" posturing was under-pinned by the Italian philosopher Antonio Gramsci's theory of "cul-tural hegemony." Zemmour argued that French institutions, especially academia and the media, had been overrun by American-style liberals, who were losing track of what it meant to be truly French.

Great Replacement—the theory constructed by Renaud Camus that immigrants with higher birth rates will one day take over from the indigenous population—was central to so much of the discourse of men like Zemmour. Camus, the leading white nationalist writer and conspiracy theorist in France, has (like Zemmour) convictions for inciting racial hatred, but (again, like Zemmour) that has made no difference to his public profile nor his ability to spread his ideas. Quite the opposite, in fact.

References to the French nation and the so-called aliens who threaten it are not only clickbait, but they also translate into millions of votes. Even brazen racism has become socially acceptable, thanks in large part to these men and women. Emptied of moral content and—some would say—even all appropriate facts, debates drop into the gutter. Even fiction has been used to demonize undesirable communities.

Author Michel Houellebecq's *Soumission* (*Submission*) of 2015 was a dystopian novel that featured the election of an Islamist to the French presidency. Enlightenment ideals were disintegrating, and the enemy was taking over. Beyond Muslims, the main target of *Soumission* was France's intellectual and political class. Houellebecq's international bestseller suggested Marine Le Pen would lose to Mohammed Ben-Abbes in the 2022 presidential election, because the mainstream political establishment wanted to keep the far-right out of power. Houellebecq, who had faced a charge of inciting racial hatred by insulting Islam before being acquitted in 2002, was again accused of bigoted provocation against Islam, leading to Prime Minister Manuel Valls saying, "France is not Michel Houellebecq—it is not intolerance, hatred, and fear." There were plenty of reasons to disagree.

There are very occasionally one or two noble exceptions to the rabble-rouser pamphleteers. Holocaust survivor Stéphane Hessel's *Indignez-vous!* (*Time for Outrage!*) is only thirty-five pages long, but coming from a writer in his nineties who was a pupil of Jean-Paul Sartre at the École Normale Supérieure in Paris, it is a commendable rallying cry for those who want to change the world. Hessel attacks indifference, particularly over key issues such as Palestine. As a former member of the French Resistance who had fought against Nazi Occupation, he regularly condemned Israel for its ongoing oppression of Palestinians. Hessel—who sold more than four million copies of his book in thirty languages—died in 2013. By this time, he had inspired protest

movements such as Occupy, which campaigned against inequality and
the system that finances capitalism.

Educating the Educators

The abiding threat to anyone who is struggling within France's sprawling national education system, and the kind of citizens it produces,
is excommunication. There is a quasi-religious fervor in the way the
system is run, and if you show any kind of dissent, you can quickly
find yourself expelled. Politicians, teachers, and inspectors uphold not
only reactionary institutions but an ideology that stretches back to
eighteenth-century philosophers who were by no means as enlightened
as everybody thinks.

The mission of the Black Hussar–style public servants is essentially
to transmit conformity in the language of Molière. A fear of making
mistakes is palpable and inhibits entire generations. Anything that is
raw and challenging is marked down, and if you are a nonconformist
failure, then you can go off and get a manual job or try unemployment.
It is in this way that elite intellectuals impose their culture—which,
they believe, should be the only one available—and treat anything that
challenges it as trash.

A good way to start improving the situation would be to encourage
teachers to teach, rather than to simply impart knowledge with a sour
face. Many have no idea how to deal with a classroom full of energetic
children or older students. They ignore the social backgrounds of the
pupils, let alone any personal problems that might be troubling them.
Little effort is made to enjoy general discussions about what is happening in the world or simply to amuse and entertain. As John Stuart Mill
would argue, honest human interaction is essential to good teaching.

The sneering brutality prevalent in French schools certainly needs
reform. Rote learning and nonstop exams do not suit everybody, nor
does having your failure exposed to the world. There is a simple marking system in France: a pass is ten out of twenty, but there is no incen-
tive to do better than that, because all you need is a pass. Those who
do particularly badly have to repeat a year. This beats all the confidence

out of them and sometimes puts them off any kind of academic activity for life. The French system stifles creativity in students very early on and leaves them terrified of failure. This is no way to educate people.

The overriding sense of aggression in many French schools and colleges manifests itself in politically motivated blockades and strikes. University riots are legendary, and *lycée* students often join in. They spray graffiti on walls, set fire to trash bins, and worse. It is by no means uncommon to see the riot squad moving in with truncheons drawn. Teachers often join in, too, and not always on the side of their students. There is no sense of pride in French educational institutions. The divide between those who run them and the students is wide. Authority figures are unnecessarily aloof or antagonistic.

There are around a million civil servants running France's education leviathan. It's a military-style hierarchy, full of people handing out orders and making sure that they are complied with. The Minister of Education is at the head of it all, rather than proper educators. Dealing with inspectors from Paris is not easy. This entire structure needs reform to hand power to the grass roots. Teachers should be making decisions about courses, financing, and timetables based on their own circumstances. Schools need to be more autonomous. Creativity, energy, and enthusiasm need to be encouraged. Learning for pleasure is what inspires people for life.

When Oxford academics came over to Paris to interview me for my job at Jesus College, they feared ending up with a standard-model French teacher who would terrify their undergraduates. We laughed about this soon after I got my contract, and I made a special effort not to come across as a tyrant. This went down very well at Oxford, but I would not have lasted five minutes at a *grande école*.

7

IDENTITY

The Great Debate

The world of reality has its limits; the world of
imagination is boundless.

—JEAN-JACQUES ROUSSEAU (1712–1778)

France is obsessed with Frenchness, to the extent that there was once
a Ministry of Immigration, Integration, National Identity, and
Co-development. It lasted for three years, up until 2010, and in that
time, it launched a "great debate on national identity" in an attempt to
codify "what it means to be French."

There was much talk about former colonies, and the buzzwords
were "assimilation" and "integration." However, the level of argument
was best illustrated by the torrent of racial abuse that flooded an official site that had been especially created by Éric Besson, the Immigration and National Identity Minister. It had seemingly been intended
to spark discussion and interesting philosophical and sociological
observations—intellectual rigor, in other words. Instead, noteworthy
contributions included comments like "France is for Christians" and
"Being French means eating pork and not wearing a burqa." The reality was that bundling "immigration" with "national identity" while

opening online forums to the public gave voice to bigotry under the guise of patriotism.

Algeria was an obvious focus of the debate because it raised the question of dual identity: French-Algerians who might not be entirely French, despite being born and brought up in France. If you had roots in Algeria, and the country was playing France at football, would you cheer for the blues or the greens? That is, Les Bleus, representing your parents' adopted homeland, or Les Verts, from the former colony where they were born?

First-generation North African immigrants and their descendants from *les banlieues* could not, according to many French nationalists, accept the tricolor's dominance over the star and crescent flag of Islam. Commentators pointed to loud choruses of "One, two, three / Viva l'Algérie!" that were heard being chanted by Algeria fans at every game involving their team before the riot squads of the secular Fifth Republic moved in with their batons and tear gas to sort out those responsible. Intended to reaffirm pride in being French, the debate was accompanied by a drive to make schoolchildren sing "La Marseillaise," and to get adults to take banal civics tests to which the multiple-choice answers were always "Charles de Gaulle" or "Austerlitz." In France, the debate about identity does more to stir up anger and resentment than any football hooligan ever could.

Officially, the common denominator related to all those living in France and its overseas territories is a very distinct form of republican unity—one that implies that everybody has common values. The French model is unique in that it asks immigrants to leave all their cultural inheritance at the point of entry. Everybody is meant to be molded into an identikit citizen. Descendants of immigrants are purged of their ancestry too.

The establishment position originates from Enlightenment philosophers such as Jean-Jacques Rousseau, whose thinking helped bring about the overthrow of the French Crown. The republican national identity evolved during the 1789 Revolution.[1] The "Marseillaise" and the blue, white, and red flag—derived from the tricolor *cocarde* (the pleated-ribbon ornament first worn by revolutionaries)—became unifying symbols of the new order, underpinned by the universal motto of *Liberté, Égalité, Fraternité.*

In modern France the *tricolore* is still seen everywhere, and the "Marseillaise" is sung with pride, despite its bloodcurdling chorus ("To arms, citizens / Form your battalions / March, march! / Let the impure blood / soak into our furrowed ground!"). The French nation continues to revere much that came out of the Revolution. In theory, Article 1 of the Constitution of the current Fifth Republic states that the Republic is "indivisible" and that it "ensures equality before the law of all citizens without distinction of origin, race, or religion." Yet in practice, France's supposed republicanism has failed to deliver the lofty promise of Liberty, Equality, and Fraternity for all. For some, the blanket republican identity forged during the Revolution covers up, rather than fixes, stark injustices.

A Digest of Anarchy

The French Revolution of 1789 is glorified today in a manner that always underplays the diabolical bloodshed involved. Instead, it is associated with the Declaration of the Rights of Man and of the Citizen of the same year, inspired by America's 1776 Declaration of Independence. There were seventeen Articles in the French document, ranging from the first that guaranteed freedom and equality to the last stating that private property was a "sacred right."

The people were the ultimate heroes of the popular uprising that changed the progress of human history, providing a radical step toward democracy, equal rights, and freedom. Peasants and urban laborers, the *sans culottes* (those without knee breeches—the silk garments worn by the eighteenth-century nobility), at the bottom of society rebelled against the wretched lives imposed on them by the Ancien Régime. Class divisions were intense before the Revolution, with the privileged having little social conscience, and certainly not in relation to the masses.

In turn, many of the republican revolutionaries were united in a hatred of the Monarchy and the established Catholic Church, because of the spiritual authority it had provided to Kings and Queens. The Roman clergy were also major landowners, meaning there were economic reasons for opposing them. Legislation removed land from priests, and the Civil Constitution of the Clergy of 1790 subordinated Christian dogma to government decrees. All priests were forced, under pain of death or exile, to swear allegiance to the new Constitution. *Laïcité*—secularism, a principle that republicans are still obsessed by— grew out of this ferocious anticlericalism.

When the *Gilets Jaunes* were rioting and bringing major cities including Paris to a halt, there was always a mobile choir rehearsing revolutionary anthems such as "La Carmagnole" (lyrics include "Long live the sound of the cannon") and "Ça Ira" ("Ah! It will be fine! / The aristocrats, we will hang them!") in between fighting the police.

The 1789 Revolution gave hope to many of the twenty-eight million people living in France at the time, as well as others around the world. Those able to read Rousseau's ideas learned about his very positive view of mankind: he considered people to be ultimately decent and capable of working together for the common good.

Democratic opinion flourished thanks to print. Newspapers that once required royal licenses, and which were heavily censored as a result, were replaced by new republican ones with titles such as *Friend of the People* (a deliberate contrast to the monarchical daily, *Ami du Roi—Friend of the King*). Pamphlets were distributed in coffeehouses, taverns, and salons. The publications were full of dissent but also optimism about the future of *la Nation*.

French citizens started to embrace nationalism—that is, the idea that the state was the best representative of the people. The old order could be discarded in favor of rallying round *la Patrie*. Rousseau outlined a touching faith in humanity in his 1762 *Du Contrat Social; ou, Principes du Droit Politique* (*The Social Contract*). It argued that people were obliged to give up their selfish independence in return for communal rights that would benefit everybody. The Declaration of the Rights of Man and of the Citizen that was adopted by the Paris National Assembly in August 1789 was an echo of Rousseau's *volonté générale* (general will). Its Article 6 reads: "The law is the expression of the general will. All citizens have the right to take part, in person or by their representatives, in its formation. It must be the same for everyone whether it protects or penalizes. All citizens being equal in its eyes are equally admissible to all public dignities, offices, and employments, according to their ability, and with no other distinction than that of their virtues and talents."

Such ideals are still held in high esteem by French republicans, however remote they are from reality. In practice, the vague "general will" never represents what all the people want. Instead, a small dogmatic minority works out what is "best" for society. The fact that Rousseau recommended the death penalty for those who refused to agree to the *volonté générale* is indicative of how intrinsically intolerant it is.

Rousseau had little interest in promoting the rights of women either. He considered them the weaker sex and almost entirely dependent on men because of their supposedly poor powers of reasoning. In *Emile, or On Education* (1762), which describes a boy's development in the state of nature, Rousseau wrote: "Once it is demonstrated that man and woman are not, and should not be constituted the same, either in character or in temperament, it follows that they should not have the same education." It would be many years before there were advances in sex equality in France.

Reactionary regimes can easily use the idea of the *volonté générale* to quash democracy. The 1789 Revolution soon turned into the Reign of Terror, led by Robespierre and the Jacobins—the most powerful Republican club of the Revolution, originally founded by anti-royalist Bretons. The Committee of Public Safety was encouraged by manipulative speeches by Robespierre, as he blithely ignored liberty, democracy, and equality in private. Instead, he built up his personal power base and killed or jailed anyone who crossed him. Counts vary, but after Robespierre took charge of the "safety" committee, around half a million so-called enemies of the Revolution were arrested, at least ten thousand died in prison, and tens of thousands were executed, many by guillotine, on the Place de la Révolution in Paris (now Place de la Concorde).[2]

Robespierre's deceit is easily exposed. Rather than a case study in the flourishing of the Social Contract, the First Republic was responsible for tens of thousands of sudden and violent killings: royals were beheaded in Paris, and massacres abounded across France. Many victims were summarily executed without trial. The September Massacres of 1792 saw more than one thousand prisoners killed in Paris alone. There were up to two hundred thousand casualties following an insurrection by Catholic royalists against the Republican *bleu* army in the southern Vendée department throughout the 1790s, resulting in 170,000 insurgents being slaughtered.

There was no real "general will," beyond the poor wanting enough food to eat and to avoid dying in squalor. Bread riots in the cities and countryside proliferated. The Revolution of 1789 ultimately ended with the military dictatorship of Napoléon Bonaparte and all-out war caused by France trying to force its Revolution on other countries.

The Anglo-Irish conservative statesman Edmund Burke used his 1790 pamphlet *Reflections on the Revolution in France* to attack the uprising as a "digest of anarchy" that failed to respect the "wisdom of the ages." Burke bemoaned the mass killings and shattering of an ancient culture, albeit one based on the hereditary principle. He also lamented the way the masses—the "swinish multitude"—entered politics as baying mobs, rather than through well-established institutions.

Plenty of French are persuaded that history is a succession of numerous dark plots. An IFOP poll on behalf of Conspiracy Watch and the Fondation Jean-Jaurès in December 2018 found 60 percent of respondents were sympathetic to at least one conspiracy theory. Many (43 percent) thought France's Health Ministry was conspiring with Big Pharma to conceal the dangers of vaccines—a theory that would have widespread implications during the COVID-19 pandemic, which started a year later.

There is a lot of talk in the modern Republic about the Illuminati working against the true France. Check online blogs and social media threads, and you'll hear and read about the globalists undermining the true wishes of the people. Apparently, the Illuminati killed JFK and made Kim Kardashian famous, as well as triggered the Ukraine

War and the coronavirus pandemic. Most of all—as far as France is concerned—they stole the Revolution and then twisted it into a warped justification for the chaos that followed. Rousseau's *Social Contract* never delivered a French Republican ideal, and its failure led to simmering grievances and bleak suspicions—hardly secure foundations for a modern state.

The American Way

France may still appear very exotic to many foreigners, with its revolutionary heritage, but the conformism of its citizens is undeniable. The psychologist Gustave Le Bon, who is best known for his 1895 work *The Crowd: A Study of the Popular Mind*, described revolutionary mobs fired up by engaged leaders such as Robespierre and Jean-Paul Marat as marking the start of "the power of the masses."

Le Bon argued that the "psychological crowd" was primarily motivated by a collective unconsciousness, as if it were a herd. Instead of individual personalities, values, and beliefs, each person became "a grain of sand amid other grains of sand, which the wind stirs up at will," as Le Bon put it.

French conformism also manifests itself in an Americanization that took root in the post–World War I era, after US soldiers and related visitors had imported jazz, bubble gum, and open-top Cadillacs. France had been *la grande nation*—the universal teacher of civilized values and refined intellectualism—until the humiliation of the Nazi Occupation battered its sense of self-worth.

The French began to dream like the consumers of Middle America. They wanted large, detached homes packed with labor-saving appliances and prestige automobiles on the front drive. The particularly affluent ones installed swimming pools in the gardens of their deluxe suburban homes (there are now more than three million private pools in France). "Sarko the American," as the former President was dubbed by some, personified the drift toward obsessive consumerism and the need to show off his success using designer goods, such as Rolex and Patek Philippe watches.

À Bout de Souffle (*Breathless*), the 1960 New Wave film directed by Jean-Luc Godard (Paris-born but, like Jean-Jacques Rousseau, also Swiss), celebrated American crime capers, Humphrey Bogart (the film's antihero, Michel, played by Jean-Paul Belmondo, wanted to be Bogie), Oldsmobiles, and the Champs-Élysées. The most famous avenue in France was developed into a vast strip full of shopping malls and car parks—a place where you could pick up the *Herald Tribune* and meet as many Americans in Paris as French.

The legacy of an older, more creative France was still present, but America and Britain started to dominate cultural life. Elvis Presley and Mick Jagger became heroes of French youth, more so than Johnny Hallyday—the "French Elvis," who was largely unknown outside his own country, despite the Jimi Hendrix Experience playing with him in France in 1966. There was very little to be excited about in Paris, which began to feel like a living museum. There was a strong feeling— still relevant to this day—that French culture was *à bout de souffle*, out of puff. Soon there was a Disneyland on the outskirts of the French capital, which would become the most popular tourist destination in a country filled with theme parks.

The *Trente Glorieuses*—thirty years of economic success starting in 1945—spread not only affluence but also Americanization. Nowadays, some French wear baseball caps and are entertained by all the big American media outlets, such as Netflix and Amazon Prime. The forward-thinking—people like Emmanuel Macron—speak English extremely well, and often with an American accent. Names such as Kevin—after the American actor Kevin Costner—have proliferated. There are Brads (Pitt), Léos (DiCaprio), and Ashtons (Kutcher).

McDonald's—the French call it MacDo—is immensely popular, along with the Buffalo Grill restaurant chain. Teenagers and older youths—often much older—wear NBA apparel and are still break dancing and producing awful urban graffiti. The popularity of Pink Floyd is as strong as it was in Britain and the United States almost half a century ago. I went to a concert by Roger Waters, cofounder and main creative talent behind the band, in Paris in 2018, when he got a number of local school children to sing the chorus to "Another Brick in the Wall." The song is about alienation, and particularly kids feeling insignificant in their neglected, underfunded schools. The suburban Parisian youngsters looked great in their black "Resist" T-shirts as they punched the air in defiance, but Waters had North London youngsters doing the same thing four decades earlier. This time around, thousands of French at the concert acted as though the entire concept was new and original.

Despite their obsession with what comes out of "Anglo-Saxon" countries, the French have by no means adopted the can-do dynamism of America. The structures of day-to-day life may have changed to some extent, but the attitudes have not. Rugged individualism—the trait that built the American republic—is not part of the French one.

Traditional Gallic conformity is the reason you see so many French people wandering around in large groups and generally getting along by agreeing about pretty much everything. There may be political arguments, but in terms of social life, the French do not like to challenge norms. There is an order to the world, and it is not their job—let alone anyone else's—to change it. Altering the seating and table arrangements in a café or asking for fries instead of rice with the fish advertised on a menu would be viewed with alarm, for example.

The French don't like thinking outside those little blue grid boxes that helped them with their handwriting early in life. If there is a way of doing something, and it works, then they will stick with it. The French mindset is stubbornly suspicious of change.

This lack of a "Let's do it!" dynamic and an overwhelming respect for the status quo do not mean a lack of politeness, however. A French person will call you Monsieur or Madame while explaining that what you want is not possible and that you should learn to conform. Formality, and indeed brusqueness, does not necessarily mean dislike. It simply indicates that the French are distanced and confident that they have found the right way of doing something. They do not appreciate anyone telling them otherwise.

Conformity also limits social mobility. A key indicator of how you are perceived as a French citizen is economic status. Social mobility is difficult, but the public education system technically gives everyone a chance of making it happen. Bright, aspirational citizens can move upward in principle, but the structural barriers to advancement are immense.

Men of Africa

Rachid Bouchareb's *Days of Glory*—or *Indigènes* (Natives)—came out in 2006 and was nominated for the Academy Award for Best Foreign Language Film. It caused a sensation by reversing the conventional portrayal of French identity after the D-Day invasion during the Second World War. The stars are Sami Bouajila, the son of Tunisian immigrants to France, and Jamel Debbouze, who comes from a Moroccan background.

Their Arab soldier characters are representatives of some five hundred thousand men from France's African colonies brought into the military to fight the fascists. The *indigènes* (a word that signifies members of indigenous populations, rather than settler communities) were mainly impoverished Algerians, Moroccans, and sub-Saharan Africans who were used as cannon fodder. The Black Africans were widely known as *tirailleurs sénégalais*—Senegalese sharpshooters— even though many of these infantrymen were forced into military service from colonies beyond Senegal. Free France enforced compulsory conscription in many territories. Preference was slowly shifted toward North Africans, because they were considered better than troops from sub-Saharan Africa. French Generals had a problem reconciling nationalist aspirations with recruitment, but nevertheless a large-scale mobilization in 1943 saw more than 132,000 Algerians, 25,000 Tunisians, and 85,000 Moroccans joining the ranks. De Gaulle had established Algiers as the capital of the Free French by this time.[3]

Beyond being a classic war film full of explosions and firefights, *Days of Glory* challenges the hero stereotypes, and indeed the allegedly universal values of the French Republic. There is a scene in the film when the featured *indigènes* sing "Le Chant des Africains" (The song of the Africans), the stirring marching anthem that includes the words:

"We come from the colonies to save the motherland / We come from afar to die / We are the men of Africa."

Toward the end of the war, close to half a million of these soldiers made up 80 percent of the Free French Forces that landed on Mediterranean beaches two months after D-Day, during Operation Dragoon. They recaptured cities such as Toulon and Marseille and pushed the Germans out of France.

Those who failed to survive the most lethal war in human history at least avoided the humiliation of being excluded from the August 1944 victory parade in Paris, which was reserved for white soldiers. Colonial soldiers made up around two-thirds of De Gaulle's Free French Forces during the Second World War, but they were erased from their units for the ceremonial celebrations.

By the time the Allies reached Paris, De Gaulle was keen to assert his authority over the leftists, including plenty of hard-line Communists, who had played such a big part in the French Resistance and were intent on seizing political power. Allied High Command agreed to let De Gaulle parade down the Champs-Élysées with the fabled Second Armored Division (*2e Division Blindée*—or, more commonly, *la 2e DB*), but only if it "could be made one hundred per cent white."[4] Photographs of the marching troops showing rows of white faces would help De Gaulle project the false impression that indigenous French had in fact liberated themselves without the assistance of their colonies, even though around seventeen thousand *tirailleurs* died fighting the Nazis.

The myth of a "whites only" Liberation was soon followed by the French authorities stripping their colonial troops of their uniforms and shipping them back across the Mediterranean to Africa. When repatriated Senegalese prisoners of war protested about pay in November 1944, up to three hundred were gunned down at the Thiaroye military camp, near Dakar, French Senegal. Details of the December 1, 1944, Thiaroye massacre are not taught in France today. *Camp de Thiaroye*, a film about the scandal, was banned in France for a decade when it came out in 1988.

Soldiers forced into service in French colonies were expected to fight and die for *Liberté*, but there was no question of them enjoying the *Égalité* and *Fraternité* that should have come with it. Discrimination against veterans continued as successive French governments froze their war pensions after their countries became independent. The closing credits of *Indigènes* highlighted this outrage and allegedly led to a change in government policy. Meanwhile, those veterans allowed to remain in France ended up in decrepit holding camps that—like the ones designed for laborers—were eventually transformed into housing estates.

A new film about colonial soldiers called *Tirailleurs* was released in January 2023. This time, Omar Sy, the French-born Senegalese director and star actor, concentrated on the *indigènes* who fought during World War I—once again opening up old wounds concerning the way colonial soldiers were treated.

The Racism Barometer

By far the ugliest form of segregation in French society is still one built on race. Whole ethnic communities live on the out-of-town estates or in the less salubrious *cités* of major cities—"apartheid" exists in France, as former Socialist Prime Minister Manuel Valls put it. In his New Year address to the press in 2015, Valls had pledged to provide "republican answers" to this rampant ill, but there were no specifics.

Racist sentiment is extremely hard to monitor or regulate, because the so-called color-blind Republic does not compile data on the subject. Instead, France's lofty universalism aims to secure social unity precisely by ignoring differences. The contradiction between fantasy equality and real-world discrimination is startling. Like most officials, public intellectuals are far more interested in propping up their weak *républicanisme* than trying to tackle insidious discrimination.

The National Consultative Commission on Human Rights does at least produce an annual poll that attempts to measure bigotry. The so-called racism barometer survey of July 2022 pointed toward "the persistence of discrimination" because of real or assumed differences related to origin, religion, or skin color. More specifically, it noted how that year's presidential campaign—the one in which the far-right made significant breakthroughs—was "marked by the obsessive return of migration and security themes."

This government-funded report said the COVID-19 pandemic highlighted "stigmatizing discourse with racist and xenophobic overtones."[5] The main reason for this was the virus arriving from China in January 2020 and there being a sizeable Chinese diaspora in France, particularly in cities such as Paris. As so often, "immigrants" were linked with the importation of all kinds of horrors, including potentially lethal disease. In short, the overall findings of the survey are typical of a supposedly color-blind nation where your race and religion actually *do* mean a great deal—when people want to discriminate against you.

The report was published on the fiftieth anniversary of the July 1, 1972, Pleven law, which created the offense of racist defamation and racial provocation, hatred, violence, and discrimination in France. The authors concluded that the "incantatory invocation of the values of the Republic is not enough" to deal with such racist sentiments. The report said there needed to be "reasoned policies to fight against racism and discrimination, involving those whose rights are violated." Diagnosing problems with comprehensive data is vital for an effective remedy.

A particularly serious problem pinpointed by the human rights researchers was with the forces of law and order. As early as the 1920s, Paris police had set up a North African brigade to deal with alleged troublemakers imported from the colonies, in this case Maghreb countries such as Algeria and Morocco. The unit—which became noted for its extreme aggression—was disbanded, but it was reformed just before the Algerian War and called the Aggression and Violence Brigade, or BAV. It retained the same mission as the North African brigade: to act as a colonial police force in the heart of Paris. It operated between 1953 and 1962.

As far back as 1948, James Baldwin, the Black American writer, arrived in Paris and reported on immigrants he referred to as *les misérables* being "treated like dirt." The unemployed and low-paid laborers from Algeria, then still the jewel in France's imperial crown, were particularly persecuted by the authorities. Those who are obviously from African and North African backgrounds still suffer abominable

abuse in France. Macron's ministers are among the many who now regularly use words such as *ensauvagement*—turning savage—to describe
those they still consider to be largely responsible for street crime.

In June 2020, the Paris police prefecture was fast to clamp down
on any shows of support for the legacy of Adama Traoré, a Frenchman from a Malian background who had died in police custody on his
twenty-fourth birthday in 2016, while fleeing an identity check. Four
years later, I attended a rally in support of Traoré and his surviving
family outside the Tribunal de Paris, the court complex in the north of
the city. Officers said the demonstration should be banned because it
might lead to mass virus contagion during the coronavirus pandemic.

Some twenty thousand people turned up anyway, just as thousands
did at later protests by the Eiffel Tower and on Place de la Concorde.
Passions were running high, not least of all because of the similarities
between Traoré's death and that of George Floyd, the African-American
from Minneapolis, Minnesota, who was killed during his arrest in his
home city on May 25, 2020. Both Black men had suffered asphyxiation
while in police hands and became symbols of institutionalized racism.

The main difference between the cases was that the Floyd case was
supported by contemporaneous video. Floyd was seen gasping for mercy
as an officer who would later be convicted of murder knelt on his neck
for almost nine minutes. Such a graphic recording was not available
in the Traoré case, and this is why allegations were vehemently con-
tested by the officers accused of killing him. In consequence, any kind
of legal conviction was impossible. In May 2020, a final official report
was released that completely cleared the three policemen involved.

Despite the obvious advancement of justice when people filmed
appalling events, there were moves underway to prohibit the broadcasting of any footage that might identify the law enforcement officials involved. Éric Ciotti, a conservative MP, proposed a bill aimed at
"protecting" those in the line of duty because "being recognized in the
media and on social media might put their lives and their families in
danger." Chillingly, the legislation would include a year in prison and
a fine approaching €45,000 for anyone who misused their cameras. In
short, anyone who captured evidence of racist brutality by the authorities would risk becoming a victim themselves.

The suggested ban came at a time when French police were regularly trying to snatch and destroy phones or—if they wanted to be less provocative—asking people to delete images. They were acutely aware that valid complaints against them had ballooned alongside the number of citizens recording with their smartphones.

The near constant use of cameras at French demonstrations by the anti-government *Gilets Jaunes* from November 2018 turned police violence into a huge issue. During the COVID-19 lockdown, there were further examples of police excesses caught on video, particularly against ethnic minorities. Three officers in the southern town of Béziers faced prison sentences after they were filmed in April 2020 dragging a handcuffed suspect along the ground and sitting on him in the back seat of a patrol car just before he died in their police station. The victim, Mohamed Gabsi, a Muslim from an Arab background, was only thirty-three and the father of three young children.

There was a time when nobody would ever have heard of Gabsi or his suspicious death, but thanks to the footage, and the ease with which it could be instantly distributed, the wider world had a very good idea of what he went through. To support documenting police abuses, the group Urgence Violences Policières (police violence emergency) provided a free app for people to send images to a secure server where they could be stored for future legal use.

The right to film police is a crucial public safeguard, particularly in the case of street protests, identity checks, and other potential flashpoints. In an age when camera technology is growing more sophisticated by the day, any attempt to ban recording is likely to be as futile as trying to outlaw demonstrations. More than that, it displays a grotesque cynicism that threatens human rights and civil liberties while putting people in lethal danger. Ordinary citizens going out and capturing the truth provides the kind of racism barometer that the authorities have never come close to creating.

French inquiries into Black and North African men who have been shot dead or otherwise allegedly killed by police seldom go anywhere. Yet at the time of the Adama Traoré demonstrations, Emmanuel Macron denied there was an institutional problem in the police and

Gendarmerie. A government spokeswoman said that Macron had told a Cabinet meeting that racism and discrimination were "a plague and a betrayal of republican universalism." Once again, a dreamy principle had prevailed over the life of a non-white French citizen.

Queen of Diamonds

There has been no stranger aspect of French identity than their love for the Queen—the British Queen. I saw it for myself when the UK monarch visited France for the seventieth anniversary of the D-Day landings in 2014. Her Majesty arrived in Paris by high-speed Eurostar train with her husband, Prince Philip. Crowds cheered as they walked up the platform at the Gare du Nord before taking their places in the back of a vintage maroon Bentley that had been driven over for them via the Channel Tunnel. The prestige British car contrasted magnificently with the poky Renaults and Citroëns used by all the French officials.

Royal duties during the state visit—the Queen's sixth to France—included laying a wreath at the Tomb of the Unknown Soldier alongside President Hollande. Union Jacks lined the Champs-Élysées and the Arc de Triomphe, along with soldiers in dress uniform forming a guard of honor and a cavalry band.

Compared to the dreary Socialist head of state, the Queen cut an extraordinarily grand figure. She was dressed in a powder pink ensemble, complete with the Williamson pink diamond brooch, which contains one of the world's rarest jewels. It was discovered by Canadian mine owner John Thoburn Williamson in Tanzania in 1947, and the rough 54.5 carat sparkler was displayed in St. James's Palace before Elizabeth's marriage to Philip at Westminster Abbey the same year. A year later, the Queen used London diamond cutters Briefel & Lemer to turn the rough diamond into a twenty-four-carat faceted gem, one that could outshine any bauble in Paris.

Cries of "Vive la Reine!" also rang out at a flower market—the Marché aux Fleurs—that was to be named after the Queen. It was on the Île de la Cité and opposite the former Conciergerie prison where Marie Antoinette, the bona fide last Queen of France, had spent her final hours before being beheaded. In stark contrast, Queen Elizabeth II—who had first visited Paris in 1948 as a young Princess—personified the ongoing prestige, massive wealth, and stability of her own monarchical system.

The savage destruction of most of France's royals and related aristocrats had a profound effect on French identity and the country's institutions. "Something is missing in the democratic process and the way it functions," is how Macron put it. "In French politics, that missing something is the figure of the King."

Macron was almost slapped in the face by a royalist during regional election campaigning in July 2021, while carrying out a presidential walkabout in the Drôme department of southeast France. Macron's assailant shouted, "Montjoie Saint Denis!" It was the battle cry of the Kings of Navarre and a slogan that also used to appear on coats of arms. The literal meaning is obtuse, but *montjoie* is thought to be a mound of earth honoring a sacred event—in this case the place where Saint Denis, the first Bishop of Paris, who became known as the Protector of Gaul, was beheaded in the second century.

There was even worse for Macron in March 2023, when he was forced to cancel a state visit to France by the late Queen Elizabeth II's son, the new King Charles III, because of widespread rioting. Millions were furious at the antidemocratic way Macron had raised the retirement age from sixty-two to sixty-four without a parliamentary vote. Protesters threatened to disrupt planned appearances by Charles in Paris, Bordeaux, and at a banquet in the Palace of Versailles itself. Charles pledged to visit France again later in the year, but in the meantime his first ever trip abroad as head of the UK and Commonwealth was to Berlin.

France's Age of Kings was supposed to end with the abolition of the Bourbon dynasty following the 1789 Revolution, but it was reinstated in 1814, after the Emperor Napoléon Bonaparte was exiled. Fifteen years later, in July 1830, there was another people's uprising and King Charles X abdicated, to be replaced by Louis-Philippe, Duke of Orléans. His July Monarchy included the invasion of Algeria. Louis-Philippe was forced to abdicate at the start of the 1848 Revolution, and he spent the rest of his life in exile in the United Kingdom.

It was then that the French monarchy appeared to expire once and for all.

There are now Legitimists who want to restore a Bourbon as King of France, and Orléanists who want a British-style constitutional monarchy. Bourbon nostalgists point to the enlightened way Louis XVI sent the Marquis de Lafayette to America to help defeat British oppressors. Others offering a pretender include the House of Bonaparte, founded by Napoléon I in 1804, when the First Republic became the First Empire. There is also an Alliance Royale that welcomes both Bourbon Legitimists and Orléanists. Their banners are common at Rassemblement National and Reconquête rallies. Many monarchists see themselves as being part of the far-right family.

Monarchists tend to be anti-globalist and anti-American, because they blame one of the largest and most dynamic republics in the world for a host of unwelcome developments, such as mass consumerism. More sinisterly, royalists rally against alleged secret societies and expressions of "foreign" cultures and religions. They also belong to often violent groups such as Action Française (AF), which lost a lot of clout for supporting the Vichy Regime during the Second World War. The man who attempted to slap Macron in the "Montjoie Saint Denis!" attack was linked to AF.

Jacques de Crussol, the Duc d'Uzès and the president of the Association for Mutual Assistance of the French Nobility, estimated that there were some four thousand French families that still considered themselves noble, compared to twelve thousand at the start of 1789.[6] Deprived of their estates and feudal fortunes, they scrape about for an identity using the past and—usually—the *de* (of) at the start of their surname to emphasize their sense of historic importance.

One of the reasons France is the biggest tourist destination in the world is because millions arrive to visit the aristocratic piles across the country—in particular Versailles, former palace of Queen Marie Antoinette and her husband, Louis XVI, west of Paris. The sheer decadence is as extraordinary as the British Queen's Williamson pink diamond brooch.

Marie Antoinette created her English Gardens there from 1777 and included a Love Monument folly, with a statue of Cupid and his bow.

A mock rural settlement—the Queen's Hamlet—was built around an artificial lake, complete with a quaint working farm and cottages full of rich furnishings. There was a dairy, stables, pigpen, henhouse, sheep grazing land, and even a fishermen's cottage. Up to ten million people a year now flock to such follies, along with other lavish mansion houses across France that are relics of the Ancien Régime.

Elizabeth II did not quite pass the longevity of the reign of Louis XIV—who was King of France for seventy-two years, having ascended the throne when he was four—but she did preside over the British Crown changing from a divine right to a service monarchy. The survival of the monarchy in Britain meant there were no bloody revolutions, as democracy was left to develop under the auspices of a benign figurehead. Both France and Britain were imperial powers—the kind that could go diamond hunting in Tanzania. Both countries have traditionally viewed themselves as civilizing forces, ready to spread their know-how around the planet.

The main difference is that the British were far more pragmatic: trade and Empire involved building up spheres of economic influence that could be exploited to create vast wealth. The private companies that were installed in countries such as India were driven by commercial ambitions, even though they supported them with violence when required.

The French, in contrast, believed that their culture—the French way—was worth expanding per se. Hence Algeria was viewed as an actual part of mainland France, complete with its own *départements* and hôtels de ville (town halls). Just as during the Napoleonic Wars—when Bonaparte wanted to export the Revolution around the globe—a strong sense of nationalism was essential. Overseas conquest was like revolution: a chance to disseminate universal ideals. As Jules Ferry wrote, "France cannot only be a free country. . . . France must also be a great nation . . . and carry anywhere it can its language, its mores, its flag, its arms, its genius" and "civilise inferior races."[7]

Jules Ferry was not only the architect of the secular education system but also a colonizer. Secularism and colonization were pillars of the French nation that emerged in the nineteenth century. British

India—the jewel in the imperial crown—was a different type of colony. While the Raj was ruled directly by the British, it was mainly local entrepreneurs who "managed" regions for the Crown, rather than capturing them. The sheer horror of France's so-called *mission civilisatrice* in Algeria continued right up until the 1960s.

The largely peaceful process of decolonization that accompanied Elizabeth II's reign is typical of the evolution of the British nation. There was none of the gassing, napalming, and torture that characterized the French conquest of and ultimately withdrawal from Algeria. The French republican experience has been a savage one. Even as crowds celebrated victory over fascism on the streets of European capitals on May 8, 1945, French forces slaughtered up to forty-five thousand men, women, and children in and around the towns of Sétif, Guelma, and Kherrata in northeastern Algeria. They were ruthlessly subdued in retaliation for some of them taking part in pro-independence protests. It was not until February 2005 that Hubert Colin de Verdière, France's Ambassador to Algeria, finally described the bloodbath as an "inexcusable tragedy." Despite this, we can be certain that VE Day will remain a date for Algerians to mourn a genocide.

Pseudo-monarchs have helped the French feel more certain about their identity. Napoléon Bonaparte and Charles de Gaulle remain the Frenchmen that most fascinate the nation. Books about them pack bookshops, and their legacies are discussed constantly. Bonaparte became an Emperor-dictator, while De Gaulle remodeled the entire nature of the French Republic to reflect his ego.

People are impressed by such strong men, and that is why monarchical flags are still prevalent all over France. A people unsure of their identity as they face an uncertain future harken back to a "glorious" past. Of course, the French will never restore a King or Queen, but such roles still intrigue them. Charles de Gaulle explicitly based the institution of the Fifth Republic presidency on the long-gone monarchy. He said he wanted to revive "the stability and continuity which [France] had been deprived of for 168 years."[8] As Emmanuel Macron has pointed out, all that was missing was the "figure of the King," but that hasn't stopped successive Presidents trying to fill the void.

After years of policy angst between Macron and the United Kingdom, the French President emerged as a royal superfan during the mourning period for Elizabeth II. The man who called Brexit "a crime" and who regularly went to war with British ministers over issues such as English Channel fishing rights sounded completely different. He made it clear that he absolutely loved history's second-longest reigning monarch, telling the British people, "To you, she was your Queen. To us, she was *the* Queen." Macron also said Her Majesty "touched French hearts" and "represented eternity."

I've spoken in person to Macron about his admiration for Britain, and it is absolutely genuine. One of his paternal great-grandfathers was a butcher from Bristol who joined the British Army during the First World War and ended up marrying a Frenchwoman. Before the demands of state intervened, Macron used to spend regular holidays and weekends in the United Kingdom with his wife, Brigitte.

More than that, Macron is absolutely obsessed by constitutional monarchy. This was why, in the run-up to his election in 2017, he spoke about a metaphorical void in French life caused by the absence of a King, suggesting that Frenchmen such as Napoléon Bonaparte and Charles de Gaulle had acted as substitutes for the long-dead monarchs, but that the "deep emotional abyss" endured.

They Put an Algerian in to Please the Arabs

As France struggles to pin down its national identity, at least there is football—a game that the French have become masters at, and which creates a sense of unity. There is very little to match the outpouring of patriotic fervor that accompanies a successful cup run, especially when Les Bleus become World Champions.

The national squad is made up of players from diverse ethnic and religious minorities: North African, West African, Caribbean, and even Armenian and Basque. The poster boy of the so-called rainbow team that first won the World Cup for France in 1998 was Zinedine Zidane, who was born in the Marseille suburbs to Algerian parents who had moved to France in the 1950s. Zizou—one of the greatest players ever—was said to personify an inclusive nation. On the night of France's victory against Brazil, his image was projected on two giant screens on the Champs-Élysées accompanied by the caption: "Zidane for President."

Les Bleus last became World Champions in Russia in 2018, and Emmanuel Macron took full advantage of the victory's unifying potential. As with the triumph on home soil twenty years earlier, tricolors were waved at gatherings across the land, and the team once more became the apparent symbol of a dynamic, egalitarian country in which those of immigrant descent could be loved and respected. The sense of pride was summed up by a photo of Macron, still wearing formal shirt and tie, punching the air inside the Moscow stadium where France beat Croatia. Macron was so overcome with happiness that he then forced his wife, Brigitte, to join him in hugging and kissing their players on the rain-sodden pitch.

Kylian Mbappé, France's most formidable player, is the son of an Algerian mother and Cameroonian father. Stars such as Paul Pogba, N'Golo Kanté, and Blaise Matuidi all come from African families and were born and brought up on the rundown estates around Paris—an area said to be the greatest pool of footballing talent on the globe after the São Paulo favelas. These players were feted as heroes who seemingly personified the very best of French values.

Beyond the handful of multimillionaire footballers, the reality for men and women of the same origin was, of course, very different. During the World Cup in the summer of 2018, non-football-related violence broke out in the Breil quarter of the western city of Nantes. It was far more indicative of the actual state of modern France as it pertained to the young and the disadvantaged.

A CRS riot control officer shot dead Aboubakar Fofana, a twenty-two-year-old Frenchman from a Guinean background, after trying to arrest him in Breil. The allegation was that Fofana had reversed his car quickly into a group of officers, causing a knee injury to one. The police shooter was placed in custody. He initially claimed he had fired his gun in self-defense, but changed his version to "accidental shooting" after video evidence showed what he had done.

The killing prompted thousands to take to the streets, throwing Molotov cocktails, burning cars and buildings, and attacking the forces sent out to quell the fire. Disturbances went on for almost two weeks. Apart from signaling the start of yet another summer of urban disorder, Fofana's death said everything about what really happens to a disturbingly high number of people with African and Arab roots.

Men like Paul Pogba—a tall, powerfully built, Black Muslim who, like Fofana, has Guinean parents—are just the kind who are routinely demonized. Politicians and media commentators whip up hatred against *banlieusards* who are given next to no opportunity to join the mainstream or to access the decent housing and jobs that go with it. It was no coincidence that, twenty years on from France's 1998 World Cup win, the *banlieusards* still had very little chance of advancing in a rigidly exclusive society.

It is noticeable that Marine Le Pen does not "do football." Her Rassemblement National party is far more comfortable with viewing *banlieusards* as potential criminals. It was Le Pen's father, Jean-Marie Le Pen, who first spoke out against the 1998 rainbow team. Noting the number of footballers from "foreign countries," Le Pen regularly questioned their suitability to represent France. In a statement in 1996, after Les Bleus qualified for the Euros semifinals, he said, "It's artificial to bring foreign players here and baptize them the French team, although I could think of other names for them." Then, two years later, when Les Bleus won the World Cup, he snarled, "They put an Algerian in to please the Arabs, a Kanak who won't even sing 'La Marseillaise,' and Blacks to satisfy the Antilleans. None of this has anything to do with a French team!"

Such discourse was still going strong in Le Pen's party when France won their second World Cup. At the time, in July 2018, Grégoire de Fournas (the Rassemblement National politician who would later shout "Go back to Africa!" at a Black MP) took part in a Twitter discussion about the way ethnic minority players in Les Bleus were getting too much praise. Fournas tweeted: "And when this team loses, it's no longer the fault of the blacks and the Arabs?"

Before the European Championship finals in 2016, France striker Karim Benzema accused Didier Deschamps, the France trainer, of taking the lead from Le Pen's "racist" Front National by refusing to play him. Benzema was being investigated by prosecutors and police in connection with an alleged sex-tape blackmail case, but he felt he was being excluded from the national squad because of his Algerian background. Retired French footballer Eric Cantona—a legend at Manchester United—had also claimed Benzema and Hatem Ben Arfa, whose father was an international footballer for Tunisia, were being kept out of Les Bleus because of their North African Muslim heritage.

Cantona taunted Deschamps with the words: "Benzema is a great player. Ben Arfa is a great player. But Deschamps, he has a really French name. Maybe he is the only one in France to have a truly French name. Nobody in his family mixed with anybody, you know. Like the Mormons in America." Asked directly if he thought Deschamps—a former France teammate—was guilty of discrimination, Cantona replied, "Maybe no, but maybe yes. The debate is open."

Cantona's accusations prompted the threat of a defamation claim from Deschamps's lawyers. Then, Benzema, whose club team was Real Madrid, told Spanish daily sports newspaper *Marca* that Deschamps had "bowed to pressure from a racist French party"—a clear reference to the Front National. Benzema suggested that other powerful figures inside the French Football Federation might also have been involved in a campaign against him.

The Le Pen party is not the only one that wants to keep perceived outsiders in their place. Les Républicains remain reactionary, while Macron himself has frequently displayed a bigoted streak. Macron was happy to have a winning "soccer" team, but he was less happy to support the communities that had produced it. As US Secretary of State Antony Blinken opined in the *New York Times* following France's last World Cup win: "The larger test for Mr. Macron is whether he can do for the banlieues what the banlieues have done for French soccer." Suggesting that elite sports should not be the only option open to deprived young people, Blinken wrote that what was needed was "a sustained, focused national effort to find, nurture, train and place future Mbappés in France's newly vibrant economy."[9]

France Is Sick

The Future of French Identity was a grandly titled document published by the government's Planning Secretariat in 1990. Pointing to endemic pessimism, it stated: "We have the impression that many French people have doubts about the capacity of their country to meet successfully the dangers, opportunities and uncertainties which the future holds," while highlighting "a disarray of the national identity at the same time as a loss of legitimacy of a state that traditionally took on responsibility for mobilizing national energies."

Michel Noir, then a Member of Parliament and the Mayor of Lyon, resigned from the Gaullist Rally for the Republic party around the same time, saying, "France is sick, sick of seeing politicians of all denominations dedicated to their favorite game of internecine battles for power, sick of crises in justice, education, safety and health, sick that France no longer holds its historic role on the international stage."

Noir placed his hope in a new "grand design," suggesting France needed nothing less than a "new democracy." MPs were already blaming so-called progressive ideas being imported from America for the identity crisis—not least of all rampant individualism and the omnipotence of consumer society and the mass media. It all added up to the impoverishment of the state, it was argued. At the time, Socialist President François Mitterrand was into his tenth year in office and had been severely criticized for his monarchical aloofness. Future President François Hollande was a young MP then and said: "For the first time, when people ask me what my profession is, I don't dare reply MP."

There is a clear thread between such exasperated comments from more than three decades ago and what is happening today. Big business continues to look after the Paris establishment, and the prosperity of the bourgeoisie in cities such as Paris and Lyon, but millions feel alienated from a highly centralized state with little interest in grassroots democracy. Paris-based industrialists top global rich lists, while their lackey Presidents push the retirement age up and the cost of living rockets, along with inflation and unemployment, especially in the vast swaths of flyover France.

In the meantime, politicians join pop philosophers in equating economic and physical insecurity with unwanted immigrants. Those who vote Rassemblement National are mainly spread across depressed northern and south coast areas, where traditional industries are disappearing. There is no route back to the African colonies that once provided an escape to a prosperous life enhanced by the pride of being linked to an imperial power.

Huge segments of society feel let down and ignored. Hence the anger and violence of the *Gilets Jaunes*, the disturbances accompanying attempts at pension reform, and the endless strife in the *banlieues*. Alarm bells were already ringing loudly in 1990. A polarizing election in 2022 showed how far France has been moving to the extreme, as an identity centered on disillusion, frustration, and rage dominates.

8

FEMINISM

And God Created Woman

I was made for another Planet. I mistook the way.

—SIMONE DE BEAUVOIR (1908–1986)

Women's rights have developed extremely slowly in France, despite successive revolutions. The country's expertise at overthrowing rulers in 1789 certainly didn't extend to defeating the patriarchal system, but at least there was Marianne: the incarnation of freedom who would come to symbolize the Republic. This fantasy figure was given the most popular girls' names of the late eighteenth century—Marie and Anne—and was not afraid of taking to the barricades.

The most famous version of Marianne is in *Liberty Leading the People*, the painting by the romantic artist Eugène Delacroix, which is now in the Louvre. Marianne is waving the *tricolore* flag and holding a musket with a fixed bayonet during the July Revolution of 1830. Dressed in a Phrygian bonnet and exposing her bosoms, she is meant to personify powerful Gallic femininity. Marianne also now takes pride of place in most official buildings across France. There are depictions and sculptures of her in law courts, prefectures, and city halls. The Marianne bust that was smashed to pieces in the Arc de

Triomphe by the *Gilets Jaunes* was typical of those placed in venerated national monuments. She is also on the official government logo and stamps.

Up until 1969, the identity of this superwoman was deliberately mysterious. Anonymity created an aura of universalism, in line with France's values. But then President De Gaulle approved a sculpting workshop in the Louvre turning international sex symbol Brigitte Bardot into the national image. De Gaulle had met Bardot once, at a dinner at the Élysée Palace at the end of 1967. The head of state said he admired the actress and model for her simplicity, her outspokenness, and her good humor. Her high cheek bones, plump lips, and—yes—her clearly defined breasts and slightly menacing expression (Don't mess with me, I am French!) all perfectly suited a new depiction of a classic symbol.

Bardot ostensibly united the country—north and south—because she was a Parisienne who had spent summer holidays with her prosperous parents on the Riviera, in Saint-Tropez and La Baule. Instead of becoming a ballerina—her childhood ambition—she was spotted by the film director Roger Vadim and became his teenage bride in 1952. A minor role in the romance *An Act of Love* (*Un Acte d'Amour*) alongside Kirk Douglas followed a year later and, in 1956, Bardot became world famous thanks to *And God Created Woman* (*Et Dieu . . . Créa la Femme*), the sexually explicit Mediterranean romp that had to be heavily censored for American audiences. The press portrayed BB—as she became known—as a blonde bombshell rival to Marilyn Monroe, as well as the personification of French womanhood.

How unfortunate, then, that BB now has multiple convictions for racism and a record of mocking women who complain about sexual harassment. She particularly detests Muslims and wants to see "foreigners" deported. BB has also been reprimanded for insulting members of the LGBT community.

BB, older and nastier, might certainly still qualify as a Marianne bust. She epitomizes a country with a far from impressive gender equality record, and one in which thousands of complaints about sexual violence are made every year. Police reported a 10 percent increase in the number of domestic attacks in 2020, with 159,400 victims. Eighty-seven percent of them, or 139,200, were women. Of these, 5,400 filed complaints for rape or sexual abuse. A total of 102 women died as a result of an attack by a violent partner in 2020, and in 2019 the figure was 146—meaning that a woman was murdered every two to three days.[1]

Bardot is a Le Pen voter who has watched the success of the far-right increase in line with attacks on women, especially Muslim ones. BB's criminal record has by no means prevented Marine Le Pen from proudly posing for pictures alongside the BB Marianne bust. An exhibition dedicated to the Bardot legend in Boulogne-Billancourt lauded her for freeing women from "the rigid codes of the austere and conservative France of René Coty," the country's President from 1954 to 1959. Bardot "embodied the Republic by offering her features to the bust of Marianne," according to the exhibition blurb.

Patriarchal structures remain very strong in France, particularly in politics, and there can be as many votes in sexism as there are in racism. There has never been a female President, and only two distinctly low-key women have ever been Prime Minister. Édith Cresson resigned in April 1992 after a disastrous ten months and eighteen days in the job. Thirty years later, Élisabeth Borne was appointed. Meanwhile, France's obsession with its own brand of secularism, and indeed an often absurd form of feminism, oppresses a huge section of the population. This includes Muslim women who are literally criminalized for their choice of clothing.

The great contradiction in French feminist discourse—whether argued by the Left or the Right—is that it uses *laïcité* as a tool to "protect" and "emancipate" Muslim women from allegedly repressive males while also stigmatizing and penalizing those same women. There are plenty of perfectly liberated French Muslims who choose to wear headscarves and modest clothing, yet they are branded as victims of an oppressive culture and religion. France thus excludes female citizens from public spaces because of their clothes, using fines and the threat of prison to enforce its diktats. How and why did this come about? And what is the state of feminism in a country where a rigorously macho culture still dominates all walks of life, not least of all politics?

A Glorious Chance

The reluctance of French revolutionaries to take up the cause of female emancipation was called out by one of Britain's greatest writers as early as 1792. Mary Wollstonecraft traveled across the English Channel to see how the biggest historical event of her life might have advanced gender equality. She originally called the French Revolution a "glorious chance to obtain more virtue and happiness than hitherto blessed our globe."[2] Wollstonecraft saw the Revolution as a daring social experiment that might be repeated in Britain, but it soon became clear to her that women were excluded from the new "universal" republican ideology.

The Declaration of the Rights of Man and of the Citizen only applied to men over twenty-five who paid an appropriate amount of tax. This was despite a women's march to Versailles in October 1789 campaigning against the high price and scarcity of bread. There was also a women's petition to the National Assembly that called for a decree confirming equal rights; it was not even discussed by Parliament. The Enlightenment philosopher Nicolas de Condorcet advocated women's suffrage, while Dutch feminist Etta Palm d'Aelders delivered her celebrated "Discourse on the Injustice of the Laws in Favor of Men, at the Expense of Women" address to the National Convention in 1790, but to little effect.

Wollstonecraft arrived in Paris in December 1792, a month before Louis XVI was guillotined in Place de la Concorde. After observing the King at his trial before the National Assembly, she admitted to crying when she saw "Louis sitting, with more dignity than I expected from his character," as he was transported to his death in a hackney carriage.

Despite her disgust as the bloodshed intensified, Wollstonecraft was still able to focus on female emancipation. She particularly wanted to reply to a pamphlet on plans for France's new educational institutions by the French statesman Charles Maurice de Talleyrand-Périgord—better known as Talleyrand—whom she had met in London. He had become a member of the post-revolutionary National Constituent Assembly, but he suggested that "men are destined to live on the stage of the world," while women should be managing "the paternal home."

Talleyrand would become Chief Diplomat for the warmongering Napoléon Bonaparte, at a time when France was carving up huge parts of Europe as it built its empire, so he was always likely to have a highly misogynistic view of life. Beyond answering Talleyrand's reactionary opinions, Wollstonecraft also wanted to counter points made by Edmund Burke in *Reflections on the Revolution in France*, particularly those about women being the weaker sex.

The result was Wollstonecraft's *A Vindication of the Rights of Woman*, an extraordinarily radical work of literature that argued, "It is time to effect a revolution in female manners—time to restore to them their lost dignity—and make them, as a part of the human species, labour by reforming themselves to reform the world. It is time to separate unchangeable morals from local manners."

Wollstonecraft's book suggested that enlightened societies needed an education system that viewed female students as being just as important as male ones. Without the appropriate teaching, women are conditioned into a subservient position, which allows them, at best, to become homemakers or to carry out menial tasks. Dreamy romance becomes a woman's main motivation in life, rather than anything that might require an intellect. The difference between Wollstonecraft's thinking and that of male Enlightenment philosophers such as Jean-Jacques Rousseau was that she wanted women to be educated into becoming rational beings. If a woman is not "prepared by education to become the companion of man, she will stop the progress of knowledge and virtue," Wollstonecraft argued. She was especially critical of Rousseau because his concept of equality extended only to men, no matter their backgrounds. He stated in *Emile* that women needed to be supported by men at all times, because women were less rational.[3] Wollstonecraft, in contrast, called for radical political change to create schools and colleges that would benefit both sexes. Her book would have a profound impact for years to come.

The treatment of women by the Jacobins—the most ruthless political grouping to come out of the 1789 Revolution—disturbed Wollstonecraft. The Jacobins expected "Amazons"—a reference to the female warriors of Greek mythology—to conform to Rousseau's thinking. Wollstonecraft ends *A Vindication of the Rights of Woman* with a proposal to establish free, national, coeducational schools committed to equality between the sexes. She also calls for a women's "revolution" that will allow them to take up roles in all sectors of public life. Wollstonecraft argues, "Men have superior strength of body, but were it not for mistaken notions of beauty, women would acquire sufficient to enable them to earn their own subsistence, the true definition of independence."[4]

Wollstonecraft's ideas were frequently attacked after her death. Many Englishmen were horrified by the bloodshed that followed the 1789 insurrection, and they thus considered any kind of revolution to be extremely dangerous. As far as France was concerned, it would also be many years before Wollstonecraft-style theories were finally acted upon.

On Becoming Women

It was not until the second half of the nineteenth century and so-called first-wave feminism—a period of intense activity focused on overturning legal obstacles to gender equality throughout the Western world—that militant feminist ideas had some effect. The Paris Commune of 1871 involved women founding political groups to fight for equal pay, the right to divorce, and the closing of official brothels. Women also got involved in fighting against the state forces that crushed the insurrection.

Louise Michel was one of these women: a progressive teacher who joined the revolutionary National Guard and ran the Montmartre women's vigilance committee. "Oh, I'm a savage all right," Michel wrote. "I like the smell of gunpowder, grapeshot flying through the air, but above all, I'm devoted to the Revolution."[5]

The Suffragette movement, founded in Britain under the banner "Votes for Women," was replicated in France by the establishment of the French Union for Women's Suffrage (Union Française pour le Suffrage des Femmes, UFSF) in 1909. The members of the UFSF were more moderate than their UK counterparts—there was to be no throwing themselves under racehorses—but they were nonetheless highly committed to the cause. As early as 1914, more than five hundred thousand women said "yes" in a referendum calling for universal male suffrage—which had been granted in 1848—to be extended to their sex. The UFSF campaign was stepped up when Britain passed the Representation of the People Act 1928, allowing all women the vote, but it was not until 1944, at the end of the Nazi Occupation, that France finally became one of the last countries in the world to introduce female suffrage—twenty-four years after the United States and fifty-one after New Zealand.

Two world wars had challenged traditional gender roles, and demands for equality could no longer be ignored. Women had fought with the Resistance, but, at the time of their enfranchisement, there were plenty of conservative women who objected to having a constitutionally guaranteed right to vote in a country where traditionally subservient stereotypes, including that of the uncomplaining housewife, were respected. By 1958, the number of women in the National Assembly and Senate was less than 2 percent. The figure was still just 6 percent in 1993.

Simone de Beauvoir published *The Second Sex* in 1949, focusing on the disadvantaged position of women in society and suggesting remedies. Two sections—entitled "Facts & Myths" and "Lived Experience"—provided much of the intellectual backing for the second-wave feminism movement, which started in the '60s and lasted two decades. Then, feminist activity concentrated on issues such as reproductive rights, inequalities in the workplace, and domesticity—particularly domestic violence, including marital rape. The second wave coined the slogan "The personal is political."

Beauvoir was an existentialist who accepted Jean-Paul Sartre's maxim that existence precedes essence, and so she argued that "one is not born a woman but becomes one." Women made up a historically oppressed "other," Beauvoir contended, and even philosophers such as Mary Wollstonecraft had got it wrong when they claimed that women should aspire to be just like men.

Married French women were permitted to work without their husband's agreement only from 1965, while birth control was officially legalized in 1967. A year later, the Mouvement de Libération des Femmes (MLF) began to emerge out of the May '68 riots, and its creation was formalized in 1970. Many MLF members had first become activists during campaigns against the wars in Algeria and Vietnam, and a period of genuine civil unrest on mainland France empowered them even more. MLF was connected to the American women's liberation movement, so it benefited from global momentum.

Women serving in government in France in the 1970s included Simone Veil, who advanced women's rights considerably. In 1974, Françoise Giroud became the first Minister for Women's Affairs. Male-only responsibility for making legal decisions about children was abolished by Parliament in 1970 in favor of joint parental authority. In 1971, Simone de Beauvoir and Gisèle Halimi, the prominent Tunisian-French lawyer, cowrote the "Manifesto of the 343"—a front-page headline and title of a petition inside the liberal weekly magazine Le Nouvel Observateur. In it, 343 women spoke openly about having illegal abortions. It constituted an act of civil disobedience that exposed the signatories to criminal prosecution. This led to a period of protest and public debate that resulted in the 1975 Veil Act, which legalized abortion.

Third- and fourth-wave feminists celebrated legal breakthroughs such as workplace sexual harassment becoming an offense in France in 1992, along with marital rape being outlawed in 1994. The term mademoiselle—for Miss—was removed from official documents in 2012, and in 2018 a law combatting sexual harassment in the street was introduced. Despite all this, there was still a lot lacking in France's approach to feminism.

In 1995, President Jacques Chirac set up the Observatoire de la Parité entre les Femmes et les Hommes—a monitoring authority on gender inequality—but this did not stop a shocking purge of his own female ministers. On a single November day—dubbed Black Tuesday—Chirac's Prime Minister, Alain Juppé, dismissed eight out of twelve female ministers. They included Secretaries of State as well as junior ministers, and, just six months into the job, each was given five minutes to clear her desk. All had originally been called the *jupettes*, in reference to their boss, Juppé, and a pun on the French word for miniskirts. Juppé is said to have been heard calling them "old biddies." This was the real face of French feminism, critics argued. François Mitterrand had made Édith Cresson the first ever French female Prime Minister in 1991, but she resigned after a calamitous ten months as her popularity rating collapsed. Despite clear economic problems, she blamed institutional sexism for playing a large part in her demise.

By 1996, when women still only made up 6 percent of *députés* in the National Assembly, ten women politicians from all parties published a manifesto demanding political parity between the sexes be enshrined in the Constitution. "From condescending indifference and contempt to open hostility," wrote the signatories, "we have been able to measure the gap between public principles and reality in the behavior of the political class."

Despite this, other women were against forced parity. In February 1999, fourteen prominent women argued that it would undermine republican universalism, thus opening the door to requests for equality from other groups, such as ones focused on race and religion. The opposers said that "gender blindness" was essential. Among them was the philosopher Élisabeth Badinter, author of a three-volume history of the Enlightenment. Badinter is typical of self-styled Enlightenment feminists. She lobbied hard in support of banning clothes associated with Muslim women, for example. While being interviewed about her book *Fausse Route* (The wrong way), Badinter conceded that women were overwhelmingly the main victims of domestic abuse, saying, "Admittedly, there are many more women victims of men than the reverse." But she added, "There are also female executioners and shrews of all kinds."[6] The words were straight out of the classic "on the other hand" French establishment playbook.

When former French Trade Minister and then International Monetary Fund (IMF) chief Dominique Strauss-Kahn was arrested on suspicion of attempted rape in Manhattan, Badinter remained conspicuously tongue-tied before saying two months later, "I was not heard because I thought the only appropriate attitude was to be silent for the moment." Referring to the #MeToo-style campaigners who did speak out against DSK's alleged sexual misconduct, Badinter said, "It's unacceptable to use a possible injustice to advance a cause."[7] It turned out that Badinter, a multimillionaire heiress, was a close friend of DSK's wife, Anne Sinclair—another hugely wealthy member of the Paris establishment.

In 2000, France introduced a gender parity law, meaning candidate lists for proportional representation elections to the Senate, to regional and municipal legislatures, and to the European Parliament had to be 50 percent female. For parliamentary elections at home, fines were introduced for parties that dropped below the desired 50 percent, but many parties were happy to pay them. In 2018, Les Républicains were fined the most, with a €1.78 million penalty for not meeting the threshold for women on their lists in the previous electoral year. The new measures by no means stopped France's political establishment from being dominated by men, nor did they change the insidious macho culture. As is so often the case in France, the new law may have improved the situation in principle but certainly not in practice. Sexism remained as commonplace as ever.

This became clear in 2017 when Emmanuel Macron suggested that poor African women were having too many babies. Rehearsing a canard that is popular among nostalgic colonialists who regularly criticize the "dark continent," the newly elected President used a press conference at the G20 Summit in Hamburg to say that wanton reproduction often made foreign aid pointless. "Seven or eight children per woman," were Macron's exact words. There was even the classic racist trope about the alleged "civilizational" problems that result from an escalating birth rate, especially mass immigration to Western countries such as France.

Macron's crudeness was torn apart on social media, but there was generally silence from the Paris establishment. This is because sexist and imperial attitudes prevail in a country that has not altered its condescending approach toward those it once subjugated. Macron made the comments just after elevating Simone Veil to the status of secular sainthood by awarding her a final resting place in the Panthéon, alongside Jean-Jacques Rousseau and Victor Hugo. Veil's greatest achievement was the legalization of abortion, said Macron. It was a poignant contrast between a beyond-criticism (white) national heroine devoted to keeping population numbers down and all those unnamed, feckless (Black) mothers who were incapable of controlling anything, least of all their own bodies.

He's Killed Me

When crime statistics showed that sexual assaults on women increased by 33 percent in 2021, France's Interior Minister suggested the figure was mainly due to more people talking about the subject. Gérald Darmanin wrote, "These trends are part of the context of freedom of speech and better consideration of this subject by the police."[8]

Darmanin was quite right. Women are talking far more about rape, sexual assault, and harassment, and a great deal of it is going on in France. Police and gendarmes recorded 75,800 complaints from victims of such violence in 2021. This meant that the number of declared victims of sexual violence had risen by 82 percent since the beginning of the Macron presidency, and there is plenty of evidence that many other women are still suffering in silence. Registered complaints were still well below the United Kingdom, however, where police logged 183,587 sexual offenses in the same year. This by no means pointed to the situation being better in France; it just showed that plenty of women were still reluctant to deal with the authorities. Even when they did go to the police, justice was hard to come by.

This reality came into sharp focus in France following the horrific death of Julie Douib, a thirty-four-year-old mother of two who was killed by her former partner in March 2019. He fired a 9 mm pistol at her shortly after learning that the criminal case she had initiated against him for threatening behavior, harassment, and assault had been dropped. This was very typical. Just 18 percent of domestic abuse complaints are investigated, while 80 percent are abandoned, according to French Justice Ministry statistics.

Warning signs in Douib's case were nonstop. She reported her problems to the police ten times and tried to express her fears to those closest to her. No one quite understood how grave the situation was, however. Detectives evidently did not take her seriously, even though she repeatedly told them her attacker had a gun. They said they could not do anything unless he used it. By that time, it was far too late, of course. Douib's last words to the neighbor who found her dying from bullet wounds at her home in L'Île-Rousse, on the Mediterranean island of Corsica, were, "He's killed me."

Douib's murder was not an isolated one. She was one of 146 women who were killed in similar circumstances the same year. To this figure, we must add millions more who have suffered in other ways, including physically and mentally. In 2020, only 0.6 percent of rapes reported by adults resulted in a conviction—equivalent to a derisory 683 convictions out of 112,000 complaints.[9]

A "sexism barometer" survey—the first of its kind in France, released by the French government to mark International Women's Day in March 2022—exposed widespread abuse. The High Council for Equality between Men and Women revealed that 61 percent of French women had been the victim of a sexist action or insult in the street or public transport, 46 percent in the workplace, and 43 percent at home. Sexist remarks were often dressed up as "humor," according to 57 percent of respondents. As many as 20 percent of eighteen- to thirty-four-year-olds said they had been sexually harassed, as had 13 percent for older women. This was all despite a new law making sex and personal development education compulsory in 2021.[10] Women's groups, supported by the World Health Organization, have pointed to an epidemic of domestic violence globally, which was amplified by the COVID-19 lockdowns and has continued unabated.

In addition to using the Internet, campaigners are adopting more rudimentary means of communication in order to raise awareness. A group called Les Colleuses (the gluers) sticks messages on walls. Their main message about the Douib case simply read, "Justice for Julie." Another feminist organization persuaded bakers to wrap some of the ten billion baguettes produced in France each year in bags that contain the numbers for abuse hotlines. This is not about tokenism. It is about seeing existing anti-abuse laws enforced and tougher ones introduced. The issue should not be politicized either; there needs to be more cross-party work in Parliament dealing with it. The hope is that the thousands of women who report being victims of physical or sexual violence in France every year will be heard and protected—sooner rather than later.

The Paris Wife

What Interior Minister Gérald Darmanin did not mention in his press release about crimes against women was that his boss, President Macron, had allowed him to carry on working when he was being investigated for rape. The case against Darmanin was dismissed when the complainant stopped cooperating with police, but not before Darmanin admitted to taking her to a swingers' club and then to a five-star hotel for sex. This was all while Darmanin was officially offering professional advice to the woman over a legal dispute dealing with a housing issue. Nicolas Hulot, Macron's former Energy Transition Minister, and Damien Abad, Minister for Disabled People, were also kept on while being investigated over rape allegations by the media and, in Abad's case, the judiciary.

Macron's first campaign meeting before the 2022 presidential election was in Poissy on March 7, the eve of International Women's Day. Asked about the rape and sexual assault accusations against his lieutenants, he replied, "These ministers have never behaved like this in front of me."

There was zero sensitivity displayed toward women's rights when the previous five Presidents of France had highly publicized difficulties with their personal lives. Socialist François Hollande infamously evicted his First Lady, Valérie Trierweiler, from the Élysée Palace after being caught sleeping with his then mistress, TV actor Julie Gayet, in a nearby love nest. The clownish Hollande was pictured arriving on the back of a moped for liaisons with Gayet at the flat in Rue du Cirque (Circus Street). Nicolas Sarkozy devoted the first few months of his single term in office pursuing the supermodel Carla Bruni, whom he married at the Élysée after being rejected by his second wife and at least one journalist lover.

Jacques Chirac, another philandering conservative, was notorious for his affairs. On the night Diana, Princess of Wales, died in a Paris car crash in 1997, nobody could raise Chirac, because he was allegedly spending the night with the veteran Italian actor Claudia Cardinale rather than his wife.

François Mitterrand infamously kept a second family a state secret using public funds. The existence of his illegitimate daughter, Mazarine Pingeot, only became public in late 1994, a few months before he left office the following year. A picture of Mazarine appeared on the front cover of *Paris Match* on the eve of her twentieth birthday. A year later, Mazarine and her mother, Anne Pingeot, were among the mourners at Mitterrand's funeral, alongside the President's wife, Danielle Mitterrand. In a 2016 radio interview on France Culture, Anne Pingeot blamed twenty years of subterfuge on a childhood in the conservative French heartland. She recalled being told that "a woman should be submissive and have no intellectual life," adding: "At the same time that submissive side led me to accept the unacceptable."

Valéry Giscard d'Estaing, Mitterrand's predecessor, had real and fantasy affairs. He entertained the myth that he had a liaison with the late Diana, Princess of Wales, in his 2009 book, *The Princess and the President*. Giscard cultivated a reputation as a Casanova, to the extent that he used to leave a sealed letter indicating the whereabouts of his latest love nest only to be opened in case of emergency. In an infamous incident in 1974, the married father of four crashed a borrowed sports car in the early hours of the morning with a woman said to be the actor Marlène Jobert in the front passenger seat (like many of the President's alleged paramours, Jobert later denied the rumors).

First Ladies of France are a particularly sorry example of the state of sex equality in modern France. They usually end up as state-sponsored doormats—slapstick figures who are routinely humiliated, either by their cheating husbands or by a misogynistic electorate. The abuse of women by Presidents is a throwback to the monarchical tradition of powerful men being allowed to keep courtesans hovering in antechambers.

When I spoke to Brigitte Macron just before her husband's election, she seemed to have no idea that she was about to join an excruciating soap opera. She was optimistic and upbeat back in May 2017. "I'm ready to fit in with anything that's expected of me, whatever is involved," she told me. "Being with my husband has meant extraordinary things happening—there is always an adventure around the corner. He works extremely hard, and I want to support him in everything."

Madame Macron certainly had no inkling that this would include enduring constant speculation about the twenty-four-year age gap between her and Macron, snide comments about plastic surgery, and—most extreme of all—a concerted media campaign that tried to make out that Madame Macron had been born a Monsieur. Detractors wanted to reduce her to another upstart, a presidential wallflower who should be locked away in a quiet salon while her husband sorted out domestic and world affairs.

Valérie Trierweiler suffered in silence before being callously kicked out of the Élysée Palace because of Hollande's two-timing. It was only afterward that she spilled all the embarrassing details of her ordeal in a best-selling kiss-and-tell autobiography. In turn, Julie Gayet—the actor Hollande left Trierweiler for—continues to observe an omertà about her own covert experiences in the Élysée and other official homes. She married Hollande in June 2022 in a low-key ceremony and is now seldom seen in the spotlight.

Such incidents highlight the strange position of the *première dame*. She has up to five personal assistants, six offices located in the "madame wing" of the Élysée, a team of security agents, and numerous perks, from the use of state jets to on-call hairdressers and florists. This adds up to a budget easily passing the €1 million mark, yet—as with the

First Lady of the United States, the hostess of the White House—the role is unofficial and tokenistic. It is an ill-defined, awkward position which is not regulated by statute or codified in any way. Instead, it is mainly characterized by public displays of empathy and charity fund-raising. Former US First Lady Michelle Obama summed up the confusion when she wrote in her memoir *The Light We Carry*, "Being the First Lady of the United States is a strange and strangely powerful sort of non-job. . . . It comes with no salary, no supervisor, and no employee handbook."

As has been the case throughout history, First Ladies around the world are largely required to be presentable escorts when called upon and to make their husbands look good. This says everything about the abject sexism and feebleness of the First Lady concept. Highly educated, talented women such as Madame Macron are effectively told to suspend their careers to become hollow public figures, knocking about the corridors of power—and indeed the international stage—with an alarming lack of direction.

Macron initially spoke about elevating the position from mere "partner of" to something far more relevant to an egalitarian society, but his opponents were far from impressed. An online petition against the creation of an official First Lady gathered around three hundred thousand signatures within a week, and the plan was canned. The opposition was boosted by Macron proposing a law against parliamentarians employing spouses or any kind of family member, so his proposal for the "First Lady job" smacked of hypocrisy.

Critics who did not want wives or girlfriends being paid by politicians cited Penelopegate, the scandal that surfaced in early 2017 during the presidential race, which saw British-born Penelope Fillon accused of earning a fortune in taxpayers' cash over three decades while posing as the parliamentary assistant of her husband, would-be conservative President François Fillon. As the accusations against her intensified, Penelope Fillon did not utter a single word in public. This was while Fillon was still convinced he could become French President, standing on a platform of fiscal rigor, absolute probity in public life, and the slashing of some five hundred thousand civil servant posts. If the allegations about her had remained hidden, Penelope Fillon would undoubtedly have emerged as a First Lady in the traditional mold: compliant and for the most part hushed up (or "discreet," to use the euphemism favored by François Fillon).

One of the pillars of project Fillon was the image of a selfless wife concentrating on bringing up her five children on the family's rural estate, and thus sacrificing any chance of a professional career. She portrayed herself as an exiled Anglo-Welsh housewife, riding horses and studying Shakespeare in between household chores. As she said in an English-language interview in 2007, which was broadcast on France 2 as part of an investigative documentary, "I have never been actually his assistant or anything like that. I don't deal with his communication." This was despite the couple later claiming she was a go-getting political executive all along—at one point earning the equivalent of around $10,000 a month for her fantasy expertise.

Fillon continually presented his wife as a problem. It was as if he was her white knight—pressing on with his state duties while he tried to sort out his silly spouse's self-inflicted woes. As we have heard, the Fillons became convicted criminals subject to endless appeals. They siphoned off the equivalent of more than $1 million and were found guilty of charges including embezzlement and misusing public funds.

Fillon was, like his wife, a devout Roman Catholic. All his social policies were rooted in a traditional view of family life. The Penelopegate scandal also involved allegations about the couple's two oldest children appearing on the public payroll while they were still studying, even though their father originally claimed they were qualified lawyers.

Interestingly, Fillon's daughter, Marie, received 27 percent less than his son Charles in these questionable monthly payments. This was consistent with a gender pay gap that (according to Eurostat) was still as high as 16.5 percent in France in 2019. Despite having the same job and experience, women are invariably paid less than men. Suggested measures to combat this have included pay raises in sectors where mostly women work. Another proposal was for firms to be certified as having fair pay schemes as a condition of retaining government subsidies and winning public contracts. France introduced quotas to force large companies to appoint more women to their boards in 2011, and this was later extended to executive committees, but—as with initiatives to stop street harassment—enforcement is not easy, and positive results are by no means guaranteed.

Giant Orgies at the Élysée

When Hollywood film mogul Harvey Weinstein faced multiple allegations of sexual assault and harassment in October 2017, women publicly recounted their experiences under the hashtag #MeToo. The French version was #BalanceTonPorc, which can be translated as "Call out your pig."

France's first Weinstein-style moment was in 2011, with revelations about Dominque Strauss-Kahn, then head of the IMF and the unofficial Socialist front-runner to become President of France in 2012. DSK was arrested in Manhattan on suspicion of a brutal sex attack on Nafissatou Diallo, a hotel cleaning lady. The case raised up all kinds of class issues: DSK was very rich and influential, Diallo from a poor immigrant background; DSK was married to the Paris heiress and journalist Anne Sinclair (as we have heard, a great friend of philosopher Élisabeth Badinter), while the Guinea-born Diallo was a single parent struggling to pay her rent in the Bronx. DSK was white and highly educated, and Diallo Black and illiterate.

DSK was an unreconstructed, old-school French libertine who made no attempt to disguise his vast sexual appetite. In mid-2011 he had attended an orgy in Washington, DC, shortly before chancing upon Diallo in the Manhattan Sofitel. Uncontested court evidence, including DNA, suggested that he attempted to strip Diallo of her underwear and forced her to perform fellatio in the corridor of his suite.[11] Diallo said that she felt she had to comply with the wishes of a $3,000-a-night VIP guest or else she might be fired. She was angry when DSK didn't even leave a tip.

Following a complaint by Diallo and DSK's arrest at John F. Kennedy Airport in his first-class cabin just ten minutes before the plane was due to depart for France, the IMF chief initially went through the full perp ordeal. This included being led into court from his cell in Harlem in handcuffs as charges of attempted rape, sex abuse, forcible touching, and unlawful imprisonment were filed.

As soon as the self-styled *grand séducteur* was arrested, Anne Sinclair, his wife, immediately started her new career as his apologist-in-chief. She declared, "We love each other as much as we did when we first met." Such platitudes continued throughout the court process and a succession of disturbing allegations, including from prostitutes, as DSK owned up to his "uninhibited sex life." Sinclair posted her husband's substantial bail and later won a "Woman of the Year" award for sticking by her man. Readers of *Terrafemina*—an online magazine—lauded Sinclair for the "tenacity and unwavering support" she provided to DSK. Sinclair's citation praised her "loyalty and courage," saying she had become "both a heroine and a kind of anti-heroine for women in France. Women look at the problems they face in their own lives and seem to identify with her."

The claim that Sinclair was a role model for put-upon women (a kind of universal female victims' victim) was not only repulsive, but it also glossed over the fact that she showed absolutely no sympathy for the women her husband had allegedly assaulted.

Criminal prosecutors decided that they would not have been able to convince a jury "beyond reasonable doubt" that Diallo had not consented to the coupling. That is to say, there was no chance of a criminal conviction. This was despite the fact that Diallo had never met DSK before and did not even know who he was until his face appeared on the television news.

The case became a civil one, and both parties agreed to DSK paying a sum to close the matter. Beyond this settlement—rumored to be as high as $6 million by some, but more likely around $1.5 million—DSK lost his IMF job and any hope he had of becoming President of France. The case had brought typical predatory behavior by a powerful Frenchman out in the open. Whether legal or not, it was the kind that, until then, had been largely ignored by French officials and the media.

"We are all chambermaids!" was the chant out on the street at women's marches in Paris held soon afterward. There was talk of "before and after DSK" as French women poured out their experiences.

Abuse disguised as gallantry was called out, along with rape apologists, including plenty of establishment men and women. Former Socialist minister Jack Lang had called for DSK to be released on bail because "no one had died," while the philosopher Jean-François Kahn (no relation) said the case was merely a *troussage de domestique*—a phrase once used to describe French aristocrats having sex with servants.

There was particular anger within the Paris establishment at the way a would-be President of France was perp walked, manacled and unshaven, in front of media photographers and TV crews in Manhattan, including inside the courthouse as his appearance before a judge was televised. Lang further compared DSK's treatment to a "lynching" that had "provoked horror and aroused disgust," while Robert Badinter (yes, Élisabeth Badinter's husband)—a former Socialist Justice Minister (who had enacted the abolition of the death penalty in France in 1981)—said that his friend had been subjected to "death by media."

American newspapers such as the *New York Post* and *Daily News* had a field day with puns referring to "le perv" and his "perv walk." Many suggested it was all a conspiracy theory to keep him out of power in France. Calls to rape crisis lines exploded after the DSK case as a code of silence was broken. Meanwhile, some said DSK had been a victim of puritanical America. There was a strong argument that if the alleged rape had been reported in France, DSK would not have been arrested in the first place.

DSK was also at the center of a trial in Lille in 2015, in which Paris establishment figures were shown to have submitted women to sex acts while referring to them as "livestock." DSK was once again acquitted of any crime—the allegation that he was a pimp could not be proved—but not before he had admitted to an appetite for group sex and an approach to sex that was "rougher than the average man's." The so-called Carlton affair, after the Carlton Hotel in Lille, was about a sex ring that organized "festive afternoons" in Europe and the United States involving women from poor, immigrant backgrounds.

DSK's defense was that he "never suspected" any of the women involved were prostitutes because he "only saw them naked," but when they gave evidence, they all admitted that they were. Fabrice Paszkowski—a Lille entrepreneur and a close friend of DSK—told the court that he looked forward to one day organizing "giant orgies at the Élysée." When asked by the judge if it was not odd that he had sex with strangers who provably turned out to be prostitutes, DSK replied that sex with strangers was "the whole point" of his "swinging lifestyle."

The difficulty of getting sexual assault allegations to stick in France was made clear after Paris prosecutors opened a preliminary inquiry in 2011 into an alleged attempted rape by DSK on Tristane Banon. In 2007, Banon, a young writer, had spoken openly on French TV about DSK allegedly attacking her in 2003, while she was interviewing him for a book project, and how he had acted "like a chimpanzee in heat."

Banon later told me that she had pulled back from filing a formal complaint because of the expected "hostility" she would receive, not least of all from powerful allies of DSK. Banon's own mother, Anne Mansouret—a regional official in DSK's Socialist Party, who even said she had an affair with DSK herself at one stage—had actually advised her daughter to stay quiet. "I now regret this," Banon said.

DSK himself admitted to trying to kiss Banon but said there was no attempt at rape. Less than two months after New York prosecutors withdrew the attempted rape case against DSK there, their French counterparts did exactly the same thing with the Banon case, but not before they had officially recognized that Banon had been sexually assaulted—albeit past the statute of limitations for a successful prosecution.

Banon even referred to Sinclair as "an accomplice" who stuck with her husband "because of clan pride." Poignantly, Banon was last on *Terrafemina*'s list of ten "Women of the Year" in 2011. Banon only just made the bottom of the ranking because of the allegation that she was attacked by a man, while Sinclair came in at the top because of her support for the alleged attacker. It was a bizarre and confusing equation, and—most of all—it was a very disturbing one.

The French #MeToo Paradox

Like DSK, the film director Roman Polanski was left to carry on with an untroubled life in Paris, despite a load of sexual allegations against him. Polanski, known for films such as *Chinatown* and *The Pianist*, admitted forcing a thirteen-year-old girl to have sex with him in California in 1977. The director pleaded guilty to one count of unlawful sexual intercourse with a minor but fled to France before a sentencing hearing and has been a fugitive from US justice ever since. There is no extradition treaty between France and America, so Polanski can lead a perfectly normal family life with his wife and two children while also fulfilling professional commitments.

The #MeToo movement prompted other women to come forward with historic allegations against Polanski. One alleged he sexually assaulted her when she was ten, but he was not arrested or charged. Instead, the French arts establishment celebrates Polanski as much as Hollywood does. He has received many awards, including an Oscar for *The Pianist* and three Golden Globes, as well as a Cannes Palme d'Or and multiple Césars. Before his own legal difficulties mounted, Harvey Weinstein used to write Polanski letters of support.

I last saw Polanski with a VIP badge on as he entered a Rolling Stones gig at Longchamp Racecourse, west of Paris, in July 2022. His entourage included his wife, the actor Emmanuelle Seigner. Shortly afterward, Seigner started defending Polanski, convicted of sex with a minor, on TF1's prime-time TV show, *Sept à Huit* (Seven to eight). She made out that Polanski was ultimately misunderstood and should be "left in peace."

Worse, Seigner said Polanski could not have been guilty of such a heinous crime because "all the young girls wanted to sleep with him." She intimated that what he did was somehow acceptable in a "more permissive age" and that the gruesome details of how Polanski, then forty-three, had forced himself on a schoolgirl had never shocked her. Polanski was accused of other sexual crimes, but Seigner called his critics "mad."

If all that was not bad enough, Seigner even attacked the #MeToo movement. She said it had been responsible for "a lot of abuse, lies, which discredit victims and do them a disservice." In short: women were being far too hard on rich, powerful men like Polanski.

Earlier in 2022, Jean-Luc Brunel, a model agency boss and associate of the late American sex offender and financier Jeffrey Epstein, had committed suicide by hanging himself in his cell at La Santé prison in Paris. He had been arrested at Charles de Gaulle Airport on his way to Senegal in December 2020 and placed under formal investigation for "rape of a minor over fifteen and sexual harassment." At the time, the prosecutors said, "He is suspected of having committed rape, sexual aggression, and sexual harassment on different victims, underage and adult, and in particular of having organized the transport and housing of young girls or young women for Jeffrey Epstein." Many of Epstein's victims were said to have been "sourced" in France, where Epstein retained a massive luxury apartment by the Arc de Triomphe in Paris.

Epstein, already a convicted pedophile, committed suicide in a Manhattan cell in 2019 after being arrested on US federal charges of trafficking underage girls. As in the Epstein case, there were no cameras to record Brunel's final hours in prison—something that inevitably inspired conspiracy theories. His suicide also came just days after Prince Andrew, the Duke of York, agreed to settle a lawsuit with Virginia Giuffre accusing him of sex abuse after they met through Epstein and his girlfriend, the Anglo-French socialite Ghislaine Maxwell.

Giuffre, an American who had moved to Australia, also alleged that she was raped on numerous occasions by Brunel, who was close to Maxwell—by now a convicted sex trafficker herself and in prison in the United States. Following Brunel's suicide, Maxwell's family described the news as "shocking" and said they were scared for Maxwell's safety at the Metropolitan Detention Center in Brooklyn. Maxwell's brother Ian told the *New York Post*: "Another death by hanging in a high-security prison. My reaction is one of total shock and bewilderment." Conspiracists who suspected a plot were once more inspired.

Numerous former models waived their anonymity to make their allegations against Brunel public. Among them was Dutch model Thysia Huisman, who said she was raped by Brunel as a teenager in Paris in 1991. She was represented by Anne-Claire Le Jeune, a Paris barrister who said Brunel's death was a source of "frustration" for her clients. Le Jeune added, "Epstein and Brunel died in their cells and Prince Andrew has struck a confidentiality deal. All that leaves the impression there are lots of gray areas and it will be hard to get to the truth about this ring." Both Prince Andrew and Brunel had vehemently denied all claims against them.

The deluge of accusations prompted Macron's administration to introduce tokenistic legislation. Sexual harassment, including such vague indiscretions as "long stares" and wolf whistles, became punishable by on-the-spot fines starting at €90. When I asked a government spokesman how exactly such laws are enforced, he replied, "With difficulty." The truth is that when alleged abuse extends as far as the highest offices of state and across so many other spheres of privileged French life, it is very hard to combat.

BB for Bardot Bigotry

The meeting between Charles de Gaulle and Brigitte Bardot at the Élysée Palace in December 1967 also included Jean-Paul Belmondo, the *À Bout de Souffle* star. De Gaulle said he had seen BB in *Babette Goes to War*, the 1959 film in which she played a Second World War Resistance hero who travels to London. De Gaulle was name-checked a few times in the movie, something that always impressed *le Général*.

De Gaulle's wife, Yvonne de Gaulle, had feared BB would turn up at the dinner "completely naked," but in fact she wore a black pantsuit, as opposed to the kind of cocktail dress that was normally de rigueur at such events. "Ah, it's you! From afar, I took you for a soldier," De Gaulle told Bardot, as the two most internationally famous French icons of their age came face-to-face.[12]

At this time, Bardot was being celebrated as one of the first truly liberated women of postwar France. Simone de Beauvoir wrote about her as a catalyst for radical change in women's roles. Fast-forward to 2018, and Bardot was going for the #MeToo movement in a *Paris Match* interview, saying that a lot of young actors were "hypocritical nobodies, ridiculous, and uninteresting." Bardot was by now married to her fourth husband, Bernard d'Ormale, a former adviser to Jean-Marie Le Pen, and lived with her husband and other stray animals at La Madrague, her seaside property in Saint-Tropez.

Bardot continued in *Paris Match*: "Lots of actresses will try to play the tease with producers to get a role, and then—so we will talk about them—they say they were sexually harassed." She added, "I was never the victim of sexual harassment, and I found it charming when men told me that I was beautiful, or I had a nice little backside."

Bardot's comments came the same week that fellow French movie star Catherine Deneuve was among one hundred prominent women who triggered a worldwide feminist backlash by defending the male right to "hit on women." They all signed a letter in *Le Monde* in January 2018 attacking #MeToo for what they viewed as a man-hating brand of feminism. Another signatory was Catherine Millet, the art critic who wrote *The Sexual Life of Catherine M.* The letter implied that women who were touched up on public transport should just get over it. They criticized a perceived "new puritanism" as if it was a totalitarian outrage, rather than an attempt by women to share unpleasant, unsolicited, and unlawful experiences and indeed do something about them.

The *Le Monde* letter stated: "As women, we do not recognize ourselves in this feminism, which beyond denouncing the abuse of power takes on a hatred of men and of sexuality." There was even a clumsy reference to the "freedom" men allegedly had "to pester women."

Deneuve later made a semi-apology, agreeing that there was "nothing good" about harassment, but the damage was done. A group of overprivileged grandes dames and their cronies—some of whom were a lot younger—had shown how out of touch they were with the ordinary women who were suffering daily attacks. French actor Adèle Haenel summed up the woeful "#MeToo paradox in France" when she told the *New York Times* that her country has failed to draw the line between "libertine behavior" and "sexual abuse."

Haenel, star of the 2019 movie *Portrait of a Lady on Fire*, also said she was giving up cinema "because the film industry is absolutely reactionary, racist, and patriarchal." In a May 2022 interview with German magazine *FAQ*, Haenel stated, "By leaving this industry for good, I want to take part in another world, in another cinema."[13]

In contrast to such enlightened thinking, Bardot devoted a section of her memoir *Le Carré de Pluton* (Pluto's square) to an "open letter to my lost France." It mainly involved Bardot mourning her homeland, because it had been "invaded by an overpopulation of foreigners, especially Muslims." Bardot was occasionally punished for such big-otry with token court fines: 30,000 francs (approximately $4,000) in June 2000 for "incitement to racial hatred" in *Le Carré de Pluton*, and previous ones in 1997 and 1998 for the very same racist claims.

Bardot's second book, *Un Cri Dans le Silence* (A scream in the silence) even warned of an Islamic takeover of France: "Over the last twenty years, we have given in to a subterranean, dangerous, and uncontrolled infiltration, which not only resists adjusting to our laws and customs but which will, as the years pass, attempt to impose its own." Bardot attacked all forms of racial mixing and praised previous generations who "gave up their lives to push out invaders."

Un Cri Dans le Silence also introduced Bardot as a homophobic bigot. She made disparaging remarks about homosexuals, saying some "behave like fairground freaks." Predictably, Bardot tried to defend such views by saying she was "entirely surrounded" by gay friends, but no such defense of her views about Muslims was ever attempted. A fourth conviction for racial hatred came in 2004, along with a €5,000 fine, and in 2008 Bardot was once again convicted of inciting racial and religious hatred after she sent a copy of a letter conveying her disdain for Muslims to Nicolas Sarkozy when he was Interior Minister. The letter stated that she was "fed up with being under the thumb of this population, which is destroying us, destroying our country, and imposing its habits." Bardot's fine this time was €15,000—the largest to date.

In 2021, Bardot, by now eighty-seven, was fined €20,000 by a court in La Réunion, France's department in the Indian Ocean, over March 2019 correspondence in which she had described the place as "the devil's island" and its inhabitants as "savages." She had sent an open letter to Amaury de Saint-Quentin, then police chief of Réunion island, in response to what she saw as the mistreatment of animals by its inhabitants. Bardot wrote, "The natives have kept their savage genes" and were still "degenerate savages." Bardot was particularly unhappy about La Réunion's Hindu Tamil population sacrificing goats, referring to these practices as "cannibalism from past centuries," and attacked "a degenerate population still soaked in barbarous ancestral traditions."

By this time, Bardot and her myth were still widely admired and loved across France, even though the BB bigotry was getting worse.

Life Reduced to a Headscarf

As violence against women worsens and numerous powerful men are implicated in alleged sex crimes, the French remain obsessed with what Muslim women put on their heads. They agonize about it all the time, especially when discussing national identity and feminism. Any garments that might have something to do with Islam—however tenuously—are viewed with intense suspicion. The hyperbole extends to calling them an affront to human rights and, at times, a terrorist threat. Even basic headscarves whip up intense hatred—whether the kind worn by the late Queen Elizabeth II when she was riding her horses or sports bandanas tied at the back, which allow a woman to show off her face. Defending the wearing of the hijab is compared to excusing misogyny or worse. As we have learned, Muslims are frequently unfairly targeted by the forces of law and order in France because of their looks, whether their skin color or the clothes they are wearing. Discriminatory laws based on secularism have formalized such prejudice, and they are primarily aimed at women.

The word *laïcité*—the French form of secularism—originally referred to the laity, which is to say everyone who was not part of the clergy. The current form of *laïcité* is based on the 1905 Law on the Separation of the Churches and the State. This technically ended government funding of religious groups and declared that all their buildings were state property. In other words, the State—rather than individuals—was deemed secular. The law enshrined secularism in education, but it did not ban religion nor religious symbols and clothes. On the contrary, it guaranteed the freedom of religion. Priests and nuns could still wear cassocks and veils, for example.

Despite this, three Muslim girls were expelled from their middle school in the suburban Paris town of Creil in 1989 for refusing to remove their headscarves. The Council of State argued that religion-linked clothes were fine as long as they did not disturb the classroom or constitute "pressure, provocation, or proselytism." Fifteen years later, however, in 2004, Parliament banned "conspicuous religious signs" in state schools. Any display of religious or ethnic identity was said to be interfering with a collective Frenchness and was against "republican values." This was despite Catholic schools not only being allowed to operate but also receiving state funding as long as they taught the national curriculum. It did not feel as though laws based on secularism were being applied fairly. The law technically prohibited large Christian crosses in public, non-private schools, but there is no evidence of such a ban ever having been enforced. Crucifixes can absolutely be displayed anywhere, including in schools, and this freedom is protected by European Court legislation.

In 2010, the so-called burka ban outlawed face veils in public. "The burka is a sign of subservience, a sign of debasement which is not welcome on the territory of the Republic," is how Nicolas Sarkozy put it. Law number 2010-1192 meant that France became the first European country to criminalize the burka. It was disingenuously claimed that a range of other face-covering garments, from balaclavas to motorbike helmets, would also be banned if worn inappropriately, but it was clear that the legislation was only really concerned with Muslim-linked dress.

Coverings had to be vaguely Islamic for the authorities to take an interest. Women who were wearing the full-face veil in France at the time, around two thousand of them, and men caught forcing them to wear it were the only potential suspects. Later on, when everybody got used to covering up their faces during the COVID-19 pandemic, the burka ban remained intact.

There was an outcry in February 2010, when twenty-one-year-old Ilham Moussaïd dared to cover her hair in a fitted white headscarf while standing as a regional election candidate in the Vaucluse department representing the New Anti-Capitalist Party (Nouveau Parti Anti-capitaliste, NPA). Moussaïd insisted that there was no conflict between her clothing and her effectiveness as a politician, but this did not stop *Le Figaro* from running with the outraged headline: "The NPA puts up a veiled candidate."

Media delirium also included constant references to a burka— a word that is horribly manipulated in all these kinds of debates.

Moussaïd was in fact not wearing a burka at all, but this was considered unimportant by those who wanted to demonize her. Moussaïd said in a statement, "Try as I might to explain that I am not oppressed and that it shows, there's still a lack of understanding. It is with great sadness that I watch my life reduced to my headscarf. It is with great sadness that I hear that my personal beliefs are a danger to others while I advocate friendship, respect, tolerance, solidarity, and equality for all human beings."

Despite the NPA being a fringe party, Left and Right united against Moussaïd. Socialist Party MP Aurélie Filippetti advised Olivier Besancenot, Moussaïd's party leader, to "reread Marx" in order to understand why the headscarf was unacceptable. "Religion is the opium of the people," said Filippetti. "Perhaps we should remind the NPA that workers in France don't need to be told to go and read the Koran or the Bible or I don't know what."

Critics from the Right said the NPA was an "Islamo-Leftist" party—one that courts the Muslim vote in packed housing estates at any cost. Besancenot was accused of putting a veiled woman on his team for this very purpose. This completely missed the key point, which was that a grounded young woman could be both politically active *and* wear a headscarf. What was really happening was that the headscarf was cynically being associated with a so-called dangerous ideology and "immigrants" from Africa.

A 2012 Senate bill also attempted to turn nannies working in private homes into criminals if they wore headscarves. The proposal was rejected by the National Assembly, but the message was clear: Muslim child carers presented a threat. Luc Chatel, then Minister of National Education, formalized such prejudice in the same year when he signed a circular prohibiting women in headscarves from accompanying their children on school outings.

Then, in 2016, municipal decrees published during the summer banned women in *burkinis*—swimsuits that cover the whole body—from public beaches. Yet again Muslim women were criminalized. Fines were issued and any modest beachwear with "religious connotations" was prohibited on the grounds of "security concerns" and "respect for secularism." Thus, Islam was being cynically linked with everything from sexism to terror threats.

The marketing of *burkinis* by high street brands such as H&M and designer labels such as Dolce & Gabbana was attacked by the then Women's Rights Minister Laurence Rossignol. She accused *burkini* manufacturers of being solely interested in another lucrative line of business (as if profitable commerce was to be frowned upon) and compared Muslim women who dare to shop in the "Islamic garment market" to "negroes who supported slavery." Beyond the odious, colonial-era language, the Socialist politician's argument was absurd considering that France, the country of haute couture, is a center of world fashion that makes billions out of the clothing industry.

The truth was that public figures like Rossignol who raged against the behavior of minorities they disliked were hiding their prejudices behind feminism. Rossignol has not uttered a word about Catholic nuns, or Orthodox Jews, or any other group of women who like to wear modest clothes. Celebrities—from British TV chef Nigella Lawson to Hollywood star Lindsay Lohan—were also wearing *burkinis* at the beach, but the French still used such garments to demonize and criminalize an entire faith and its followers.

In 2021, President Macron's own party reduced another educated young Muslim woman to her headscarf. Sara Zemmahi, a twenty-six-year-old laboratory technician, was barred by En Marche! from running to become a councillor in her home city of Montpellier after she was photographed in a hijab for their campaign flyer. French law does not prohibit such images on election posters, but Zemmahi was nonetheless expelled.

This came after Macron himself was found to have misled readers of the *Financial Times* by writing in a letter to the newspaper that "small girls aged three or four" in the *cités* were being forced to wear the burka while being "raised in hatred of France's values." The *FT* complaints commissioner said he was "highly sceptical" of the French President's claims, especially in the absence of any evidence, but still argued that the public had the right to know about "falsehoods spouted by global figures." In other words, fake news was somehow justified when the source was the President and the targets were Muslim children and their parents. That Macron—who came to power as a liberal centrist apparently committed to tolerance and respect—had joined in the poisonous politicking should have concerned everyone.

Even in 2022, a year dominated by the Ukraine War, related economic catastrophes, and the lingering coronavirus pandemic, France was not spared its annual Muslim dress saga. Angry Senators devoted parliamentary time to debating whether the state should ban sportswomen from wearing the hijab. Their suggestion failed, but—in the run-up to the 2024 Paris Olympics—it was clear that they were trying to apply anti-Muslim bigotry to sport.

France considers itself the home of human rights, but clothing choice is somehow excluded from the protections these rights are meant to provide. Certain feminists (by no means all of them) support such bans, because they see any kind of garment that relates to Islam, however vaguely, as being a symbol of oppression.

Annie Ernaux, the French writer who won the Nobel Prize for Literature in 2022, was among the few influential voices who railed against the absurdity of the hijab ban. She wrote in a column for *Libération*: "Everything happens as if there was no one under the 'veil,' no human being capable of thinking, feeling, and expressing themselves. The woman as an individual disappears. She is purely and simply reduced to an object."

Ernaux asked female politicians, "Why refuse to grant individuals a right that takes nothing away from others? How can we, feminist women, who have claimed the right to dispose of our bodies, who have fought and who still fight to freely decide our lives, can we deny the right of other women to choose theirs?"

She went on, "Where is the sisterhood that has allowed, for example, the meteoric expansion of the #MeToo movement? Empathy, solidarity cease when it comes to Muslim women in hijab: they are the dark continent of feminism. Or rather of a certain feminism that makes war on other women in the name of a secularism that has become the mantra of a dogma that dispenses with any other consideration."[14]

On December 9, 2017, Education Minister Jean-Michel Blanquer marked the anniversary of the 1905 law by introducing "*laïcité* units" in schools. Monitors tasked with "managing" incidents that challenged secularism were first set up in the Paris suburb of Créteil. They bred enormous suspicion and, if anything, eroded patriotism among disillusioned youngsters. So it was that *laïcité* has been manipulated to promote a dogmatic view of citizenship while "justifying" all kinds of tensions. Discrimination is allowed to flourish, while ordinary Muslims are stigmatized.

At all times, the very concept of *laïcité* became deliberately vague, flexible, and easily weaponized in any situation that might allow Muslim subjugation. It is all an echo of the colonial "civilizing mission"—in this case, aimed at assimilating people into a secular culture. Dress is disingenuously projected as a manifestation of the "Islamist threat," one of the great menaces to French society. According to this warped logic, clothes represent the failure of the state not only to integrate an allegedly alien culture but also to ward off related evils such as terrorism and—in the case of feminism—the oppression of women. (The conceit, of course, is that women only wear headscarves because men force them to.)

Cynical arguments ranging from "protecting national security" to "liberating women in a secular society" are invariably advanced. The very word "emancipation" is used as a cover for rampant bigotry. Are members of the country's five-million-plus Muslim minority somehow excluded from enjoying the principles of "Liberty, Equality, Fraternity" that underpin the French Republic? The truth is that the consequences of such constant, high-profile debates about bans can be devastating. Muslim women are regularly assaulted, both verbally and physically, for wearing hijabs. Poisonous rhetoric about dress certainly provokes horrendous attacks.

Macho France

The battles for women's *Liberté* and *Égalité* were often won in a stuttering, unsatisfactory manner. French women got the vote in 1944, for example, but the "indigenous Muslim women of French Algeria"—as these citizens who were considered second-class were called—did not get it until 1958.

The Internet has allowed for the increased visibility of social and political issues around the world, and complaints about discrimination and violence against women have quite rightly proliferated. A country that can allow an Interior Minister to carry on with his work as normal while under investigation for rape clearly has a lot of problems to resolve. This is despite Emmanuel Macron describing himself as a feminist in an interview with *Têtu* magazine in February 2017. "I was raised by women, my grandmother, my mother. My wife is also my best friend," said Macron. "It's very cheap not to be a feminist. To change politics, you have to be a feminist; it's a moral obligation."

More than this, Macron actually described sex equality as the "great cause" of his mandate when he first came to power.[15] It was the first time a President of France had prioritized feminist issues so forcefully. He said equality, education, support for victims of male violence, and stronger anti-harassment laws were all essential. Macron also described the "feeling of horror" when reading testaments that followed the Weinstein scandal and acknowledged that a woman was killed by domestic violence once every three days in France. As well as targeting problems in his country, the President said he wanted to pursue a more feminist foreign policy—boosting women's rights in impoverished parts of Africa, for example.

Has Macron's time in office brought about major changes in all these respects? Not according to a 2022 Oxfam France report, which concludes that "power remains a male affair" in the republic.[16] The Gender Equality Ministry saw its budget almost double from €27 million to €50 million during Macron's first five-year presidency, but this was still considered "insufficient" for the work needed, according to key groups that helped compile the report. The government budget specifically allocated to combating domestic violence was considered "three times lower than what is needed." The government's principal equality watchdog also reported in January 2023 that France "remains very sexist in all its spheres," and that an "emergency plan" should be set up to counter growing violence against women. A voyeuristic social media culture, and especially sites providing easy access to extreme pornography for young men, compounded the problem. Relationships were being reduced to expressions of forced domination, while femicide was increasingly being featured in music, film, and literature as part of the entertainment industry. This dark situation ultimately meant that even more lives were being threatened.[17]

The statute of limitations for assaults on minors was extended under the Macron administration, but such measures were small steps, given the minuscule number of men who were actually brought to court. The implementation of new policies was also criticized. Little use was being made of ankle bracelets aimed at locating and controlling male offenders. Even when judges did ask for them to be worn, many malfunctioned. Magistrates were also given the power to confiscate knives in cases where they might be used as weapons in domestic disputes, but this prerogative was seldom enforced, according to the Oxfam report. The Gender Equality Ministry also revealed that only 90,000 out of 250,000 police officers and gendarmes—36 percent—had been trained to deal with female victims of male violence.

While almost 50 percent of Macron's own party were women, men still held the "strategic and prestigious positions." More than 80 percent of ministerial offices were headed by men. One of the few exceptions was the Armed Forces Ministry, led by Florence Parly and Sylvie Goulard before her. On average, two-thirds of senior advisers at the Élysée Palace and in Matignon (the residence of the Prime Minister) were men. "The verdict is final," the report reads: Macron's record was "insufficient." Women have certainly become more vocal about their rights, but bold participation in public demonstrations, either on the street or online, cannot cover up the shortcomings. As in all other parts of the world, feminism in France still has a very long way to go.

Following the June 2022 parliamentary election, there were 215 women in the 577-seat National Assembly. This 37.3 percent representation was down two percentage points from 2017, when Macron first came to power and championed gender balance. The Gaullist conservative Républicains had 29.5 percent female MPs, while the far-right Rassemblement National had 37.1 percent. The newly formed left-wing NUPES alliance had 43.6 percent. Macron's Renaissance coalition was at 40.4 percent, down seven points compared to 2017.

Despite this, Élisabeth Borne became France's first female Prime Minister in thirty years. She meekly dedicated her nomination by

Macron to a still scandalously underrepresented sex. "Follow your dreams," said Borne. "Nothing must slow down the struggle for women to be prominent in society." There were no references to structural or cultural problems. The implication was that women merely lacked ambition.

Édith Cresson, France's first ever female Prime Minister, was eighty-eight by this time, and she was quick to highlight how sexist the Republic still was. When it became clear that Macron was going to name a woman as Prime Minister, she said, "Only in France is there any question raised about appointing a woman to Matignon. To my eyes this is scandalous. Has the question been asked in the United Kingdom, where Margaret Thatcher was in power for eleven years? In Germany, where Angela Merkel was Chancellor for sixteen years? Never. The same goes for Portugal, where a woman was appointed Prime Minister long before me."

Referring to France, Cresson said, "It's not the country that is macho: it is its political class. There were the same attacks as there are today. I was under permanent criticism. They commented on my dress. We would never allow the same thing, the same comments, on the dress of male politicians. When we talk about women, we have no problem talking about their clothes or their appearance."

Cresson concluded: "The post of Prime Minister is a very difficult position in any case. . . . And then if the difficulties are increased by the fact that the head of government is a woman, it complicates the political situation even more. If another woman is appointed, I won't be giving her any advice. To her I simply say, you'll need a lot of courage."[18]

9

ECONOMICS
Winners and Laggers

Man is incapable of understanding any argument that
interferes with his revenue.

—RENÉ DESCARTES (1596–1650)

F rench heads of state are given all kinds of unimaginative names,
but the bland "President of the rich" is the one that you hear most
often. It is not particularly insulting—not in a personal way, anyway—
but it is highly appropriate. Street demonstrators use it all the time,
whether they are referring to a former merchant banker like Emmanuel
Macron or an alleged wealth-hating leftist like François Hollande.

I once asked Hollande about the inappropriate link between the
most senior public servant and immense amounts of easy wealth
and privilege. At first, he did not want to talk about it. This is very
French. Unlike in America and Britain, there is traditionally a Gallic
repugnance toward obsessing about personal gain. This can perhaps
be traced back to the country's roots in Catholicism, which tends to
extoll the virtues of the poor. France was once a country mainly populated by rural folk whose simple lives were considered more worthy than those devoted to acquisition. After killing their monarch,

along with the fabulously rich absolutist regime he headed, French republicans called for a fair distribution of the national wealth, with modesty technically expected of everyone. That said, Hollande was reluctant to deny that Presidents of the Republic live like modern-day Kings. How could he? Hollande undoubtedly had the air of a very well-resourced *gauche caviar*—the French equivalent of a champagne socialist. Nevertheless, he did envisage that getting into the most privileged establishment position of all was at least a chance to attack it from within.

"I will not be looking to make friends among the very rich," he told me as he contemplated becoming the second-ever Socialist President of France. "There will be a lot of new measures aimed at making society far more just. This will include very high taxes on the very rich." There was no ambiguity involved. As Hollande later put it in a speech at a campaign rally in 2011: "My true enemy has no name, no face, no party. He will never stand for election, and he will never be elected. Despite all this, he is in charge. My enemy is the world of finance."

Hollande blamed a failing capitalist system, and particularly the rotten banking sector, for many of his country's woes. There were too many fat cats lapping up the cream while doing everything they could to avoid paying taxes. Hollande had pinpointed his foe, and becoming head of state—however unexpectedly—meant he was ready to attack.

How did that go? Well, not very well at all. Hollande's much vaunted 75 percent supertax on earnings of more than $1 million was pure tokenism—the kind of dismal measure that Presidents introduce to try to appear new and radical, and to capture the interest of the media, before it all falls apart. Wealth creators rushed to leave the country—or at least pretended to leave the country—along with celebrity icons such as Oscar-nominated and Golden Globe–winning actor Gérard Depardieu, who also conveniently held Russian and Emirati citizenships. Players at football clubs with massive fan bases, such as Paris Saint-Germain, threatened to go on strike while contemplating moves to rival clubs. David Cameron, the Prime Minister in the United Kingdom during the Hollande administration, offered "to roll out the red carpet" to French tax exiles (of which there were many), particularly in London's more salubrious districts such as South Kensington.

The Hollande supertax was meant to raise the equivalent of around $260 million in its first year—a tiny sum compared to a budget deficit of some $85 billion. The measure was regularly challenged in the courts as being punitive before a watered-down version was gradually phased out within two years. This was after Hollande's bright young Economy Minister, Emmanuel Macron, had laughed it off as an attempt to turn France into "Cuba without the sun."

Other failed Hollande initiatives included weakening Paris as a financial center—meaning it would struggle to challenge the City of London—pouring millions more into civil service jobs, and trying to renegotiate the EU pact to replace austerity with spending aimed at encouraging growth. Angela Merkel, the then German Chancellor, was so unimpressed by Hollande that she threatened to campaign on behalf of his hated rival, Nicolas Sarkozy.

What Hollande's slapstick adventures tell us about the French economy is that, yes, it keeps the very wealthy happy, and that even a determined left-winger who hates the rich has next to no chance of reforming it. On the contrary, the default position of all new administrations is to maintain the status quo: a small tycoon industrialist class at the top and the vast majority at the bottom earning significantly less.

The French State is enormous and costs a fortune. As a country, France spends more heavily than any other in the developed world. Attempts to downsize always lead to social unrest. When Macron came to power in 2017, he pledged to reduce spending, which was at a record 56 percent of GDP. Instead, it went up by about 5 percent. Yes, the COVID-19 pandemic had much to do with this, but it was still indicative of a nation in denial.

Much of the heaviest spending goes on welfare payments per se, not on specifics such as housing. Numerous regulations protect "insiders" with pampered public service jobs, many of them closely linked to a Paris establishment that dominates resource allocation across the country.

Resentment against the billionaire class that does best out of the republic's economy fuels anti-capitalist protest movements as inequality grows. In the words of a 2021 government-backed report: "Technology and globalisation have created a class of winners and a class of laggers. There is growing polarisation between those who are benefitting from technology and globalisation and those who are left behind. At the same time, the traditional 'middle class' is hollowed out."[1]

The report adds, "A lack of good jobs and deeply unequal opportunities carry potentially large social, political, and economic costs. Social costs manifest themselves in the form of exclusion, broken families, drug and substance abuse, addiction, and crime. Political consequences emerge through declining trust in government, experts, and institutions, partisan polarisation, the rise of populist nationalism, and backlashes against globalisation and immigration." Essentially, the failing French economic model cannot possibly meet the expectations of the majority of its citizens. Inequality is accelerating, along with corruption among the ruling classes. Plans to fight climate change inevitably lead to taxes on those who can least afford it, such as happened with the "green" surcharges on fuel that Macron tried to introduce. They caused particular damage to those living in rural communities, who rallied within the extremely violent *Gilets Jaunes* movement.

Macron was also portrayed as an out-of-touch Republican monarch when he used a presidential decree to raise the pension age two years to sixty-four in March 2023. He had little chance of winning parliamentary approval so simply ignored the National Assembly, causing nationwide rioting along with strikes and other protests. The perception in foreign countries was that the French were revolting against joining the "real world"—a place where many were working past sixty-eight—while there were comparisons between Macron and Louis XVI. These did not abate when the President was due to sit down with King Charles III for a state banquet at Versailles. It was canceled, along with an entire state visit by the British monarch, because of the violence and acts of disorder, including the words "Death to the King" being scrawled on walls close to the Élysée Palace. The intense anger across France was all related to criticism of the kind of capitalism that increasingly supports a tiny elite that controls the majority of the world's wealth.

The 0.1 Percent

In July 2022, the wealthiest person in France was industrialist Bernard Arnault, who was worth $163 billion. He had started out working for his father's civil engineering company, Ferret-Savinel, before building up a retail empire that now includes the luxury goods group LVMH. By the end of the year, thanks to a slump in the tech sector and some bizarre actions on the part of the spaceflight tech magnate Elon Musk, Arnault was the richest man in the world. *Égalité* only goes so far, it seemed. Next on the French rich list was L'Oréal heiress Françoise Bettencourt Meyers, whose fortune was valued at $74.8 billion.[2] She is the daughter of the late Liliane Bettencourt, the richest woman in France before her.

The Paris homes of these Gallic tycoons look as luxurious and secure as the Élysée Palace itself. Arnault's own eighteenth-century hôtel particulier is on the Left Bank of the Seine and full of artistic treasures. Postmodernist paintings sit alongside Louis XVI furniture in the grand salon, while rare manuscripts in a mahogany-paneled library include poetry dating back to the Middle Ages. A near neighbor is François-Henri Pinault, husband of Hollywood star Salma Hayek and owner of the retail company Kering. Pinault is an industrialist who also considers his taste for high culture to be as refined as his business acumen, and his pile reflects this. I often walk past such buildings in Paris and contrast them with the rows of tents for the homeless that are dotted along the nearby Seine quays.

Many list-topping American multibillionaires, such as Microsoft founder Bill Gates, have done it all by themselves, but in France inherited wealth produces far greater returns than start-ups. Despite the meritocratic ideas championed by the French Revolution, up-and-coming members of the Bettencourt and Arnault dynasties will certainly earn a lot more by creaming off profits on family capital rather than trying to build up their own reputations. This Gallic emphasis on exploiting a well-established golden goose guarantees low economic growth as well as vast inequality in a land where the minimum wage in July 2022 was the equivalent of $11.60 an hour.

French economist Thomas Piketty's *Capital in the Twenty-First Century* references the novels of Jane Austen and Honoré de Balzac to highlight how lucrative a good marriage could prove in the nineteenth century and onward. The meritocratic notion of achieving success through your own efforts less so. Inherited wealth will still generally "dominate wealth amassed from a lifetime's labour by a wide margin," Piketty argues.

French multinationals such as L'Oréal and LVMH export capitalism brilliantly, but conditions for doing business domestically can be a lot more restrictive, not least of all because of the high cost of hiring staff and the protection they receive once employed. Bureaucratic regulation, a vast civil servant class, and an overall distrust of entrepreneurship also work against economic aspiration. This is particularly disastrous for those trying to break out of housing estates or isolated rural areas. As these people struggle, France pours multimillions into the world's third oldest space program, after America's and Russia's, as rockets and satellites are prioritized over those finding life difficult on Earth. In September 2022, Prime Minister Élisabeth Borne said $9 billion would be allocated to space activities over the next three years—an increase of 25 percent.

At the start of Macron's first term, some nine million people—a third of them children—lived in poverty, which is defined as 60 percent of median income. This figure of 14 percent of the French population remained consistent throughout Macron's period in office, despite attempts to reduce it.[3] "I don't want a plan that leaves the poor living in poverty, only more comfortably," Macron said in 2018, but inequalities were as stark as ever.[4] They are most clearly evidenced in cities such as Paris, where the homeless set up squalid encampments close to unoccupied mansions bought as investments by the superrich.

Such material injustices are of course prevalent the world over, but—along with ennui and film noir—economic pessimism is a staple of French culture. Marine Le Pen, Macron's greatest electoral rival, described France as "the world champion of debt," "the world champion of unemployment," and even the "world champion of poverty."[5] None of this is true—Le Pen should spend some time in Burundi or Mozambique—but it is a perception that says much about the sclerotic nature of economic development in France.

Le Pen herself calls for mass state investment to alleviate poverty among her base—many are from forgotten communities in former industrial areas and barren countryside—while pledging to cut taxes and the cost of living. One of her presidential campaign slogans was "Give the French their money back," but she never explained how this fitted in with increased spending. Similarly, Macron came to power in 2017 promising to cut costs and create a country that was better equipped to deal with challenges from emerging economies, such as China, Brazil, and India. Soon, however, he was forced to spend even more than his predecessors as inflation and the cost of living soared.

During a visit to Denmark in 2018, Macron himself spoke about the kind of French celebrated in the Asterix cartoons: ones who are proudly resistant to change. Macron referred to "Lutheran Danish people who have been open to the changes of the last century, as opposed to the defiant Gauls who resist all change."

Speaking to Queen Margrethe II, Macron said he was impressed by the pragmatic Danish labor system, which involved "flexi-curity" (flexibility and security) and allowed bosses to sack workers by text, sure in the knowledge that those leaving would be supported by an easily accessible social security system. The situation in France was far more complicated, meaning management were wary of offering long-term contracts.

Macron's dismissive comments (he tried to pass them off as banter) about Gauls were accompanied by policies that reduced taxes for the wealthiest and undoubtedly led to the superrich becoming even richer. In 2018, Macron abolished the wealth tax known as ISF—*impôt de solidarité sur la fortune*, or tax on fortune. There would be no more tax on share dividends either. This was "runoff" economics—the French version of "trickle-down"—which is meant to see the very rich pouring their saved money into the economy rather than hoarding it for a rainy day. As Macron's Finance Minister Bruno Le Maire put it: "Overtaxing capital did not lead to more tax justice, but to more investors and creators of wealth leaving."[6]

An official report published in 2020 pointed out that the incomes of the 0.1 percent—the wealthiest people in France, amounting to just 3,800 households—had risen sharply under the Macron administration.[7] The number of people benefiting from company dividends was also up. *Le Monde* called the report "highly inflammable" at a time when "more and more households are being pushed into poverty."[8]

In another report, the France Stratégie policy unit clearly pinpointed the *cités* and the way the economic situation for those living in them has remained unaltered since the riots of 2005. The report explained, "One of the visible and harmful consequences of these trends is a scarcity of what could be called 'good jobs'—good pay, relative security, some career progression, access to adequate (re)training, safe working conditions, and the possibility of sustaining a normal 'middle-class' life with a reasonable level of economic security and the scope for some savings."[9] While economic fortunes could fluctuate for communities up and down the land, they were invariably rock bottom for those on the suburban estates.

Golden Years

Nostalgia is very important to the French, and, economically, the most recent golden age was made up of the postwar decades that lasted from victory in 1945 until just before Emmanuel Macron's birth in Amiens in 1977. The basis of this triumph was *dirigisme*—the economic doctrine that involved the state directing market economics, rather than simply regulating from time to time. Instead of being laissez-faire about market failures and production problems, the government intervened directly. This meant state investment and production incentives such as subsidies and tax breaks.[10]

De Gaulle first introduced a *dirigiste* economic plan months after Liberation in 1944 and was backed by funds from the 1948 Marshall Plan. The postwar reconstruction was the start of three decades of prosperity that included high wages, a vast increase in available goods including cars and TVs, and a sophisticated social welfare system.

In addition to the billions transferred from America as part of the European Recovery Program, debts to America from the First World War were wiped out. The United States became a role model for the aspirational French consumer. A coalition of Gaullists, Socialists, and Communists in De Gaulle's provisional government nationalized sectors including energy, so creating Électricité de France (EDF) and Gaz de France. Air France was taken over by the state, along with the Bank of France; the four biggest commercial banks, including Société Générale; and Renault (the car manufacturer had been linked with producing trucks for the German army of Occupation, meaning it was considered worthy of government takeover, unlike Peugeot and Citroën).

The nationalization program was a great success. Public investment stimulated growth and created new industries, as four-year governmental economic plans defied capitalist orthodoxy. These strategies were used as a tool to restructure companies and to create jobs. A welfare state was set up by the postwar administration, while the private sector managed key services on behalf of the government. The French motorway system started to appear thanks to public investment, for example, but concessions were sold to private or semiprivate organizations to operate and maintain the new network.

A rapidly growing population caused by *le baby boom* and increased immigration was integral to the "Glorious Thirty." Initially, a new workforce needed to rebuild more than a million buildings destroyed or damaged during the war years, along with transport infrastructure. France's population became an increasingly youthful one too. By 1967, a third of the country was under twenty.[11] Better nutrition and medical care ensured people lived a lot longer. Belief in a sovereign economy that standardized working methods and won France global prestige inspired both management and workers as, beyond organizing public services, the state regulated the production of goods like never before.

Living standards improved significantly as the French moved out of their rural smallholdings into more prosperous suburbs. There were some six million agricultural workers in France in 1955, compared to around eight hundred thousand by 2020. Farming methods changed, meaning large companies bought small farm owners out, and productivity soared. Finding a market for all that French cheese, meat, and wheat was a primary reason for founding the European Economic Community in 1957. Tariffs were abolished and free trade with countries such as West Germany and Italy boomed.

It is easy to romanticize a disappearing France full of jolly, God-fearing peasants, but actually a home with modern conveniences and nearby supermarkets was, for many, preferable. The French remain very nostalgic about *la France profonde*, perhaps because it is not just a physical place but a reference to a simpler life away from the chaos of the city. This did not prevent them embracing an American-style dream as their country became far more urbanized and—thanks to new technology—far more connected. The positives that grew out of the *Trente Glorieuses* were undeniable. A nation shattered by war had, by the 1970s, become renowned for its world-class industries, excellent transport system, and booming tourism sector.

The prosperity yielded by *dirigisme* came to a crashing halt following the oil crisis of 1973, however. The Saudi Arabia–led Organization of Arab Petroleum Exporting Countries announced an oil embargo to punish Western states for supporting Israel during the Yom Kippur War. By 1974, the price of oil had risen by 300 percent, and so-called oil shocks continued throughout the '70s, with disastrous repercussions. Increased energy costs meant production became hugely expensive, and instability followed.

As the crisis intensified, France had to diversify its energy sources, and so accelerated its nuclear program, which had started in the 1950s. Atomic testing had controversially taken place in Algeria in the 1960s—the first French A-bomb went off in the Sahara in February 1960—and also in French Polynesia, where there were some two hundred nuclear explosions over three decades until 1996. Thousands of people developed very serious health problems, leading to claims of crimes against humanity, and environmental damage was also immense. Despite this checkered past, French nuclear power companies such as EDF and Areva became majority owned by the French State. Billions were poured into the sector by successive governments, as taxpayers funded bailouts. By 2022, nuclear power was generating up to 70 percent of France's electricity and employing around 220,000 people. Faced with the energy crisis caused by the war in Ukraine, France pledged to open all of its fifty-six aging reactors, all run by EDF.

In reaction to the economic turmoil created by the oil crisis of the '70s, price freezes and wage control were used to try to defeat spiraling inflation, right up until Mitterrand's first Socialist administration in 1981. Mitterrand endeavored to force a recovery with another range of nationalizations in 1982. His government swooped on banks, steel and pharmaceutical companies, defense manufacturers, and computer businesses such as ITT-France. Mitterrand projected this "common program" as a continuation of the work started by De Gaulle's provisional government, but the postwar consensus was fast disappearing. Growth stalled, there was a recession, and the franc had to be devalued.

The French, meanwhile, were becoming ever more pampered. If they were not on strike, then they were taking the whole of August off. Mitterrand's Socialist administration gave people five weeks of paid holidays in 1981 and took the legal retirement age down from sixty-five to sixty. Mitterrand also reduced the working week to thirty-nine hours (Socialist Labor Minister Martine Aubry further lowered it to thirty-five hours in 2000). When a bank holiday fell on a Tuesday or Thursday, French employees took the Monday or Friday off as well. The practice became known as *le pont*, or bridge. If two bank holidays fell conveniently, then this double whammy turns into a viaduct—a whole week off.

Trade union membership was surprisingly low in France—about 10 percent of the workforce—but they have always fought tooth and nail to oppose new initiatives. What was certain was that the amount of money being spent on welfare and the bloated public service was unsustainable. As is still the case, the French government was the largest employer in France by a long way. The wage bill was enormous.

Mitterrand chose austerity and closer European integration as the way out of trouble. When he came to power on May 10, 1981, it was the first time in the twenty-three-year history of the Fifth Republic that a Socialist had taken over from the Gaullist Right. He promised a break with the established order, but things did not go according to plan. Realizing the failure of his first set of nationalizations, he applied a *ni-ni* policy during his second seven-year term starting in 1988. This officially meant "neither nationalization nor privatization," but in fact led to wholesale privatizations. This was the period of the Big Bang deregulation of financial markets presided over by British Prime Minister Margaret Thatcher, when privatizations appeared irresistible.

France slowly started to emerge out of recession in 1994, after government spending had reached 55 percent of GDP. This compared to 37 percent in the United Kingdom for the same year, and 21 percent in the United States. Then there were mass strikes in the winter of 1995 during Jacques Chirac's first term of office. Three weeks of nationwide disruption included a complete shutdown of the public transport system. Chirac's new Prime Minister, Alain Juppé, announced welfare cutbacks as a means of reducing the budget deficit from 5 percent to 3 percent, as required by the Maastricht Treaty of 1992, which committed EU member states to the monetary union.

Maastricht imposed strict free-market rules that ensured more privatizations. The strikes were a success for the unions, who in particular forced Juppé to abandon his attack on so-called special retirement schemes that enabled railway workers, for example, to give up work at age fifty-five. Juppé had pledged he would never back down, but his bluff was called.

Chirac, meanwhile, tried to reverse years of decline by eliminating the wealth tax and the need for bureaucratic approval before firings. Incremental reforms achieved little, however, and nothing was done about structural change. Instead, botched reforms strengthened the view among the pessimistic French that any kind of tinkering inevitably led to trouble. It was only thanks to the threat of the far-right Front National delivering a President, Jean-Marie Le Pen, that Chirac got his second term in 2002, but the economic crisis continued. Chirac failed to heal the social divide—the mass riots in the *cités* came in 2005—while policy *immobilisme* remained the norm. Vague efforts were made to press domestic reforms, but the government always backed down in the face of protest.

Moné, Moné, Moné

Nicolas Sarkozy, whose early mentor was Jacques Chirac, reveled in material wealth. The "bling-bling" President wore Patek Philippe and Rolex watches and never hid his love of *le moné*, as he famously mispronounced the English word while trying to attract foreign investors into France when he was Chirac's Finance Minister.

One of Sarkozy's first actions on taking office in 2007 was to award himself a pay rise of 172 percent, to €240,000 a year, but this sum barely equaled a day's earnings of the big business beasts who were his closest allies. Many of them had piled into Fouquet's, the mahogany-paneled restaurant on the Champs-Élysées, for a celebratory party on May 6, 2007—election day, when Sarkozy came to power while being projected as a radical visionary who could impress wealth creators from Britain and America. Slogans including "The new Margaret Thatcher" and "Sarko the American" were bandied about before his miserable single term fizzled out with next to nothing accomplished.

Sarkozy's gold-star allies included Bernard Arnault, who was already the wealthiest man in France, and other industrialists such as Martin Bouygues, François Pinault, Serge Dassault, and Vincent Bolloré. Their combined wealth was approaching the size of France's national debt. The dress code at the dinner had been relaxed excess, blazers and jeans instead of starched suits and stiff collars. Attendees embraced and joshed. All were practically rubbing their hands at the chance the new President would provide them: the opportunity to make even more *moné*.

Detractors described the bash as a shocking example of Sarko's vulgar inclinations. Macaroni stuffed with Périgord black truffles (€95) was on the menu, along with fifty grams of *caviar impérial* (€180) and

grilled sole meunière (€85). White wine included Chablis costing €200
a bottle and Château Haut-Marbuzet AOP at €380. Perrier-Jouët Belle
Epoque champagne was €300. "President of the rich" read the inevitable headlines, along with references to the "Fouquet's gang."

Sarkozy spent much of the meal talking to Bolloré, a corporate
raider who always wore handmade blue shirts embroidered with his VB
initials. Assets owned by "the little prince of cash flow"—as he was
nicknamed in the French press—included two private jets, a beachside
home in Saint-Tropez with its own vineyard, and the entire island of
Loc'h in the Glénan archipelago, in Bolloré's native Brittany. Bolloré's
main home was a town house in the Villa Montmorency, the private
enclave in the 16th Arrondissement of Paris popular with showbiz stars
including Gérard Depardieu, Isabelle Adjani, and Carla Bruni, soon to
become Sarkozy's third wife.

Bolloré had started his own independent career in 1981 by buy-
ing out his family's cigarette and Bible paper-making company for a
symbolic franc. Highly aggressive takeovers during the next three
decades enabled him to build up the Bolloré Group—a conglomerate
that seemingly covered every field of human activity that made *moné*,
from transport to telecommunications. Hostile takeovers could make
Bolloré extremely unpopular, but the financial gains were enormous.
By 2017, his empire encompassed 338 companies, 45 of them situated
in tax havens as they turned over some $7 billion a year. "The secret
is to find a new fishing spot that nobody else has yet discovered," was
Bolloré's key business advice. It was an old Breton saying, and one that
was designed to appeal to risk-takers.

Some of the Fouquet's guests brought modest gifts for the new
President, while Bolloré's offering was an instant, all-expenses-paid
holiday on his sixty-five-meter yacht, *La Paloma*—a floating palace
bought and then renovated for a total cost of some $9 million, which
was rentable for up to $200,000 a week. Bolloré had heard that Sar-
kozy and his then wife Cécilia were going through a rough time and
thought a few days of absolute luxury on the Mediterranean might
help them patch up their difficulties, especially after such a stressful
election campaign.

Accordingly, the day after Sarkozy had pledged to be "the President of all the French people" and then dined at Fouquet's with the gang, Bolloré flew him, Cécilia, and their ten-year-old son, Louis, from Paris to Malta on his Falcon 900EX. Opponents back in Paris attacked the trip the moment the paparazzi pictures started to roll in.

François Hollande, then leader of the Socialist Party, said, "The problem is the style of this holiday—the fact that it is on the yacht of a rich businessman, and we don't know today if it was the Republic that covered the expense of this trip." Referring to Jacques Chirac's penchant for luxury, Hollande added: "We thought the Chirac presidency was over, and it was what Mr. Sarkozy doubtless called a rupture, but I see that it is more a question of continuity."

Ségolène Royal, Hollande's former partner and the Socialist candidate who had just lost to Sarkozy in the second-round head-to-head of the presidential election, was particularly sneering as she sent her spokesman out to castigate the new President describing the voyage from Malta to Sicily as a "form of arrogance, insult even." Royal continued, "We have never seen, to this extent, someone show off in such a provocative way his taste for money and his closeness to business, having just been elected."

On his return from Malta, Sarkozy had told reporters that the trip "had not cost taxpayers a *centime*," adding, "I'll tell you one thing: I have no intention of hiding, I don't intend to lie, I don't intend to apologize." Pressed on his links with Bolloré, Sarkozy said, "He has been inviting me for twenty years and I've refused. Vincent Bolloré is one of the great French industrialists. He has never worked for the French State."

The deception was that Bolloré, a self-made businessman known for working fifteen hours a day, carried out all his profiteering in the private sphere while delivering huge tax payments and not taking anything back from the state. This was simply not true. Even a brief perusal of BOAMP (France's Official Bulletin of Public Procurement Announcements) revealed how Bolloré had made millions from government contracts, many of them linked to Sarkozy. Shortly before the Fouquet's dinner, SDV International Logistics, a company owned by the Bolloré Group, had, for example, won a contract worth up to $5.6 million to deliver diplomatic bags for France's Foreign Ministry. Another lucrative Bolloré deal signed in December 2006 was with Sarkozy's own Interior Ministry and involved the "installation of modular security rooms at the Grenoble Police Headquarters."

Sarkozy's earlier position as Budget Minister between 1993 and 1995 had also been extremely useful to Bolloré when he was exploiting France's historical ties with West Africa to sell billions of cigarettes to often impoverished Africans. Gauloises and Gitanes were among the iconic brands associated with SEITA (Société d'Exploitation Industrielle des Tabacs et des Allumettes), the state-owned company that had first made enormous profits from selling tobacco and matches to France's colonial subjects at the beginning of the 1900s.

Bolloré's own empire was hugely reliant on money from such sales a century later. His Tobaccor company owned nine factories and had a quasi-monopoly of the tobacco market in countries from Congo to Senegal. Bolloré moved to buy up SEITA at a time when Sarkozy was its supervising minister. The privatization of the state company, finalized in 1995, provided a massive windfall for Bolloré.

Details of behind-the-scenes negotiations were later made public by an American civil court, and they revealed that Bolloré was considered "politically very influential" and indeed the key to privatization because of his close links with Sarkozy. This was especially the case because Jean-Dominique Comolli, the chief executive officer of SEITA, was also a good friend of Sarkozy. As ever, Bolloré was able to buy shares for extremely low prices and sell them later on—in this case to Imperial Tobacco in the early 2000s, achieving a profit of some $200 million.

Sarkozy never had any problem with men who could create such easy wealth, saying, "I wish for the French economy a lot of Vincent Bollorés, that is to say men who are able to invest to create jobs. You know, it's not shameful to have worked hard, to have created a great group, to have provided employment." There was in fact little evidence of corporate raiders like Bolloré actually boosting job numbers. Streamlining newly acquired businesses to make them more profitable often meant redundancies.

The Paris home Sarkozy shared with Bruni was raided by the fraud squad within a few days of the end of his presidential term. Corruption allegations swirled. They ranged from accepting laundered millions from the Libyan dictator Colonel Muammar Gaddafi to trying to bribe a senior judge. Meanwhile, Sarkozy thought nothing of attempting to become head of state again in 2017. One of his rivals for the Républicains ticket in 2016 was Alain Juppé, by now a convicted criminal himself after receiving in 2004 an eighteen-month suspended prison sentence for misuse of public funds (it was reduced to fourteen months on appeal).

Sarkozy's former Prime Minister, François Fillon, won the ticket to contest the 2017 election on behalf of Les Républicains, despite Fillon and his wife, Penelope, having to defend themselves against corruption charges. Both Sarkozy and the Fillons were found guilty of corruption in separate trials and received custodial sentences, subject to multiple appeals.

Les Républicains were the latest incarnation of the Gaullist party that was meant to represent the upright politics of wartime leader De Gaulle. Fillon's fall from grace—the decisive factor in him losing the 2017 presidential election to Macron—could not have been more humiliating or telling.

Hollande's own Budget Minister, Jérôme Cahuzac, was convicted of tax fraud after being tasked by the President with clamping down on tax evasion when the Socialists came to power in 2012. Cahuzac resigned from his job fighting the charge in March 2013 and then admitted that there had been a secret Swiss bank account in his name for more than two decades. It then emerged that he had been using an offshore company in the Seychelles to further launder his millions, many of them earned through his lucrative career as a plastic surgeon specializing in hair transplants. Cahuzac was eventually jailed, as was his ex-wife, Patricia Menard, who had been stashing undisclosed cash profits in an undeclared Isle of Man account.

One limited success of the Hollande administration was the creation of the Central Office for the Fight Against Corruption and Financial and Fiscal Offenses. This was part of a crusade that would ultimately bring men like Sarkozy and Fillon to justice. The new Office certainly brought more probity into the running of the country, even though punishments were by no means as tough as they could have been.

Another Sarkozy crony who ended up with a criminal conviction also happened to be the most powerful woman in world banking. Christine Lagarde's judicial ordeal is a textbook example of how the great and the good of the Paris establishment get their few days in court and face prison but are never actually punished, even after being found guilty.

In February 2016, Lagarde was appointed to her second five-year term as Managing Director of the International Monetary Fund. The reappointment was unopposed by anyone on the IMF's executive board, despite the fact that Lagarde was due to face trial in Paris for "financial negligence" and was facing up to a year in prison.

This unusual state of affairs was barely commented upon in France. AFP, the national news agency, did not even mention the former Finance Minister's problems with the law. Its report of the vote of confidence in Lagarde instead focused on "new challenges" and the need to direct the IMF's $1 trillion budget and staff of 2,672 to "support struggling countries."

Lagarde had initially been acquitted in September 2015, but a court specializing in ministerial misconduct subsequently ruled she should be charged. In turn, the IMF said this was "incomprehensible" and announced an appeal. Lagarde herself argued there was "no basis for a charge" and that she had "acted in the best interest of the French State and in full compliance with the law."

In December 2015, Lagarde was in fact indicted for approving a $360 million payment to support a struggling tycoon. She had been Sarkozy's Finance Minister when, in 2008, businessman Bernard Tapie was awarded the cash in compensation for disposing of his majority stake in Adidas. Tapie had to get rid of his sizeable investment in the German sports multinational in order to become a French Cabinet minister in the 1990s, but he accused the partly state-owned bank Crédit Lyonnais of defrauding him during the sale of his shares. There was widespread dissatisfaction among ordinary French people when Lagarde gave Tapie such a huge amount of taxpayer money, especially when it emerged that he had backed Sarkozy during his 2007 election campaign.

Despite the question mark over her financial probity, Lagarde considered herself best qualified to steer the world out of the 2009 financial crisis, handing out multimillions as she saw fit, and nobody in any kind of position of power or authority in the banking world disagreed. This was still the case when, on December 19, 2016, Lagarde was convicted by three professional judges and twelve politicians from the Paris Parliament at the Cour de Justice de la République, which can only judge ministers and public officials. However, the judge ruled that Lagarde should not be punished or maintain a criminal record. She was not even in court for the verdict, instead choosing to fly back to her office in Washington, DC. The IMF gave Lagarde its full support, and she carried on as Managing Director as if nothing had happened.

An intriguing aspect of the Lagarde scandal was her bizarre "use me" letter to Sarkozy. It was leaked to the French press in 2013, after being seized during a police raid on her Paris home. In the undated letter, Lagarde appeared to tell Sarkozy to "use me for as long as it suits you and suits your plans." As well as subjecting Lagarde to ridicule, it called her impartiality into question. Extracts also included the words: "Dear Nicolas, very briefly and respectfully, I am by your side to serve you and serve your plans for France. I tried my best and might have failed occasionally. I implore your forgiveness." Lagarde never discussed the letter and instead blustered on as eleventh Managing Director of the IMF.

The political elite's inclination to corruption did nothing to instill confidence in their economic management. Chirac was immune from prosecution throughout his twelve years as President of France, despite being accused of paying members of his own political entourage to do fictional jobs while he was Mayor of Paris. It was not until 2011 that Chirac was finally given a token two-year suspended jail sentence for diverting public funds, abuse of trust, and illegal conflict of interest. The convictions came with no discernible hint of public ignominy at all. Chirac continued to be viewed as a much-loved veteran statesman. Like all former heads of state, both Chirac and Sarkozy kept hold of a wide range of benefits including a very generous pension, personal security, and lifetime membership of France's Constitutional Council. Each living head of state costs the French taxpayer the equivalent of at least $1 million a year.

One of the truisms of French economics is that corruption is rife, especially among conservative administrations. While radical institutional and economic reforms are long overdue, such abuses show that complacent Presidents who literally live in a palace are not inclined to carry them out. Governmental institutions, and the private companies linked to them, need greater scrutiny. As it is, the World Bank and the World Economic Forum estimate that bribery and misappropriated funds around the world amount to around $3.6 trillion, or 5 percent of the world's GDP. At the time of Sarkozy's criminal conviction in 2021, France was ranked 22 out of 180 on Transparency International's corruption index, with a score of seventy-one out of one hundred. For one of the world's top ten economies—and one associated with a universal sense of morality—this is appalling.

Sarkozy tried to portray Hollande as an incompetent leftist who would "bankrupt France," but nothing so dramatic was attempted. Hollande's administration of 2012 to 2017 failed to take any extreme measures to restore competitiveness. Timid tinkering aimed at reducing public spending infuriated the tax-and-spend Left and did not stimulate the economy. Hollande reacted by ditching the genuine Socialists in his Cabinet and employing Macron. There were protests from within Hollande's party, but Macron's new policies were pushed through in spite of Parliament. In 2016, new labor laws were passed without the agreement of a majority in the National Assembly.

Whatever It Costs

By the time Macron came to power in May 2017, France was still viewed by its Anglo-American critics as being an economic basket case: a nation of big taxes, and even higher expenditures, not least on the public sector. It all evoked the words of former Prime Minister Georges Clémenceau, who joked that his country was "so fertile that you plant civil servants and taxes grow."

Early retirement, shorter working hours, and long holidays cost a lot of money, as does universal childcare and one of the best resourced health services in the world. The French are obsessed with their rights to social care. Throw in all the green measures made necessary by the Paris Climate Accords, and costs were astronomical. It was actually incredible that France was not facing a crippling financial crisis, but hefty taxes were used to offset this, together with borrowing enabled by low Eurozone interest rates.

Macron said he wanted a reset. He projected himself as a free-market disrupter who would slash $60 billion in public spending with pension and labor reforms. He was a technocrat, not a man of the Left or the Right, and he was backed by plenty of coherent centrist economists, he argued. During his first election campaign, there was the promise of a "Marshall Plan for the reindustrialization of areas where the economy has collapsed." Deregulation was needed in the private sector, especially for small- and medium-sized companies struggling with red tape. Start-ups in cutting-edge sectors, such as robotics and cryptocurrencies, needed backing. The retirement age had to rise from sixty-two to sixty-five—Macron ideally wanted to merge forty-two separate pension schemes into a single system—and thousands of civil service jobs would also have to go.

Making training a condition of social assistance in times of unemployment was also a Macron necessity, as was lowering taxes for individuals and businesses, so as to boost purchasing power. Full employment required increased mobility in the job market. Such measures were all associated with Anglo-American economic liberalism—the kind that many in France detest. They were still talking about Reaganism and Thatcherism, and pledging to defend France's traditional social model to the hilt.

The *Gilets Jaunes* movement was soon on the street, reacting to the new President's initiatives with violence. There were swift U-turns by Macron, and then the coronavirus pandemic kicked in properly at the beginning of 2020. This led to Macron having to spend heavily, just like his predecessors. The beginning of the Ukraine War in February 2022, and all its related costs, soon meant inflation was soaring. There were crisis policies to try to keep down the cost of living. As Macron admitted, "We are creating debt for our children. Do we have any margins for manoeuvre? No. We increased our debt during the COVID-19 crisis."[12]

Solid growth levels and a relatively low unemployment figure helped Macron enormously. The jobless total within the adult population fell to 7.3 percent during the first three months of 2022, a figure not seen since 2008.[13] Public debt, however, was still at 111.6 percent of GDP, compared to an EU average of 93 percent.[14] Macron's COVID-19 strategy was dubbed "Whatever it costs," as billions were spent on keeping businesses afloat and making sure employees held their jobs. As lockdowns and other measures ended, there was also a radical Parliament calling for very expensive new measures, such as price caps on fuel and the protection of low retirement ages—the issue that had caused Chirac so many problems, including a general strike, back in 1995.

Meanwhile, the main criticism of Macron was that he was still fixated on making the rich richer, even if he did not flaunt his own wealth. (Macron spent four years working as a banker for Rothschild in Paris, when he is said to have earned around $3 million for advising Nestlé during its $12 billion acquisition of a unit of Pfizer in 2012, but there has never been any sign of Ferraris or penthouse flats.) Flexing the enormous power that came with his job, Macron bypassed Parliament and used presidential decrees to loosen employment laws. He made it easier to hire and fire, while simplifying negotiations between bosses and employees and curbing the power of trade union collective bargaining. Attempts at liberalizing the economy were the main reason for the *Gilets Jaunes* street protests. Even if he didn't socialize with them, Macron was viewed as a puppet of the superrich. His main opponents—Le Pen's Rassemblement National and Jean-Luc Mélenchon's La France Insoumise—liked to portray themselves as enemies of bankers, just as Hollande had done.

In fact, politicians who understand economics know full well that they are beholden to the world of international finance. Institutions such as the World Bank and the IMF are crucial to domestic success.

ECONOMICS: WINNERS AND LAGGERS 271

According to figures from Christine Lagarde's IMF, up to 60 percent of France's government debt is held overseas. This compares to under 25 percent in the United Kingdom. There is no patriotic sentimentality involved in these French figures—the Republic has to retain the goodwill of overseas banks, hedge funds, and sovereign wealth funds to finance its ever-maturing budget deficit. If the lending stops, then France would have to rely on EU bailout funds or the IMF.

The nature of work in France is also changing rapidly. Jobs for life are disappearing, as entrepreneurial start-ups outsource to workers based abroad because of the high social charges involved in hiring anyone in France. Traditional clock-in factories are vanishing, along with the kind of laborers who used to be worn out by the time they reached their fifties.

If you had to name a country that likes thinking about work more than doing it, then modern France might well be it. The nation is built on refined ideology rather than toil. In grisly Soviet republics, rough-handed laborers were glorified, but the Gallic version celebrates sloth. Accordingly, the great philosophical conundrum posed by visitors to the land of Descartes, Montesquieu, and Voltaire is invariably: "How on earth does anything get done?" The question—if not the answer—came into sharp focus during the coronavirus lockdowns, when people had even more downtime than usual. The pensive settled down in their comfiest armchair—or Louis XIV chaise longue—and considered that, yes, they really were losing the will to work. This was the conclusion of an IFOP/Fondation Jean-Jaurès poll in September 2022, which demonstrated that the laziness bug that has always lurked across France has turned into a full-blown national epidemic.[15] Only 24 percent of the country described work as "very important" in their lives. This compared to a frankly exhausting figure of 60 percent back in 1990. In the words of high-profile Green MP Sandrine Rousseau, the French have earned "the right to idleness," although she did not say how.

The French are sick of all the buzzy expressions that have been imported from the "Anglo-Saxon" countries and reflect drastic changes in old working practices. Terms that further encapsulate the horror of

the new order include "sandwich at your desk" and "giving 110 percent." They represent attacks on treasured Gallic rights that relatively
new technology has made impossible to defend.

The majority of French workers take social media for granted nowadays, but before around 2010 many did not touch it, and there were
very few ways of telling what workers were up to in their spare time.
Now they complain that the reverse is true. In a time before email
and cell phones, the basics all used to get done—shops opened, businesses did fine, and public services were available to all, just as they
are today. The difference was that nobody was able to impose obsessive
Anglo-American work mania through never-ending communication.

Now, the clear line of demarcation between work and leisure has
disappeared completely, and joie de vivre is the main casualty. Work
has become a way of life, rather than a part of life, and everybody is
meant to be chasing results and profits 24-7, like they do in London
and New York. As the global economy and ever faster and more intrusive tech threaten Gallic culture, it is little surprise that so many French
have had enough of it all and want to spend their precious time doing
something a lot less productive.

Macron said he wanted to pour billions into retraining those who
have lost their jobs, but this does nothing for disaffected suburban
youths who are just starting out. Institutional problems such as huge
payroll taxes have not been touched. Like all his recent predecessors,
Macron has just tinkered. Look at his approach to environmentalism.
A climate bill introduced by his administration was aimed at reducing
greenhouse emissions, but there was immediate opposition. The lack of
commitment in this area became clear in December 2018 when Macron
caved in to the *Gilets Jaunes* rioting within three weeks and abandoned
green taxes on petrol and diesel. This was followed by Macron delaying
the banning of the most polluting cars from 2025 to 2030, scrapping a
flight eco-tax, and watering down legislation ending the advertising of
polluting products. This was despite France's ambitious stated agenda
to cut emissions and Paris lending its name to the benchmark Climate
Accords of 2015.

Nothing is being done to reverse the crisis in France's once
gold-standard health service either. Health care costs represent more

than 12 percent of GDP, and the country spends hundreds of billions reimbursing medical charges.[16] People are prepared to pay for it via taxes and social charges, but the system is looking increasingly rickety. Despite all the cash available, it cannot cope with spiraling demand. Staff are being asked to do more for less pay, and burnout rates are high. Strained emergency services are just part of the overwhelmingly bleak picture, too, as hospitals report shortages of gynecologists, geriatric nurses, and numerous other vital specialists.

A serious historical problem is that France severely limited the number of medical student places available from the early 1970s until 2021. Demands for health professionals to be trained more quickly are increasing, especially as it can take up to seven years before a doctor can practice. There are plenty of so-called medical deserts in the countryside, where vulnerable people have to travel miles to find somebody to look after them. Many staff are quitting altogether to join a private health sector in France that offers attractive packages. Some are also moving abroad to take up lucrative jobs in countries such as the United States, United Kingdom, Canada, or Gulf states. Those who have worked in the French system for decades know that the coronavirus pandemic has exacerbated difficulties that have been intensifying for years, but little is being done to address them.

Macron certainly listens to people talking about France's endemic economic problems—he remains affable and approachable—but he does not do much. He falls back on crony conservatism while triggering the anger of struggling workers. There is no doubt that extremist politicians such as Le Pen and Mélenchon are channeling this discontent to significant electoral success.

Start-Up Nation

One area where the French economy seems superficially dynamic is in the very Anglo-American realm of start-ups. There were a record 995,900 businesses created across the country in 2021, up 17 percent from the year before.[17] Popular sectors included transport, storage, green tech, and crafts. Economy Minister Bruno Le Maire boasted about a million new businesses as "quite simply a new record." Yet many of them are very small-scale and overwhelmingly unambitious. A lot of them are sole traders, or *micro-entreprises*, and they have nothing like the kind of venture capital available to start-ups in Britain and the United States. Very few, if any, will go international.

Macron said in 2017 that he would "liberate work and the spirit of enterprise," but he mainly favored big companies by dropping their tax rate from 33.3 percent to 25 percent, for example. Hiring and firing staff became easier for them thanks to a reduction on social security contributions paid by employers. Macron's labor code changes mean employers can now lay personnel off without grounds.

As a result, job insecurity is greater than it has ever been. Short-term contracts and appalling conditions added up to 3.3 million people in low-security jobs in 2020—that is to say, 12.4 percent of those with a job.[18] The figure was further skewed by close to two million people who were no longer actively seeking a job being knocked off unemployment numbers.

Meanwhile, the huge class of have-nots has contributed to anti-rich sentiment expanding across France. There were calls for higher taxes and a fairer distribution of the windfall profits enjoyed by those running companies such as oil giant Total. These agitators objected to the exorbitant compensation being paid to executives and asked how much salary cash, stock options, pension money, and golden parachute payments anyone needed in a lifetime.

Macron launched a "great national debate"—in which he invited people to voice opinions on policy issues such as whether public spending or taxes should be cut further—but wild expressions of democracy seldom solve complex economic problems. On the contrary, politicians need to stop listening to the street at crunch moments. Backing down from much-needed initiatives—such as slimming down the bloated size of the French State—should not be abandoned because of one too many Saturday riots or thousands of expletive-ridden online comments.

More effort needs to be put into integrating immigrants into French society, rather than ignoring them or banishing them to a lifetime of welfare dependency. *Chibanis* and *chibaniates* are the North African Arabic words referring to the "elderly" retired men and women workers from the Maghreb and sub-Saharan Africa who arrived during the *Trente Glorieuses* to help rebuild the republic after the war. Almost a million of them had to fight for their social rights when they were working, and injustice continued when they left their jobs. Dumped in inadequate social housing and given a pittance in pensions and other benefits, these workers formed the Chibanis Cooperative in Roubaix, northern France, in 2021 and pledged to "raise awareness of the deplorable situation of vulnerable elderly people, in particular immigrant seniors." Founder Hamza El Kostiti said, "Their vulnerability, sometimes coupled with a language barrier, makes them miss out on their fundamental rights."

The insidious anti-migrant sentiment prevalent across the French political divide—including within Macron's own ranks—spells economic and social disaster. This is especially so in an EU giant that is meant to be committed to the free flow of services and goods and creating business premises and homes for a highly mobile, transnational workforce.

Encouraging such workers—there are millions of them across the world—will be far more beneficial to French society than letting the same old families dominate business year after year. There is every reason to increase the tax on inherited wealth. Redistributing wealth should also involve a fairer income tax system that helps entrepreneurs but that curtails the excesses of greedy executives.

Cuts to government spending, which is consistently higher than in other developed nations, are essential. The size of the public payroll is unsustainable, especially as France has to compete with increasingly dynamic rivals. France's richest 0.1 percent saw their purchasing power leap by 4 percent under Macron. The richest 1 percent of the French population enjoyed an average gain of 2.8 percent in total revenue. There was little evidence of speedy and effective trickle-down. According to an Institute for Public Policies survey, the total average rise in the standard of living for the French as a whole over the past five years was around 1.6 percent. The least privileged—the bottom 5 percent—were the biggest losers: their purchasing power sank 0.5 percent on average under Macron.[19]

The France Stratégie report from 2021 presents a clear diagnosis, stating that "levels of economic insecurity remain large, socio-economic gaps across different strata have not closed, many regions lag behind in creating good jobs and economic opportunity, youth unemployment remains very high, and social mobility is low. . . . Economic inequality manifests itself not only in differences in income and wealth, but also in gaps in health, education, opportunities, mobility, and access to quality work."[20]

The report recommends

> that for economic opportunities to be widely and fairly distributed, France needs to take action in multiple ways and at several stages of people's economic lives. It must equalise access to quality education and revise the core pillars of the welfare state in terms of social protection and progressive taxation to take into account the changing realities of the labour market and the international landscape. It needs to ensure an adequate supply of productive, high-quality jobs by focusing on labour market policies that partner with businesses and industrial policies that target employment specifically. Finally, it must foster communication and feedback between different levels of governments and employers, as well as between the government and citizens.

There is no doubt that the French economy delivers spectacular results for a supremely privileged minority. The richest man and woman on earth in 2023 were both French and based in Paris—LVMH boss Bernard Arnault, and L'Oréal cosmetics heiress Françoise Bettencourt Meyers. The focus of such multibillionaires was on exporting hugely expensive goods that the vast majority of ordinary French citizens struggling with growing financial woes and attacks on their social system could not hope to afford.[21]

10

FOREIGN POLICY
Post-Empire State

We cannot claim to be a great nation if we are not capable
of giving the world what it expects from us, from France.

—FRANÇOIS HOLLANDE (1954–)

Those of us who spent time in Tahrir Square, Cairo, during the
Egyptian revolution of 2011 watched up to a million people forcing the resignation of long-term President Hosni Mubarak. All rejected
the brutal authoritarianism of the military dictator and called for him
to be replaced by a civilian government that would uphold the universal
values associated with stable democracies such as France. Protesters I
spoke to were using relatively new online platforms to great effect, to
communicate and then unite peacefully in shows of strength that terrified their oppressors. After less than three weeks of demonstrations,
Mubarak's seemingly invincible regime toppled.

On a return visit to Egypt two years later, everything had changed
completely, however. State-sponsored death squads were on the streets,
and another ruthless army commander was giving the orders. General Abdel Fattah el-Sisi, the new Mubarak, had succeeded in oust-
ing Mohamed Morsi, the first ever democratically elected President of
Egypt.

Tahrir was by now a place of anger and bitterness. The injustices of the Sisi era had included the Rabaa massacre on August 14, 2013, when at least one thousand people were killed and thousands more wounded during attacks on two squares full of protesters. Many had been taking part in sit-in demonstrations, making it easy for their assailants to mow them down using bulldozers and tanks. Men with guns—and the inclination to use them against unarmed civilians—were now controlling a city that had so recently been a focal point of hope and optimism.

Sisi's Egypt became even more repressive than Mubarak's. New legislation shielded soldiers from prosecution for crimes against humanity, including the mass murder of civilians. Public services were under martial control, as was much of the economy. Widespread abuse of human rights included arbitrary imprisonment, torture, and more extrajudicial killings.

Among Sisi's biggest international supporters was France, to the extent that President Emmanuel Macron would invite him to the Élysée Palace in December 2020 to receive the Légion d'Honneur, the country's highest state order of merit. Other recipients returned their awards when they heard about this, but Macron cared little. Arms sales to the third biggest country in Africa by population were of more interest to Macron—a classic French statesman who would gladly ignore atrocities in return for some form of "stability" in an allied country.

It was just like the period leading up to the start of the Arab Spring, when French ministers enjoyed exotic holidays as the guests of North African despots, including in Tunisia and Egypt. Nicolas Sarkozy, President at the time, spent Christmas in Morocco, courtesy of the King. French weapons were offered as a means of propping up dictators across the Arab world, even when the revolts were underway. As for Michèle Alliot-Marie, the Minister of Foreign Affairs at the time, she had proposed reinforced security cooperation with the Ben Ali regime, which was carrying out a ferocious repression against the first demonstrations of what would become the Jasmine Revolution. Alliot-Marie even enjoyed a family holiday in Tunisia at the beginning of the uprising, when a private jet plane owned by a friend of Ben Ali was placed at her disposal.

When Macron came to power, he had promised to ditch such callousness while attacking the interventionist policies of his immediate predecessors, Hollande and Sarkozy. As a post-empire state that was meant to have changed its ways, France needed to start showing a bit of morality. "With me, it will be the end of a form of neo-conservatism imported into France for ten years," said Macron.[1] Was this true, or—as in the disgraceful Egyptian example—was this just more fantasy foreign policy?

From Grandeur to *Déclassement*

Foreign policy is an essential facet of French identity. Whether attacking other countries or simply intervening diplomatically, the French have traditionally favored strongman aggression to assert their interests. This goes back to the way Napoléon Bonaparte exported the Revolution through conquest, and indeed to the imperial ambitions of monarchs such as Louis XIV, who made his kingdom the most powerful in Europe.

Charles de Gaulle called hardheaded French exceptionalism "grandeur." He believed that the country's essential grandness—its grounding in universal values and its maintenance of an effective military—made it more than capable of carving out its own destiny, without having to rely too much on others. A proudly independent nation was best placed to ensure its own security and the very best interests of its citizens. When he created the Fifth Republic in 1958, De Gaulle ensured that this approach was institutionalized. The President—the elected sovereign of the new system—would have absolute power to mold foreign policy in accordance with his own wishes.

In such circumstances, *déclassement*—a downgrade in status—is one of the ugliest words in the French language. Presidents have an abiding fear of failing in foreign affairs. Historical ignominies that have brought about periods of *déclassement* include capitulation to the invading Germans in 1940—the disaster that resulted in Nazi Occupation and collaboration in the Holocaust. Defeat in the Battle of Dien Bien Phu in 1954 meant France had to withdraw from all its colonies in what was once called French Indochina. The Suez Crisis two years later heaped further humiliation on France and severely damaged relations with key allies, not least of all the United States. Worse was to come in 1962, when Berber and Arab Muslim nationalists won their War of Independence in Algeria.

Like all those in his position, Emmanuel Macron broadly sticks to the established playbook as a way of avoiding *déclassement*. In his speeches and interviews, he references a version of civilization mainly built on the Renaissance and the eighteenth-century Enlightenment that led up to the 1789 Revolution.

Macron seeks to champion market economics, individual freedoms, democratic regimes, and the French version of humanism. It is not just conventional threats—other nation-states—that worry Macron either. He is very concerned about Europe's dark past, including its history of colonialism and slave trading, and wonders whether we should be tearing down statues of former French heroes. Macron has been a victim of cyberterrorism; he told me about the Russian hackers who were targeting him just before he came to power. He is also very suspicious of multinationals, particularly the digital ones that use ever-improving technology to exert power over all our lives. *Le numérique* (information technology) fascinates Macron but also makes him extremely fearful.

Macron wants to maintain France's strong position in the world, but—as the globe shrinks—he also knows how important it is to honor alliances and to work within increasingly powerful global institutions. He is Commander-in-Chief of the only military force in the European Union with nuclear weapons, and one that is a leading member of NATO and the UN Security Council.

First on France's list of close friends is Germany, followed by the rest of the twenty-seven EU member states. Then there is the ever-crucial Atlantic alliance that must be worked on constantly. France was the first official ally of the United States following independence from Great Britain in 1776. An enormous amount of help with the American Revolution came from the French aristocrat and military commander Gilbert du Motier, the Marquis de Lafayette. He went on to name his only son Georges (with a French *s*), after George Washington, first President of the United States.

Macron is also a great admirer of the United Kingdom and its shared history with France. One of his great-grandfathers was a British soldier. There are numerous Franco-British spats, especially since the UK left the European Union, but the *entente cordiale* generally remains strong.

Rather than a grandeur based on French exceptionalism, Macron has pushed for a strengthening of the European Union so that it can stand up to countries such as Russia and China while also competing economically with the United States. Yet what has become very noticeable is the sense of impending catastrophe that Macron introduces into so much of his discourse.

Macron told the UN General Assembly in 2018: "We are currently experiencing a deep crisis of the Westphalian liberal world order, and as a result, we are witnessing the emergence of an increasingly bipolar and illiberal world."

The worry, according to Macron, is that great civilizations such as France are under existential threat. The world order is crumbling as rival ideologies grow stronger. An aggressive Russia is a case in point. Macron traveled to Moscow on February 7, 2022, just before President Vladimir Putin's forces invaded Ukraine on February 24. Macron was convinced he had the charisma and diplomatic skills to make Putin back down, but—as far as stopping the war was concerned—French efforts came to nothing.

There was no little humiliation involved, especially when Putin insisted on putting Macron at the opposite end of a giant table in the Kremlin. The official reason was coronavirus social distancing, but it was also clear that Putin simply didn't want Macron getting too close for geopolitical reasons. Back in Paris, Macron continued to have long phone chats with Putin, even as Russian missiles rained down on Ukrainian cities such as Mariupol and tanks rolled across the border.

Prior to the invasion, Macron tried to persuade Putin to pull his army back from Ukraine. In scenes that evoked the 1938 Munich crisis, Macron's shuttle diplomacy involved rushing from Moscow to Kyiv via Berlin. Macron certainly had the look of a Neville Chamberlain about him—he was ineffective.

When Macron's negotiations with ex-KGB man Putin ended in embarrassing failure, there was a great deal of disquiet, especially from Ukrainians who wanted to carve out their own foreign policy. As usual, Macron had vacillated between appeasing Russia and supporting Ukraine, because he was reluctant to choose one side.

NATO allies were furious when Macron declared in a TV interview in October 2022 that France would not respond in kind if Putin fired tactical nuclear missiles at Ukraine. The whole point of an effective nuclear deterrence policy is that you do not reveal your hand, but Macron appeared oblivious to this. When, in 1986, Mitterrand was asked how France would respond in the event of a Soviet attack on West Germany, he pointedly refused to answer.

Energetic monologues are typical of Macron. I've observed him at numerous foreign policy events, and he comes across as supremely focused and very well briefed. He understands every detail and is extremely eloquent. In his usual dark blue suit and tie with crisp white shirt, he is a classic representative of the traditional Western elite. Macron is ostensibly set on dealing with global warming, migration, terrorism, health provision, and all kinds of other matters that need to be addressed urgently. The former merchant banker and taxman talks about economic inequality and the crisis of contemporary capitalism. Macron frowns and emotes like the world is on the verge of caving in and only he can save it.

How much of this act is honest, though? There were undoubtedly personal reasons for Macron's failed appeals to Putin to back down from attacking Ukraine. After announcing his candidacy to stand for a second term as President in 2022, Macron wanted to shift his campaign focus from parochial issues to global ones. He aimed to reassure an increasingly divided electorate that he could manage the national security state and the military-industrial complex that drives it. A willingness to pinpoint threats in the world, and to go out and deal with them, was essential to the persona he was trying to project.

Opponents such as Marine Le Pen—who got to meet Putin around a very small coffee table during her own trip to Moscow—united in accusing Macron of being a pompous windbag with little talent for dealing with realpolitik. The principal accusation was that hot air remained an integral component of the foreign policy of a brutally pragmatic nation.

The Frenchman's Burden

The most ruthless expression of France's foreign policy has always been its colonialism. France had a presence on the African continent from the seventeenth century, but the invasion of Algeria in 1830 was the starting point for a wave of colonization. France's alleged justification for expanding its empire was its devotion to universal values. The foundation of this *mission civilisatrice* was the dissemination of French culture and language. Technically, this kind of paternalism would be accompanied by philanthropic acts such as providing health care, transport infrastructure, and the like, but of course funds for indigenous populations were always limited, while the promotion of France's own interests remained paramount.

Both sides of the political spectrum supported colonialism at different times. The French Left was very keen on it during the 1880s, for example. In line with the revolutionary tradition, the Left believed that the homeland of the Enlightenment should be spreading its universalist message around the world. Colonialism was a way to globalize the ideas of 1789. It was nothing less than racism dressed up as a republican and revolutionary duty. Thus, Jules Ferry, France's Prime Minister twice during the 1880s, used oxymorons such as "emancipatory colonialism." In a July 1885 speech that would have landed him in court today, Ferry stated, "It must be said openly that indeed the superior races have a right vis-à-vis the inferior races; but because there is also a duty. They have the duty to civilize the inferior races."

Military force was always crucial to the exportation of republican ideals. During 132 years of colonialism in Algeria, millions of indigenous Algerians were killed, including during the eight-year independence war. Settler colonialists contributed enthusiastically to the carnage. Such barbarism was extended significantly following French invasions in West and Equatorial Africa during the so-called Scramble for Africa—the period of imperialism that started in 1884 when seven European powers divided up the continent between them during the infamous Berlin Conference. Tunisia and Morocco became French protectorates in the years leading up to the First World War. Afterward, parts of Togo and Cameroon that had been German colonies were assigned to France as League of Nations mandates. By 1930, the French Empire also included the Indian Ocean islands of Madagascar, Réunion, and the Comoros, as well as Djibouti in the Horn of Africa.

European settlers—the *pieds-noirs*—were confined to Algeria, but armed force and economic exploitation served to contradict France's "civilizing" mission throughout the empire. Occupation naturally caused dissent and resistance, and ever more violent methods were used to crush them. Beyond the bloodshed, so-called educational programs focused on erasing African culture, so as to forge a universal French one.

Even when colonies officially became independent in the 1960s, the French wanted to maintain their influence. De Gaulle believed that "French world power and French power in Africa were inextricably linked and mutually confirming."[2]

The old colonial relationship was restructured to form Françafrique—a sphere of influence involving a variety of political, financial, military, and French language links. De Gaulle's great ally in this process was Jacques Foccart, head of African affairs at the Élysée Palace, and the so-called father of Françafrique. Foccart carried on as adviser to De Gaulle's successors into the 1970s.

Outright corruption was very important to keeping the postcolonial order together. Africa's Francophone world—which ranged from Benin and Burkina Faso to Senegal and Togo—soon encompassed countries notorious for their human rights violations. Subservient African leaders were happy to bury thoughts of a democratic renaissance in return for lavish aid programs, bribes, and help with security, including arms.

France continued to interfere in the affairs of former colonies long after their independence, as it propped up corrupt and compliant despotic allies. Methods ranged from covert military operations and alleged assassinations to direct financial help. The French secret service was said to have murdered Félix-Roland Moumié, an anti-colonialist Cameroonian leader, using thallium in Geneva in 1960—the same year that Cameroon gained independence.

The assassination of Thomas Sankara, the President of Burkina Faso, in 1987, was another example of a popular, Pan-Africanist leader disappearing after apparently threatening French interests. Sankara's revolutionary idealism was such that he changed the name of Upper Volta, the former French colony, to Burkina Faso, which means "Land of Incorruptible People." He was also fiercely suspicious of the "imperialist" agenda of overseas powers and organizations such as the World Bank and the International Monetary Fund. He was shot repeatedly during a coup d'état, after which France was widely accused of masterminding Sankara's demise.

Such alleged missions are by definition shrouded in secrecy, but as recently as January 2017, *Le Monde* published leaked papers that showed how serving Presidents regularly green-light extrajudicial death sentences. François Hollande ordered the killings of at least eight Islamist terrorist commanders who were French citizens, according to official documents.

France recognized self-determination movements after the Second World War, but it wanted to retain its access to energy resources and mines across Africa. It cherished its reputation as a world power with influence in its *pré carré*, or own backyard—a metaphor used by Sébastien Le Prestre de Vauban, Louis XIV's military engineer, to define French territory that needed defending.

Jean-Bédel Bokassa, who was nicknamed "the Central African Napoléon" and who fought with the Free French during World War II, was typical of those hoisted to power by the ostensibly retreating French. A decade after becoming President of the Central African Republic in January 1966, and after much pampering from the allies in Paris, he declared his one-party state the Central African Empire and crowned himself Bokassa I. In terms of procedure and luxury, the coronation, in a sports stadium in Bangui, was an exact copy of Bonaparte's as Emperor of the French in 1804.

The Bokassa diamonds affair of 1973—when future French President Valéry Giscard d'Estaing accepted jewels from the President of the

Central African Republic—was another example of French politicians expecting largesse from former colonies. The despotic CAR leader Bokassa handed over the fabulous gifts in the expectation of favorable treatment, just as his forebears did in the age of empire. It was only when rumbled that Giscard claimed "the proceeds from these gifts" were donated to humanitarian aid charities.

Support for such French puppeteering was encouraged by the United States, as former French colonies were seen as bastions against the Soviet Union's geopolitical influence during the Cold War. It suited the Americans to see France act as the "Gendarme of Africa" by maintaining military bases in former colonies. These garrisons were originally said to be defending Africa against the spread of Communism, but French economic interests were always the priority.

The most enduring legacy of French colonialism in Africa is the African Financial Community (CFA) franc—a unit of currency that was pegged to the French franc, and then to the euro. It was a product of the Bretton Woods Conference of 1944, which attempted to set up the postwar financial order.

The principle behind this franc (originally called the French African Colonial franc when it was created in 1945) was—in simple terms—to give France economic control over African states. To begin with, CFA nations had to deposit 100 percent of their foreign reserves in the French Treasury, where this money was used as interest-generating capital for France. This percentage was reduced to 50 percent, but France continued to devalue the CFA franc so as to increase the purchasing power of the French franc within some fourteen sub-Saharan countries, covering an area bigger than the eurozone. Some countries—among them Algeria, Tunisia, Guinea, Morocco, Mauritania, and Madagascar—left the CFA zone, but there are still some two hundred million people living in it.

Macron has unveiled plans to rename this hugely exploitative currency the "eco" but has no intention of getting rid of it. Soon after winning power in 2017, he told African leaders at the G5 Sahel Summit in Mali: "If you feel unhappy in the franc zone, you leave it and create your own currency, as Mauritania and Madagascar did. If you stay, you must stop your demagogic statements making the CFA franc the scape-goat of your political and economic failures, and France the source of your problems."

There was anger at Macron's bullish words from Africans, espe-cially as they were being used to back up monetary hegemony over what should be independent nations. Countries felt they had no chance of being in charge of their own financial affairs. Leaving any long-standing, multination financial arrangement was liable to cost billions and to cause short-term chaos for the country quitting, and Macron knew it. He was also aware that political parties in France had a notorious record of financing their domestic election campaigns with suitcases full of African cash. At the time of writing, Nicolas Sarkozy remains under investigation for allegedly accepting millions from the late Libyan dictator Muammar Gaddafi.

The economist François-Xavier Verschave published *La Françaf-rique* in 1998 to expose France's neocolonialism in its former colonies. Verschave was regularly portrayed by members of the Paris establish-ment as a conspiracy theorist, but he was a meticulous researcher who also coined the term *mafiafrique*. He referred to "the secret criminality in the upper echelons of French politics and economy, where a kind of underground Republic is hidden from view."[3]

Verschave described how African dictators were secretly paid through Elf, the former French oil company that later merged with Total-Fina. "They serve Elf and France but not their own country," Verschave wrote. "They get their medical treatment in France, their children study in France—they therefore don't concern themselves with health and education at home."

Beyond the sleaze of Françafrique, there were plenty of other post-colonial scandals across the African continent. France was at the center of many of them, as a foreign policy based on militarization became ever more reckless. France transported vast shipments of arms to Rwanda in the early 1990s, for example, and sent members of the French military to train their Rwandan counterparts. Bringing "stability" to the land-locked central African state was the nominal reason for such missions. The French claimed they did not know that their support for Rwanda might also be supporting a genocide. In 1994, over one hundred days, those belonging to the Tutsi ethnic group became the main victims of a massacre carried out by Hutu militias that claimed at least eight hundred thousand lives.

Nicolas Sarkozy always pledged that he would finally end the Françafrique system, but a confidential American Embassy report from 2008 suggests otherwise. Pinpointing faults so typical of all French politicians operating in Africa, it reads: "He was tone-deaf to some of the dynamics developed over decades of France-Afrique and his pace and rhythm (let alone his policies) did not accord with that of many African counterparts. In saying openly that he wanted to end France-Afrique, Sarkozy inadvertently gave it a new spark of life."

Sarkozy angered African leaders with his overblown rhetoric, while showing no genuine appetite to abandon Françafrique. During a notorious speech in Dakar, Senegal, in 2007, Sarkozy said: "The tragedy of Africa is that the African has not fully entered into history. . . . They have never really launched themselves into the future."[4]

Colonel Gaddafi was invited by Sarkozy to the Élysée Palace for a state visit later that year. Gaddafi brought a Bedouin-style heated tent with him, and it was put up in the gardens of the Hôtel de Marigny, once the mansion of Baron Gustave de Rothschild and by now a French government official residence for visiting guests. Gaddafi's vast entourage included camels and an all-female team of bodyguards, who wore camouflage uniforms.

Sarkozy and Gaddafi oversaw the signing of lucrative contracts worth around $15 billion, including the sale of arms and twenty-one Airbus planes, all of which were funded by Libya's enormous oil wealth. The "Brother Leader"—as cronies such as Sarkozy called Gaddafi—is also alleged to have handed over millions in laundered money to the Sarkozy 2007 presidential election campaign. Prosecutors have referred the case for trial in France; Sarkozy denies any wrongdoing.

Even before the Arab Spring revolution had begun to succeed in Libya in 2011, Sarkozy had started to turn against Gaddafi. Sarkozy had ordered the French Air Force to start bombing before a UN mandate to "protect civilian lives" had even been implemented. A few months later, French fighter jets strafed a convoy Gaddafi was traveling in, before he was ultimately murdered by an armed mob, allegedly supported by French secret servicemen on the ground.

Sarkozy was also close to Gabon's Omar Bongo, a notoriously corrupt African leader accused of squandering his country's cash on French Riviera villas. Sarkozy traveled to see Bongo in 2007, when a US diplomatic cable read, "Sarkozy went to Gabon, where elder statesman and France-Afrique supporter President Bongo received him with full honors. Sarkozy reportedly hesitated before going; visiting a France-Afrique stronghold, site of a French military base, and source of valuable commerce (especially petroleum) could smack of the old-style courting and role playing he claimed he wanted to forego. In the end, he relented."

There were banners in Gabon reading "Vive la France!" and "Vive Sarkozy!" The Americans also noted: "A slow-moving French judicial investigation of the holdings in France of certain African leaders, among them Bongo, was in progress even before Sarkozy went there in July 2007. The investigation reportedly indicated that Bongo owned or was involved in the ownership of 33 properties in France, including a Paris mansion valued at 18 million euro (currently, about USD 27.15 million)."

The Gendarme of Africa

As part of his pledge to end neoconservative interventions in the affairs of other countries when he came to power, Macron specifically claimed he would reform France's exploitation of Africa. At a speech at the University of Ouagadougou in Burkina Faso in November 2017, he said he would bring about a reset by concentrating on youth, education, and e-commerce start-ups. His focus was on "global challenges" that particularly related to Africa, such as climate change and health care.

Macron said: "I am from a generation that does not come and tell Africa what to do or what the rule of law entails, but rather one that encourages young African women and men who want to shoulder their responsibilities, who want to do what they can to see the winds of freedom and empowerment blow, as you have done here."

There would be no initial climbdown on France's military engagements in Africa, however. For Macron, they related to the fight against groups such as Al-Qaeda and ISIS. The ongoing War on Terror, which started with the 9/11 attacks on the United States in 2001, gave the French the all clear to prosecute a counterterrorism war in the Sahel—the vast region that straddles numerous countries in North Africa. The French had begun Operation Serval there in 2013, which then became known as Operation Barkhane in 2014. This aggressive foreign policy adventure was initiated by Macron's predecessor, François Hollande, who saw the opportunity to "fight terrorism" as a way of countering his disastrous approval ratings at home.

Macron continued with the hawkish view that the best way to defeat jihadis was to take the fight to them on African battlefields. French forces in five Sahel nations that were also former French colonies—Burkina Faso, Chad, Mali, Mauritania, and Niger—were all there to "fight terrorism," but another key aim was to protect French economic interests, such as the exploitation of Nigerien uranium and Malian gold.

As in the days of colonialism, such interference often increased grievances among indigenous populations and led to more terrorism against what was perceived as an invading army upholding the *mission civilisatrice*. Ibrahim Boubacar Keïta was a classic example of a Malian President who had used international aid and a close relationship with Paris to prop up his administration. He was overthrown in a military coup in August 2020, after months of street protests, and then there was a second coup in May 2021 against his successor, Bah Ndaw. There was no doubt that the presence of French forces in the country had fueled a growing feeling of nationalism in Mali.

The French Army left the country for good in August 2022, and Macron put an end to the Barkhane Operation in November of the same year. Mali was meanwhile accused by the French of working with Russian mercenaries from the Wagner Group. The Russians were also said to be operating in countries such as the Central African Republic, while China and Turkey were also building up their African spheres of influence. Such countries could pour billions into chosen regions and arrive without colonial baggage.

Relations between the French and African countries continued to deteriorate. France's aerial bombing of rebels in Chad who were threatening the increasingly authoritarian presidency of Idriss Déby caused immense resentment. Déby ended up dying from combat wounds at the hands of armed opposition groups in April 2021. A coup in Burkina Faso in September 2022 (the second in the same year after the one in January) also weakened France's position in Africa, while leaving insurgents emboldened.

Gaddafi's demise in Libya caused chaos, as armed militias exploited a power vacuum and terrorist groups set up camps just across the Mediterranean from Europe. They were perfectly placed to exploit migrant routes that were no longer patrolled by the Libyans, and France was in no position to do anything about it.

Macron's election victory in May 2017 had raised hopes that Françafrique would be buried once and for all. The President's En Marche! movement was technically free of the links mainstream parties had established in Africa, but this did not stop it from conforming to tradition. Flowery rhetoric failed to disguise the customary duplicity. Force of arms and the support of "strongmen" took precedence over Enlightenment values and any realistic attempt at change.

Honoring the Strongmen

When, at the end of 2020, Macron welcomed the despotic Egyptian President Abdel Fattah el-Sisi to Paris for a state visit, he gave him France's highest civilian award, the Grand Cross of the Legion of Honor. Deepening defense and trade ties was considered more important than Sisi's chronic human rights abuses—despite an estimated sixty thousand political prisoners, including plenty of journalists, languishing in Egyptian prisons.

Gaddafi had also been given a Légion d'Honneur from Sarkozy, shortly before his demise. Before this, fascist leaders Benito Mussolini and Francisco Franco had been among a grisly cast of recipients. "It is with baubles that men are led," is how Napoléon Bonaparte—who created the Légion d'Honneur system under the imperial motto, "Honor and Fatherland"—had put it.

Egypt, historically the anchor of the Arab World and a country that was widely viewed as the epicenter of the Arab Spring of 2011, was thus horrendously betrayed by Macron. For those of us who had stood in Tahrir Square at the height of the protests and followed the progress of the revolution firsthand, his support of Sisi was a disaster.

While giving Sisi the red-carpet treatment on an earlier visit to Paris in 2017, Macron was asked why he had not raised alleged domestic crimes in Egypt. Macron sounded just like Donald Trump, who once referred to Sisi as his "favorite dictator," when he replied: "I believe in the sovereignty of states, and therefore, just as I don't accept being lectured on how to govern my country, I don't lecture others. My deeply held conviction is that it's in President Sisi's interest to accompany the defense and consolidation of human rights by the Egyptian state, in the context that only he can be the judge of."

France had concluded numerous military agreements with Egypt in 2015, including the sale of twenty-four Rafale combat aircraft, a multi-mission frigate, and two Mistral warships in contracts worth some €6 billion. France would now discuss the possible sale of twelve more Rafale aircraft with Sisi, said Macron. Groups including Human Rights Watch and Amnesty International issued a joint statement saying France had "long indulged President el-Sisi's brutal repression of any form of dissent."

Macron also routinely rolled out the red carpet for Libyan warlord Khalifa Haftar—the veteran Field Marshal supported by France, Saudi Arabia, the United Arab Emirates, Egypt, and Russia as a potential leader of his oil-rich country. France officially recognized the legitimacy of Libya's UN-backed Government of National Accord in Tripoli, but that did not stop it from championing the Benghazi-based Haftar. He was the kind of strongman who was more likely to crush dangerous militias, especially those linked to global terror groups.

In July 2016, President Hollande had been forced to admit that French Special Forces were operating in Libya after three soldiers died in a helicopter crash while supporting Haftar's army, which was fighting groups including ISIS around Benghazi while refusing to take orders from Tripoli. Libyan instability was a huge problem for France, but the French had tried to keep their logistical support for warlords such as Haftar—a former Gaddafi commander who became a dissident—a secret. His forces were said to be receiving France-sourced weaponry, despite a 2011 arms embargo imposed by the UN Security Council.

By the time Field Marshal Haftar arrived at the Élysée Palace in March 2020, his forces were being linked with killings that left mass civilian graves across eastern Libya. Attacks on Tripoli had targeted hospitals and other medical facilities. Such atrocities appeared to be of little consequence to Macron, who was more interested in keeping France's biggest weapons clients—Egypt and the United Arab Emirates—happy by endorsing their man.

Wheeler-Dealer

As far as Africa's past is concerned, Macron typically raises historical grievances, but rules out apologies and never mentions reparations. During Macron's election campaign in 2017, I was in Algiers when he traveled to the capital city, and, in a discussion about colonization with Echorouk, the local TV station, said, "It's a crime. It's a crime against humanity. It's truly barbarous and it's part of a past that we need to confront by apologizing to those against whom we committed these acts."

Yet there is always an "on the other hand" Macron. When our paths crossed in North Africa, he was clearly attempting to win over French-Algerian voters in the run-up to the presidential election. He said that France had "established human rights in Algeria" but "simply forgot to abide by them." This was in line with an interview from the October before, when he said: "Yes, there was torture in Algeria, but there was also the emergence of a state, of wealth, of a middle class. That's the reality of colonisation. There were civilised elements and barbarous elements."[5] This was typical of Macron, who was ever the inconsistent wheeler-dealer.

By October 2021, *Le Monde* was reporting Macron as saying that Algeria had an official history that has been "totally rewritten" by a reactionary "political-military system." This history was "not based on truths" but "on a discourse of hatred toward France." Macron even asked: "Was there an Algerian nation before French colonization?" Following the publication of this poisonous attack on its integrity, the Algerian government recalled its Ambassador from Paris.

Clarifying the past is a notoriously difficult task at the best of times, and France has a long record of covering up the atrocities it committed. This has prolonged anger and resentment among all victims of imperial adventures. Macron claimed he wanted to change all this, but his actions were always duplicitous. In 2021, he tasked Benjamin Stora, a Paris academic from a *pied-noir* background, to shed light on "the memory of colonization and the Algerian War." The settler profile of the Macron-appointed author of the report gives a clue as to why it was so one-sided. It was an inherently flawed mission, yet Stora's ultimate objective was to help bring about "reconciliation between the French and Algerian peoples," according to an Élysée Palace statement.

The maxim that history is written by the victors was being reversed. France lost the Algerian War but was determined to control the narrative about its history while evading its responsibility for one of the most repulsive episodes in colonial times. On a flight back from Israel, Macron had also said, "The Algerian War is today absent from our political memory and the subject of a conflict of memories like the Holocaust was." He added, "We don't talk about this. We crush it."

The difference was France had owned up properly to its collaboration in the Holocaust in 1995, when Jacques Chirac, the then President, formally admitted and apologized for the role his countrymen had played in sending Jews to their deaths in Nazi concentration camps. Crucially in Algeria, the French had not handed their Algerian Muslim victims over to anyone. On the contrary, they did the killings themselves.

The Stora report turned out to be a fudge. It mainly called for more research, including the creation of a "Memories and Truth" Commission, improved access to archives, and more Franco-Algerian collaboration on historical studies. Overall, a desire to downplay unspeakable crimes that were in living memory guided Stora's work. He admitted that he might have "passed a little too quickly on Algerian memories and the colonial trauma," and stopped short of recommending that France apologize for its barbaric colonial past.[6] The truth was that Macron already had plenty of evidence highlighting the crimes of *l'Algérie française*. Academically rehearsing what was already known was not required. If anything, it would exacerbate grievances. What was needed was an apology, reparations, and, yes, prosecutions.

Attempts to deal with the past also included Macron's visit to Kigali after France's recognition of the part it played in the Rwandan genocide of 1994. In a speech at the Kigali Genocide Memorial in May 2021, Macron conceded that "France has a role, a history, and a political responsibility in Rwanda. It has a duty—it must look history in the face and recognize the share of suffering that it inflicted itself on the Rwandan people by opting for too long to keep silent instead of examining the truth." Introducing obtuse qualifications, Macron insisted that France "was not an accomplice" in the genocide but had sided with a "genocidal regime." Compounding his insensitivity, he added, "A genocide cannot be excused. One lives with it."

In turn, genocide survivor Dan Karenzi spoke for many when he said, "We don't want to hear him talk about responsibility, about France's role in the genocide. We, the survivors, wanted to hear Macron apologizing to us officially. I am really disappointed."[7] Similarly, the opposition Rwandese Platform for Democracy party had tweeted ahead of Macron's speech that it hoped he would "apologize honestly" and "promise to pay reparations" to genocide victims. Instead, Macron mainly responded with weasel-word rhetoric and little else.

Middle East

When Emmanuel Macron welcomed the de facto leader of one of the world's largest oil producers to the Élysée Palace in July 2022, he was again prepared to turn a blind eye to unspeakable barbarity. He instead helped to rehabilitate Saudi Arabia's Crown Prince Mohammed bin Salman following the savage murder of Jamal Khashoggi, the dissident Saudi *Washington Post* journalist who was lured into his country's consulate in Istanbul on October 2, 2018, before being strangled to death and his body dismembered.

Audio recordings captured the final moments of the attack on Khashoggi, which was carried out by a Saudi assassination squad closely connected to MBS. US intelligence agencies alleged that he rubber-stamped the operation. While those close to the Crown Prince blamed "rogue operatives," a UN inquiry described an "extrajudicial killing for which Saudi Arabia is responsible." This did not stop Macron from becoming the first Western leader to visit Saudi Arabia, in December 2021, after news of the Khashoggi atrocity broke.

In Paris, Macron could not have appeared closer to MBS. The President guided the royal up a red carpet at the Élysée Palace as the pair prepared for a dinner at which oil and arms would be the main subjects of discussion. France and its EU allies were looking to Riyadh to increase oil exports as Russia threatened to cut gas supplies to Europe following the invasion of Ukraine.

France was also one of the biggest arms suppliers to Saudi Arabia, despite some ten million people being driven to the brink of famine in Yemen, where a Saudi-led coalition was fighting Houthi rebels aligned with Iran. More than ten thousand civilians had been slaughtered in Yemen using French weapons, including Leclerc tanks, Caesar cannons, and laser-guided missile systems. But—as usual with French foreign policy—such concerns were deemed secondary to the bottom line.[8] This was despite the fact that France is a signatory of the UN Arms Trade Treaty that bans the sale of weapons that fuel human rights violations or war crimes.

MBS's visit to the Élysée Palace coincided with France concluding yet another multibillion-dollar weapons deal with the United Arab Emirates, Saudi Arabia's biggest ally in the war in Yemen. Macron boasted that the $19.1 billion order to Dassault Aviation—which supplies military planes to the French armed forces—was "the biggest military contract of French equipment in our history."

France's military base in the Gulf—the Camp de la Paix (peace camp)—was inaugurated by Sarkozy when it opened in Abu Dhabi in 2009. It was the first ever French military installation built outside France or Africa. The camp was made up of a naval base, airfield, and army garrison and was designed as a bulwark against Iran, amid concern about its nuclear program. The camp would also be used to safeguard shipping lanes at a time when Somalian pirates were threatening commercial traffic.

The troubled relationship between Saudi Arabia and Qatar does not prevent France from supporting both. Qatar, the richest nation in the world per capita, buys most of its military hardware from the French, following a defense pact signed in 1994. Qatari Special Forces are trained by the French too. This is part of a Françafrique-style web of economic, political, and cultural ties that the two countries have been weaving since 1995, when Hamad bin Khalifa al-Thani led a bloodless coup against his father, Emir Khalifa bin Hamad al-Thani, in Doha.

In June 2017, states including Saudi Arabia and the United Arab Emirates cut all relations with Qatar over its alleged support of terrorist groups, mainly through financing. They also castigated Doha for its backing of the Muslim Brotherhood, the Islamist political group, and indeed for its cozying up to Iran. France tried to rise above the row, especially as the Qatar Investment Authority was still pouring billions into Paris. The sovereign fund owns Paris Saint-Germain, France's number one superstar football club, and is a shareholder in multiple French companies, including the Lagardère Media Group, Total, and LVMH, the luxury goods conglomerate.

Amnesty International was among human rights groups that pointed to widespread abuse of immigrant workers in the run-up to the football World Cup in Qatar in 2022, but France showed little interest. Arms sales were the priority for the third biggest military exporter in the world, after America and Russia. Its defense sector employs some two hundred thousand people and, as Armed Forces Minister Florence Parly put it in 2018, "Arms exports are the business model of our sovereignty."

When EU countries including Germany called for the suspension of arms sales to Saudi Arabia following the Khashoggi murder, Macron accused them of "demagoguery," saying, chillingly, that weapons of mass destruction had nothing to do with a strangling. "I understand the connection with what's happening in Yemen, but there is no link with Mister Khashoggi," said Macron utterly disingenuously.

As the United States disengages from the Gulf and its War on Terror commitments in other regions of the Middle East and Central Asia,

France has been trying to take over its position, despite fierce competition from rivals. France sees allies in Gulf states that regularly use the word "security" to clamp down on dissent, often in the most brutal way possible. The Gulf warlords view radical Islamists as their biggest enemies, and this plays into Macron's negative treatment of Muslim communities at home.

Israel-Palestine

The banning of pro-Palestine demonstrations in Paris is typical of France's conduct in one of the world's most intractable conflicts. As the Israeli military attacked the Gaza Strip in May 2021, exchanging rocket fire with Hamas, a police order in the French capital stated that a planned march in the Barbès district could not go ahead. There was a similar Paris ban in the summer of 2014, when Operation Protective Edge—Israel's murderous ground, sea, and air offensive against Gaza—claimed more than 2,000 lives and 10,500 wounded, overwhelmingly civilians, including hundreds of children. In turn, Israel lost sixty-seven soldiers and six civilians, with an injured total of just over five hundred.

Despite such horrendous figures and the widespread destruction of Palestinian infrastructure including hospitals and schools, which drew international condemnations from the United Nations and human rights organizations, the French authorities claimed protests in Paris were a risk to public order. Such manipulation defied Paris's history as a protest city—one that has been at the forefront of idealistic and extremely rowdy challenges to injustice and oppression throughout the centuries—but members of Paris's huge Arab diaspora were told to stay at home.

Sure enough, the banned marches went ahead illegally, and demonstrators fought running battles with riot police who were trying to disperse them. France's law-and-order strategies had not maintained peace and security but instead made violence far more likely.

Such an outcome has been much the same in the Middle East thanks to France's duplicitous and often highly secretive relations with the state of Israel. French plutonium-extracting technology and a nuclear reactor, also sold by the Paris government, are at the center of a subterranean arms factory hidden beneath the Negev desert in the south of Israel. It produces atomic warheads big enough to destroy entire cities. Israel has never owned up to this capability, but there have been enough leaks by senior politicians and scientists to know exactly what is going on.

In his autobiography, former Israeli President Shimon Peres explained how France covertly sold a nuclear reactor to Israel in 1956, despite this violating an arms embargo.[9] The foundation of Israel in 1948 led to an immediate state of war against a coalition of Arab states, and—like all its NATO allies—France initially feared publicly backing Israel. One of many worries was that Arab nations would support the Soviets at the start of the Cold War.

In fact, France saw Israel as a convenient ally against Egypt, which was on the side of anti-French nationalist guerrillas in its Algerian colony. France began shipping warplanes, tanks, and missiles to Israel. In return, France wanted Israel to attack Egypt, which by now was mainly armed by Communist Czechoslovakia.

A confidential deal was worked out in the Paris suburb of Sèvres between the Israelis, France, and Britain in October 1956, and a week later Israeli paratroopers dropped into the Sinai Peninsula. The ensuing conflict turned into the Suez Crisis. Britain and France joined in the invasion after Egyptian President Gamal Abdel Nasser nationalized the Suez Canal, which had been mainly owned by British and French shareholders. Nasser responded to the invaders by sinking forty ships in the canal, making it useless. The United States and USSR exerted huge pressure on the allied invaders to withdraw, in what turned out to be a blistering diplomatic humiliation for both the French and British.

Following the Suez disaster, Israel was depicted as a puppet of Western powers—a reputation it has found hard to shift—while France continued to create instability and conflict. The hope that Israel might obtain a nuclear reactor had been discussed informally at Sèvres and, in September 1957, Peres visited Paris to sign agreements that turned Israel into the world's sixth nuclear power. Hundreds of French scientists relocated to the Negev desert to build the new reactor for a country that was destined to remain in a state of near-permanent war with its neighbors. Hawks argue that Israel's nuclear monopoly in the Middle East gives it the ultimate strategic deterrence against such enemies. Others would contend that France helped make the Middle East immeasurably less secure.

Over decades of war and illegal occupation of Palestinian territories, it has been an open secret that Israel possesses nuclear weapons, but successive governments have never admitted it. Nor has France. To this day, Israel's ongoing nuclear program is treated in just the same way as its unlawful Occupation of Palestine: as a fact of life that is best played down. When there is overwhelming evidence of war crimes and other human rights abuses against the Palestinians, platitudes will be used to try to bury them. In between interactions with Palestinian Authority President Mahmoud Abbas in 2021, Emmanuel Macron told a US pro-Israel advocacy group that "Israel has a right to defend itself." Macron also highlighted "France's profound attachment to Israel's security since its creation."

Macron now uses the Israel-Palestine conflict to promote himself as a white knight, while managing to anger both sides. In February 2022, for example, he spoke out against groups such as Amnesty International, which had described Israel as an "apartheid state" because of its mistreatment of Arabs. "It is not acceptable in the name of a just struggle for liberty that organisations misuse historically charged, shameful terms to describe the State of Israel," said Macron in a speech read out for him by his Prime Minister, Jean Castex.[10]

At an Élysée Palace meeting with Abbas just five months later in July 2022, Macron opposed the eviction of Palestinian families from their homes during land grabs that were "contrary to international law." Such theft and violence happened at gunpoint in areas where Palestinians were routinely treated as an underclass and separated from settlers under a regime that bears all the hallmarks of apartheid.

As a regular visitor to the Occupied Palestinian Territories, I can tell you that the segregated roads alone sum up the situation. A number of them are visible from the hilltop town of al-Khader, just outside

Bethlehem: slick, modern highways for the Israelis, rock-strewn, dirt tracks for the poor and dispossessed Arabs. As a metaphor, these roads are not heading in the direction of peace.

This Is Why I'm Here

The white knight savior act is typical of the Fifth Republic Presidents who go out into the world to pursue their foreign policies. A prime example was the way Emmanuel Macron showboated through the ruins of the Port of Beirut in August 2020, after an ammonium nitrate explosion claimed at least 218 lives, injured 7,000, and caused some $15 billion worth of damage.

The speed and determination of Macron's entrance into Lebanon, which France once controlled under a League of Nations mandate, resembled colonial-era theater. Arriving by executive jet, the President, a Kennedy figure wearing a black tie and white shirt with sleeves rolled up, was immediately surrounded by a heavily armed entourage. Soon, he was berating the crummy local politicians and trying to project the power of the French Republic.

There were cries of "Revolution!" from crowds pleading for change in Lebanon, as bodyguards accompanied Macron through streets covered in rubble and shattered glass. Years of corruption and maladministration had led up to the blast, and a state of emergency had just been declared. The army was in control of the site where a compound equivalent to 1.1 kilotons of TNT had been stored in an insecure warehouse for some six years. The blast also left an estimated three hundred thousand people homeless, and many called out to Macron for help and justice. Macron made his way through his sizeable security cordon and told a woman, "I see the emotion on your face, the sadness, the pain. This is why I'm here."

Visually, this was a moment comparable with Macron jumping for joy inside a Moscow stadium as France's footballers were crowned Champions of the World—except it was a lot more serious. Rather than sporting distraction, this was a chance for Macron to present himself as Monsieur Solution. "I guarantee you this," said Macron. "Aid will not go to corrupt hands. I will talk to all political forces to ask them for a new pact. I am here today to propose a new political pact to them."

Lebanese politicians did not know where to turn. A convoy carrying former Lebanese Prime Minister Saad Hariri had been attacked weeks before, and most others were too scared to venture out onto the streets. Macron warned, "If reforms are not made, Lebanon will continue to sink."

As a frequent visitor to this so-called Paris of the Middle East, I associate Beirut not only with the rich and stylish heritage exemplified by its Corniche but also with near-permanent turbulence. There was the fifteen-year civil war up until 1990 and constant conflict with neighbors, not least of all Israel. I well remember seeing tanks on the street in Beirut and narrowly escaping a car bomb explosion outside my hotel there. Vast swaths of Lebanese infrastructure were decimated by sectarian guerrilla battles and misgovernment long before the Hiroshima-style mushroom cloud created a wasteland in what was once one of the busiest ports on the Mediterranean. Regional disputes by proxy have caused political paralysis too. Latterly, the most intense rivalries have been between the Shia group Hezbollah, which is supported by Iran, and Saudi-backed Sunni factions.

Macron had no moral qualms about firm intervention by France, which gave up its twenty-five-year colonial mandate in Lebanon in 1944 but has maintained strong ties. Lebanon is a leading member of La Francophonie—the international organization that links French-speaking nations—and a loyal trading partner. French leaders frequently endorse favored power players in the Lebanese maelstrom, but the sight of Macron hugging the victims of the Beirut blast in the middle of a coronavirus pandemic appeared crass in the extreme.

There was an Arab Spring–style feel to what was going on, in that an energetic populist was encouraging the masses to reject the status quo and strive for something better. Yet there was little in the way of solid explanation, least of all under which new mandate the French would be assisting in reforming a sovereign state. Would their future plans be implemented by the United Nations, or perhaps even the European Union? Nobody knew.

Macron is a polished media performer whose fresh-faced charisma has great appeal when viewed in well-choreographed, short TV segments or through equally transient social media posts. In all other aspects, he is shallow and ineffective.

What we can see with Macron is the same approach that France has taken for decades, with mostly catastrophic results. Heads of state show off about their country's mystical values, but they seldom uphold them. Instead, they desperately back strongmen in the hope that they will at least guarantee stability. When despots were threatened during the Arab Spring, the French switched allegiances in line with whoever looked likely to win power. Mubarak in Egypt, Ben Ali in Tunisia, Gaddafi in Libya—all were, at one stage or another, viewed as useful to the West and were embraced as allies. Even Bashar al-Assad, the Syrian President long considered an international pariah for the way he was murdering his own people, became a power player in the coalition against ISIS.

Even before that, I was in Damascus when the French Embassy reopened in 2008, in order to reverse Syria's so-called axis of evil status with the resumption of diplomatic relations between the two countries. While attending the Bastille Day celebrations at the Embassy, a French diplomat told me that at least Assad was a "secular ally," as he had banned the wearing of the headscarf at university. "Islamists" were seemingly the common enemy.

The Arab Spring was crucial because it highlighted such cynicism and inconsistency while drawing attention to the major challenges of a region blighted by a range of endemic problems, including economic inequality and human rights violations. The pro-democracy movements were never going to solve these issues overnight, but at least the global community is now talking about them. What we have learned beyond a doubt, however, is that the ruthless pragmatism of power politics and economic self-interest has, in the short term at least, triumphed over the people's revolutions.

The narrative is still the same in France: support a compliant dictator for as long as possible, allow him to be replaced if necessary, and then either stand back and do nothing when the new autocracy emerges or indeed help make it work. France sees one of the biggest threats to its interests as being "radical Islam," and yet it pours weapons into Saudi Arabia, the most extremist Islamist state, which is spreading its Wahhabi-Salafist doctrines throughout the Middle East and North Africa.

The French have sometimes differed from the United States on regional issues—especially on Iraq and Palestine—and this has helped them garner a reputation in the Middle East for upholding principles and human rights. One of Chirac's most famous foreign policy stances was his refusal to join the US-led coalition that invaded Iraq in 2003. It was a landmark decision that saw Dominique de Villepin, Chirac's Foreign Secretary, challenging the entire logic of war in a moving speech at the UN Security Council on February 14, 2003.

Villepin said: "In this temple of United Nations, we are the guardians of an ideal, we are guardians of a conscience. The heavy responsibility and great honor that are ours must lead us to give priority to peaceful disarmament. This message comes to you today from an old country, France, from an old continent like mine, Europe, that has known wars, occupation, and barbarity."

A month later, as Western foreign policy hawks pushed the invasion, Chirac himself declared: "Iraq does not represent an immediate threat that would justify an immediate war. France appeals to the responsibility of all to respect international law. Acting without the UN's legitimacy, putting power before law, means taking on a heavy responsibility." Opinion polls showed that three-quarters of the French population supported this anti-war stance. Even more agreed after Iraq collapsed into abject chaos.

It was also Chirac who turned on Israeli officials during a trip to Israel in October 1996, when the French President called on Israel to accept the creation of a Palestinian state, to return the Golan Heights to Syria, and to withdraw from the Israeli buffer zone in southern Lebanon. Chirac pointedly sent a diplomatic team to liaise with Palestinian Liberation Organization officials at their Jerusalem headquarters.

Angered by overbearing Israeli security during his own walk around Jerusalem's Old City, especially when they started rounding up Palestinians, Chirac turned on the most senior Israeli policeman and said, "I'm starting to have enough of this." Chirac started in French, and then said in English: "What do you want, me to go back to my plane and go back to France? Is that what you want? Let them go. Let them go."

Such an assertive approach did not hide the fact that the French pursue and protect their commercial interests in the region doggedly, including their well-developed efforts to tap into the region's energy resources. Actively funding, supporting, and pouring weapons into reviled regimes in countries such as Egypt and Saudi Arabia is the modus operandi of a country that has become one of the most unscrupulous arms dealers on earth.

Preserving sovereignty through an independent arms industry has long been a cornerstone of French foreign policy, an imperative that overrides all ethical concerns about the way these weapons are used. The French Army is too small for the number of weapons produced. To remain profitable, firms focus on exports. They might rather do business in Europe, but the market is dominated by US competitors, so they concentrate on the Middle East and Africa.

Meanwhile, a Françafrique-style mindset still lingers. Opportunities to abuse and exploit overseas territories are prioritized. Colonial attitudes encompassing prejudices and inequalities have by no means faded away, and not just in regard to what is happening abroad. The approach toward those perceived as aliens—including millions of verified French citizens—is straight out of the old empire. Neo-colonial views have come to define some of the ugliest manifestations of modern France.

CONCLUSION
The Art of Being French

One day everything will be well, that is our hope.
Everything's fine today, that is our illusion.

—VOLTAIRE (1694–1778)

Reimagining the ideas and institutions that underpin France is all part of the republican tradition. Our rules-based nation is a product of an idealistic history but also of revolution, so constant reappraisal is always appropriate. It was encouraged by Emmanuel Macron, an astute conformist who has never knowingly attended a street protest in his life, when he said, "The art of being French is both deeply rooted and universal, to be attached to our history and our roots but able to embrace the future. It's an ability to argue about everything endlessly and it is, very profoundly, an ability to refuse to adapt to a world which escapes us, to refuse to yield to the law of the survival of the strongest and to pursue a policy of resistance and ambition, for today and tomorrow."[1]

The major problem I have highlighted in this book is that the French are failing to live up to their turbulent past, not least of all in the way they resist and then reform. Dissent has become tokenistic, and bland complacency is pervading every aspect of life. There are too many wispy fantasies supporting stagnation and a system that is fundamentally unjust.

Large sections of society are being left behind, and—thanks to rapid developments in communication—they are more aware of it than ever before. In the meantime, extremism festers, as it always does when traditionally moderate political groupings focus on looking after wealthy elites and so become mired in corruption and inactivity. Poisonous dissemblers of truth with hardly any knowledge of how the world really works take the place of effective change makers. The rabble-rousers exploit cynicism, pessimism, and fear to their own ends.

Utopian slogans are still used as fig leaves to disguise the worst problems of a broken France: its revolutionary motto—Liberty, Equality, and Fraternity—sounds increasingly hollow, as do so many of the other rhetorical underpinnings of French republicanism, such as the Declaration of the Rights of Man and of the Citizen, which did not recognize women as active members of society. Such documents are grounded in illusions, and so is the 1789 Revolution itself. It is revered by those who underplay the diabolical bloodspilling involved and the warmongering despots it ultimately produced. As Robespierre summarized it: "To good citizens revolutionary government owes the full protection of the state; to the enemies of the people, it owes only death."[2]

For many French, the dreams have not just faded but disappeared altogether. The country is unable to reconcile competing forces such as rampant popular nationalism and increasing globalization. The knowledge vacuum is filled by those who are indisputably malevolent.

Macron himself personifies a huge structural problem that needs repairing, and that is the absurd reliance on a single alpha male with far too much influence over every field of national life, from the economy and state security to the non-religion of *laïcité*. The President is a quasi-king with his own palace guarded by soldiers who have a Napoleonic-style cavalry detachment and band. Every year, he watches his military forces parade down the Champs-Élysées, as if they are preparing to fight the next war. He can override Parliament and appoint anyone he likes to form a government, whether close friends or corporate cronies. There is never an influential deputy or any kind of charismatic underling who might stand up to the President. Macron goes through Prime Ministers like he would disposable razors. None of this is compatible with a serious modern democracy.

Changing the French Constitution of October 4, 1958, could be achieved through Article 89, but amendments are introduced by the

President, and he is hardly going to limit his own powers. Michel Debré, the "Gaullist Baron" Senator who led the working group drafting the original plan for the Fifth Republic, wanted to introduce UK-style prime ministerial government, but, instead, the new President was able to exploit the system to suit himself. The French feared civil war over the future of Algeria, and De Gaulle was the veteran soldier designated to hold everything together.[3]

The main difference between the Fifth Republic and earlier ones is that it favors strong executive rule over parliamentary dithering. The Fourth Republic—"the unloved one"—was characterized by *immobilisme*, or paralysis. Debré, who became the Fifth Republic's first Prime Minister, used the term "Republican Monarch" and created a state that was "strong, organised, even authoritarian."[4] Breaking through the infighting and instability of the revolving-door Fourth Republic, which saw twenty-four administrations in twelve years, was the priority. De Gaulle himself said that this "popular monarchy" had "instituted a new legitimacy which makes a link to the legitimacy interrupted by the Revolution."[5]

The Fifth Republic is a makeshift measure designed to get France through exceptional circumstances, in other words. Many believed it would only last five or so years, but it is now more than sixty years old. The Left despised it until François Mitterrand, once one of De Gaulle's most vocal opponents, came to power and was able to exploit the institution of the Jupiter presidency for selfish career advancement. Yet the current system is an anachronism that is causing a crisis in democracy. Globalization, including the growing clout of the European Union, has also considerably reduced the power of the nation. A major revamp of French *républicanisme* is long overdue, including ushering in an ambitious Sixth Republic to adapt to this changing world.

The Algerian War is over, and we are left with an apparatus that produces hyperactive showmen who skate around multiple policy fields without fixing the major faults. In a media-saturated age, heads of state focus on their own personal image while quickly losing gravitas. In the case of recent incumbents, such as Sarkozy and Hollande, they have become soap opera characters, clowns even.

This dangerous centralization of power in the head of state encourages sleaze, as shown by the criminal convictions of Gaullist Presidents, who are meant to embody the essential morality and grandeur of the Fifth Republic as exemplified by Charles de Gaulle himself. He has been gone for more than half a century, yet aspiring politicians still revere him and try to project themselves as Gaullists. It is a word that is meant to evoke greatness, but it is woefully outdated. Nothing has replaced it. The ghost of the vanished *Général* is all they have.

Another direct link with the Algerian War is the *cités*—the suburban estates that symbolize every kind of injustice, worst of all racism. Residents include those who still remember the shantytowns that housed immigrant workers viewed as insurgents. They were treated as an underclass from day one, and plenty of their far younger family members now feel the same way. There is an urgent need for their problems to be recognized. Only then can they be tackled properly.

Many of the worst-kept *cités* are in the greater Paris region, just a few miles from the historic splendor of the city center, which is associated with an intellectual, artistic, and architectural ebullience that projects past economic and social triumphs. Paris *intra-muros* is the area in between the city's long-vanished ancient walls. It is a very compact space, about forty-one square miles (105 square kilometers), with a population of just over two million. It feels like an enclosed city thanks to its ring road and the wide, grand boulevards built for armies to head north, south, east, and west.

Add the area beyond the walls, and Paris becomes the Île-de-France—easily the most populous of France's eighteen regions, with some twelve million residents. It covers around 4,500 square miles (12,000 square kilometers) and every aspect of French life lies within: from the Palace of Versailles to Disneyland Paris. The Île-de-France may be the center of France's industrial life, but it is by no means a testament to *Liberté, Égalité, Fraternité*. As in other major cities and towns, it reflects an unofficial form of segregation, not least of all between the prosperous middle classes in the center and west of greater Paris, and the impoverished immigrant classes in the east. Billionaire mansions and apartments remain empty most nights—many of their owners spend their time in countryside homes or distant tax havens—while thousands are stranded inside disintegrating social housing.

How do we fix this socioeconomic time bomb? Well, a start would be making sure that the much-vaunted Grand Paris plan works. This is a proposed expansion of transport links, housing and businesses that would significantly improve the suburbs. The emphasis is on creating low-carbon residential areas, full of affordable properties and green spaces, close to services and jobs. A planned new rapid transport system includes automated rail lines and dozens of new stations by 2035. The idea is to replace the decaying RER—including the so-called D for Delinquent line—so as to simplify travel and thus remove the distinction between the city and the suburbs. Seven regional business hubs are envisaged. The Société du Grand Paris has warned of "the risk of financial slippages," especially as it relies on borrowing and as expenses soar. As of June 30, 2020, the overall cost of the Grand Paris design was estimated at €42 billion.[6]

In some ways, such big projects sound ominously like the utopian thinking of Le Corbusier and the Communist planners. It is hoped that the new developments are more realistic and really do bring communities together. The motivation of housing policy should be nothing less than national unity.

In the meantime, those who portray people living on the housing estates as a subhuman threat to society should themselves be demonized and—when necessary—criminalized. It may sound hyperbolic to talk of France's Nazi problem, but there is every justification to link the Rassemblement National (formerly Front National) and its fellow travelers with the Third Reich. Not only were key founding members in the SS and *Milice*, but its most famous veteran, Jean-Marie Le Pen, is now a convicted Holocaust denier and anti-Semite. There are those, including his own daughter, Marine Le Pen, who try to pretend he is of little consequence, but—as we have learned—the senior Le Pen's ideas and personality still loom large across the rank and file. Marine Le Pen's staged schism with *papa* is not fooling anyone either. This legacy of fascism and an obsession with whitewashing the collaborating Vichy regime still runs through the far-right party, as does nostalgia for colonial Algeria.

Early campaigns by Jean-Marie Le Pen were supported by a few ideological allies in the French media. On October 26, 1985, *Le Figaro Magazine* ran a demographic projection under the question "Will we still be French in 30 years?" It was accompanied by an image of Marianne as a veiled and bejeweled Arab princess. *Le Figaro Magazine* claimed that by 2015 "non-European foreigners" would dominate France and destroy its traditional culture. Islam would become the prevailing religion, so tipping the Republic "over into the third world unless something is done now." Such white-supremacist thinking is now widely peddled by hate-mongers masquerading as intellectuals. They champion the Great Replacement theory, which has motivated mass murders involving minorities around the world.

Far more education is required about where "acceptable" racist discourse leads. France's recent fascist and colonial past certainly needs to be highlighted. There should be fewer lessons about "Our Ancestors, the Gauls" and many more about France's widespread collaboration with the Nazis, and French soldiers who were ordered to throw Algerian nationalists out of planes and then to obliterate their villages, along with the men, women, and children living in them.

Instead, Macron comes out with inflammatory sound bites such as this remark from an interview in October 2022: "Yes, when we look at delinquency in Paris, we can see that half of the delinquent acts come from foreigners in an irregular situation or awaiting asylum approval." With typical "at the same time" imprecision, Macron then added, "I will never make an existential link between immigration and insecurity," even though he had just made exactly that link.[7]

This is how immigrants are discussed in a society where *ensauvagement*—the word describing savages gaining influence in a once civilized society—becomes part of popular parlance. The English word "Black" is increasingly used by the French in a vindictive manner too.

Societies get the media they deserve, and the French one supports all kinds of sinister developments without doing much to challenge them. Look at the way it enabled Éric Zemmour as he warned of a "war of the races" and tried to rehabilitate the Vichy regime that collaborated with the Nazis. There was nothing new in his discourse—extremists have been pushing the same ideas in France for decades—but the difference was that he was being given almost unlimited airtime and column inches by mainstream outlets. Zemmour was a polemicist for *Le Figaro*, the conservative daily, and a prime-time pundit for CNEWS, the twenty-four-hour TV station. He had big money deals to write books that were publicized as much as he was.

Men like Jean-Marie Le Pen spent much of their careers being ostracized when they used the darkest episodes of France's recent history—assistance in the Holocaust and the Algerian War—to construct political arguments. In contrast, Zemmour is just one of numerous outspoken bigots guiding a French media that is also woefully subservient to those in power.

There are admirable exceptions. *Mediapart*, the online investigative news site, is impressively nonaligned. Its work uncovering Sarkozy's alleged multimillion-dollar financial links with the late Colonel Gaddafi is typical of its commitment to challenging a complacent establishment. *Le Canard Enchaîné* also continues to drop devastating truth bombs from time to time, but generally the French media lacks the snarling, brutish features of far more effective and influential journalistic enterprises, such as the ones just across the English Channel in Britain. Needless to say, the UK media is far more egalitarian too. I regularly write and broadcast for British outlets of widely different political perspectives in a way that would be impossible in France for those from minority backgrounds.

Physical violence prevails in France because it has become institutionalized. Multiple paramilitary units are on standby night and day to coerce the populace into obedience using rubber bullets, tear gas, and worse. Colonial law-and-order tools, such as curfews and obligatory identity checks, are still in use. De Gaulle's vision of a strong-armed security state on permanent alert persists, and rioters respond in kind, setting up regular demonstrations that always deteriorate into fighting and acts of destruction.

The French State is organized in favor of such wretchedly useless confrontations. Replacing the militaristic cohorts with community officers would not be difficult. Nor would ending the practice of regularly and indiscriminately smothering legitimate protesters, and indeed ordinary members of the public, with tear gas—a chemical weapon that is banned in war zones.

France is committed to exporting its militaristic model to other countries, including to brutal dictatorships. The Republic continues to meddle and muddle, especially in former colonies. *Déclassement* may be the end result, but if the money keeps pouring in, few are concerned. Enlightenment values, including human rights, always come second to easy dollars.

The terrorist threat in the period starting in 1958 was far greater than it is today. Ultranationalists with access to the weapons of state, including plenty of plastic explosives, tried to provoke a civil war. Many of them were professional soldiers and police officers with access to state armories. They came close to assassinating De Gaulle, and they blithely murdered train passengers and other French citizens who had nothing to do with their cause. Algerians—who were technically able to become French citizens during the colonial period—were subjected to the cruelest attacks because they were viewed as an internal enemy, just as members of ethnic and religious minorities are viewed now in an age when demonizing entire communities is remarkably easy. Drugged-up, cowardly criminals who carry out despicable deeds on behalf of fiendish organizations are deviously transformed into representatives of all those who look like them or who come from the same background. It is not only online trolls that consider all Muslims guilty by association; some politicians and so-called philosophers think the same.

The same kind of prejudice leads to Muslim women who cover up being derided by Left and Right, because they do not fit into an ill-conceived republican ideal. Such poisonous thinking is not only deeply sexist, but it is also meant to link them to a hated "other."

Republican universalism does not extend to many interpretations of feminism in France, a country that remains profoundly misogynistic in so many key aspects of life. Men dominate the executive, and they are invariably just like the macho egotists who are regularly accused of abusing women across sectors. In addition to the political sphere, the media, show business, and fashion industries have all had their appalling scandals in recent years. The constitutional principle of parity between men and women remains just that—an administrative ideal that does nothing to change a society where femicide and related crimes are still all too common.

Popular myths include France being unable to assimilate a sizeable Muslim minority. This plays into an alleged "War of Civilizations" between secular and religious cultures. It demonizes millions of French citizens and exposes the French Republic's refusal to integrate in a modern world where artificial boundaries between communities are falling all the time. France's insistence on manipulating *laïcité* to enforce stigmatizing policies is as pitiful as the way xenophobes cite Enlightenment values—including ones about tolerance and free speech—to attack those they abhor.

This kind of fiendish parochialism shames France. It harkens back to the original trick of creating an existential threat to the nation and encouraging everybody to fight it. This hallmark of French republican ideology is behind the pseudo-national identity crisis projected by successive administrations, including Macron's. All know that it can be used to political advantage far more easily than an economic crisis.

These republican illusions are not keeping up with the world. Alexis de Tocqueville, the Paris aristocrat who lost a grandfather to the guillotine of Revolution, was referring to America when he said a nation's greatness comes not from being more enlightened than any other country but being able to repair its faults. I would extend Tocqueville's theory to the broken French Republic: its major fault lines are easy to pinpoint, and fixing them is possible. Change requires more than high-minded ideals. A concerted period of action is needed, and it is about time that a bold France rises to the challenge. The Fifth Republic is dead. Vive la nouvelle République!

ACKNOWLEDGMENTS

Growing up in France and then spending a lot of time among those who have strong views about the country in Algeria, Britain, and the United States inspired me to write this book, meaning there are generations of family and friends who have helped me with it along the way, many unknowingly. All taught me to think about the workings of a fantastical Republic that so often appears to make no sense at all.

I won't mention everybody, in case I inadvertently leave anyone out, but particular inspiration—professional and personal—came from Sofia Alahiane, Peter Allen, Henry Blofeld, Valeria Debruyn Chianale-Blofeld, Michael Butcher, Edwy Plenel, Sarah Smith, Said Touama, and Claude Zurbach.

Thanks to my agent, Zeynep Sen, and to my friend Neslihan Feradov, who connected me to her. Dean Krystek at WordLink was eminently encouraging too. Clive Priddle, publisher at PublicAffairs, showed an instant interest in my work and then swiftly and expertly guided my writing forward with his incredible team. Working with such outstanding colleagues has been a joy. Mum and Dad first encouraged me to try to fix France, and that's why this book is dedicated to them.

NOTES

Introduction: Rebuilding the Dream

1. James Baldwin, *Going to Meet the Man*, 1965.
2. James Baldwin, *Notes of a Native Son*, 1955.

Chapter 1: Politics

1. Nicolas Sarkozy, TV interview, July 2, 2014.
2. Opinion Way survey, January/February 2021.
3. *Libération* editorial, November 22, 2017.
4. Emmanuel Macron, *Challenges* interview, October 16, 2016.
5. Éric Fottorino, *Macron Par Macron*, 2017.

Chapter 2: Society

1. National Institute of Statistics and Economic Studies (INSEE) survey: Foreigners—Immigrants in 2017, *Département* of Essonne (91). The 2017 data are disseminated according to the geography in effect on January 1, 2020. Report published on December 9, 2020.
2. See the essentials on Immigrants and Foreigners, INSEE report published August 10, 2022.
3. Conrad Hackett, "Five Facts About the Muslim Population in Europe," Pew Research Center, November 29, 2017.
4. Jean-Louis Borloo, *Vivre Ensemble, Vivre en Grand: Pour une Réconciliation Nationale*, April 26, 2018.

5. France 24 tabulation based on elected officials who have at least one parent from a French overseas territory, or a non-European one. Only MPs elected in mainland France counted.

6. Tweet by Sabrina Sebaihi, Member of Parliament, June 28, 2022.

Chapter 3: The Far-Right

1. Pierre-André Taguieff, *Sur La Nouvelle Droite*, 1994.

2. Pierre-André Taguieff, *Sur La Nouvelle Droite*, 1994.

3. Hamid Bousselham, *Torturés par Le Pen, La Guerre d'Algérie (1954–1962)* (Tortured by Le Pen, the Algerian War (1954–1962)), Rahma-Alger, January 1, 2000; *Journal Officiel Français*, June 12, 1957; François Malye, "Rémi Kauffer: Le Pen and Algeria," *Le Point*, February 23, 2018.

4. Léon Gaultier, *Siegfried et le Berrichon, Parcours d'un Collabo*, 1992.

5. Grégoire Kauffmann, "Les Origines du Front National," *Pouvoirs* 157, no. 2 (2016), www.revue-pouvoirs.fr/Les-origines-du-Front-national.html; Dominique Albertini and David Doucet, *Histoire du Front National*, 2013; Gilles Bresson and Christian Lionet, *Le Pen. Biographie*, 1994.

6. Laurent Joly, *Vichy dans la "Solution Finale": Histoire du Commissariat aux Questions Juives, 1941–1944*, 2006; Nicolas Lebourg, "Among the Auxiliaries of the Vél d'Hiv' Roundup, a Future Number 2 of the FN," Slate.fr, April 10, 2017; Sacha Ghozlan, "The France of the Founders of the FN Was Not in London, but in Vichy," *Libération*, April 13, 2017.

7. Alain Chouffan, "Malaguti: The Man Who Denies His Past," *Le Nouvel Observateur*, March 5–11, 1992; Christian Bidault, "August 15, 1944 in Cannes: P. Malaguti the Ex-boss of the FN Loiret, Assists the Gestapo During a Massacre," Magcentre.fr, August 15, 2014.

8. François Dufay and Charles Jaigu, "Le Pen and His Ghosts," *Le Point*, May 3, 2002.

9. Jordan Bardella, *Libération* interview, December 26, 2018.

10. BFM TV, August 29, 2021.

11. Jordan Bardella, CNEWS interview, October 6, 2022.

Chapter 4: Protest

1. S. G. Tallentyre, *The Friends of Voltaire*, 1906. (S. G. Tallentyre was a pseudonym used by Hall.)

2. Karl Marx, "The Eighteenth Brumaire of Louis Bonaparte," first published in *Die Revolution* magazine, 1852.

3. Julian Jackson, *A Certain Idea of France: The Life of Charles de Gaulle*, 2018; Charles de Gaulle, *The Complete War Memoirs of Charles de Gaulle*, 1998.

4. Institut National de l'Audiovisuel (INA), "L'attentat du Petit-Clamart" (The Petit Clamart attack), *Journal Les Actualités Françaises*, August 22, 1962, video.

5. Amnesty International, "Yellow Vests in France: A Worrying Assessment," November 18, 2019.

6. "New Round of Gaza Ceasefire Talks Takes Place in Paris," France 24, July 25, 2014.

7. Martin Evans and John Phillips, *Anger of the Dispossessed*, 2007.

8. Laurent Valdiguié, "Yellow Vests: Armored Vehicles Return to Paris on Saturday, Equipped with Their Tear Gas 'Dispersers,'" *Marianne*, December 14, 2018.

9. Radio France Internationale (RFI), "May-68 Seen by Immigrants from the Slums of Nanterre," March 22, 2018.

Chapter 5: Terrorism

1. Jean-Claude Veillard.

2. Louis Sébastien Mercier, "Paris Scenes," in *The Waiting City: Paris 1782–1788*, 1933.

3. Jean Lacouture, *Charles de Gaulle: Le souverain 1959–1970*, 1984.

4. Jean Lacouture, *Charles de Gaulle: Le souverain 1959–1970*, 1984.

5. Edmond Fraysse, *Commando Delta: Confessions d'un Soldat de l'OAS*, 2021.

6. Paul Henissart, *Wolves in the City*, 1971.

7. Paul Henissart, *Wolves in the City*, 1971.

8. Vincent Nouzille, *Les Tueurs de la République: Assassinats et Opérations Spéciales des Services Secrets* (The killers of the republic: Assassinations and special operations of the French secret services), 2016.

9. *Le Monde*, June 3, 1960.

10. *Mediapart*, May 3, 2017.

11. Communiqué du groupe parlementaire La France Insoumise—NUPES, October 21, 2022.

Chapter 6: Education

1. French Government DEPP (Directorate of Evaluation, Forecasting, and Performance Monitoring), briefing note no. 20.41, November 2020.

2. All figures in French Government DEPP, briefing note No. 20.41, November 2020.

3. Ministry of Education figures.

4. Most recently in "Rectifications de l'Orthographe: Rapport du Conseil Supérieur de la Langue Française," publié dans les documents administratifs du Journal Officiel du 6 décembre 1990.

5. In an interview with *Le Point*, December 17, 2020.

6. Interview during presidential campaign, 2022.

7. French Government DEPP, briefing note no. 20.41, November 2020.

8. John Stuart Mill, *On Liberty*, 1859.

9. *Frankfurter Allgemeine Zeitung*, July 7, 2022.

10. Sylvie Germain, *Le Figaro Étudiant*, June 21, 2022.

11. Jean-Paul Sartre, *Existentialism Is a Humanism*, 1946.

12. Alain Finkielkraut, *Haaretz* interview, November 2005, and speaking to radio stations Europe 1 and France Inter in June 2010.

Chapter 7: Identity

1. Otto Dann and John Dinwiddy, *Nationalism in the Age of the French Revolution*, 1988.

2. J. M. Thompson, *Leaders of the French Revolution*, 1929.

3. James Heartfield, *Unpatriotic History of the Second World War*, 2012.

4. Major General Walter Bedell Smith, declassified 1944 memo.

5. The Racism Barometer Survey, July 2022. The report sampled 1,352 people representative of the adult population residing in mainland France, using face-to-face interviews.

6. Jacques de Crussol, Duke of Uzès, BBC interview, October 2016.

7. Marc Fayard, "Jules Ferry, un Athée qui se Croyait de 'Race Supérieure'" (Jules Ferry, an atheist who believed himself to be of 'superior race'), *Le Point*, March 17, 2014.

8. Charles de Gaulle, *Mémoires d'Espoir* (Memoirs of hope: Renewal and endeavor), 1970.

9. Antony Blinken, *New York Times*, July 16, 2018.

Chapter 8: Feminism

1. French Interior Ministry figures.

2. Tom Furniss, "Mary Wollstonecraft's French Revolution," in *The Cambridge Companion to Mary Wollstonecraft*, ed. Claudia L. Johnson, 2002.

3. Jean-Jacques Rousseau, *Emile, or On Education*, 1763.

4. Lyndall Gordon, *Vindication: A Life of Mary Wollstonecraft*, 2005.

5. Gay L. Gullickson, *Unruly Women of Paris: Image of the Commune*, 1996.

6. Élisabeth Badinter interview, "L'homme n'est pas un Ennemi à Abattre" (Man is not an enemy to kill), *L'Express*, April 23, 2003.

7. Élisabeth Badinter, France Inter interview, July 6, 2011.

8. Crime figures for 2021 released by the French Ministerial Internal Security Statistical Department (SSMSI), and figures from the UK Office for National Statistics.

9. Rape data for 2020 released by the French Interior Ministry and INSEE in its report "Cadre de Vie et Sécurité" [Living environment and security].

10. Sexism Barometer Study carried out by l'Institut Viavoice based on the responses of three thousand French people over fifteen, February 2–16, 2022.

11. Sara Frazier, "A Timeline of the Dominique Strauss-Kahn Case," NBC New York, July 1, 2011 (updated August 23, 2011); BBC News, "Dominique Strauss-Kahn: How cracks appeared in the case," July 2, 2011; Ed Pilkington, "Dominique Strauss-Kahn DNA 'found on maid's clothes,'" *The Guardian*, May 24, 2011.

12. Patrice Duhamel and Jacques Santamaria, *L'Élysée, Histoire, Secrets, Mystères*, 2017.

13. Christian Zilko, "Adèle Haenel Stopped Making Movies Because Industry Is 'Reactionary, Racist, and Patriarchal,'" *IndieWire*, May 15, 2022.

14. Annie Ernaux, column in *Libération*, March 13, 2019.

15. Emmanuel Macron, live TV speech, November 17, 2017.

16. Oxfam France, *Egalité Femmes-Hommes: Grande Cause, Petit Bilan*, March 2022.

17. Haut Conseil à l'Égalité entre les Hommes et les Femmes, *Rapport Annuel 2023 sur l'État du Sexisme en France*, January 23, 2023.

18. Édith Cresson, *Journal du Dimanche* interview, May 15, 2022.

Chapter 9: Economics

1. Olivier Blanchard and Jean Tirole, "Major Economic Challenges," France Stratégie, June 2021.

2. *CEOWORLD* survey July 22, 2022.

3. INSEE figures.

4. Emmanuel Macron, speech at the Museum of Mankind, September 13, 2018.

5. Marine Le Pen, speaking to the Anglo-American Press Association of Paris, videoconference on March 30, 2021.

6. Bruno Le Maire, *France Culture* interview, January 9, 2019.

7. Report by the Tax Reform Review Committee for France Stratégie, the analysis group set up by François Hollande in 2013.

8. "Après la Suppression de l'ISF, les Revenus des 0,1 % les Plus Riches ont Explosé en France" (After the abolition of the ISF, the income of the richest 0.1% exploded in France), *Le Monde*, October 9, 2020.

9. Olivier Blanchard and Jean Tirole, "Major Economic Challenges," France Stratégie, June 2021.

10. Jean Fourastié, *Les Trente Glorieuses: Ou la Révolution Invisible de 1946 à 1975*, 1979.

11. United Nations, Department of Economic and Social Affairs, "Population Pyramids of the World from 1950 to 2100," updated in 2022.

12. Emmanuel Macron, Bastille Day interview, July 14, 2022.

13. INSEE figures.

14. Eurostat figures.

15. IFOP and Fondation Jean-Jaurès, *Les Français, l'Effort et la Fatigue*, September 2022.

16. INSEE figures from 2022.

17. INSEE figures from 2021.

18. INSEE figures from 2020.

19. Institut des Politiques Publiques survey, November 2021.

20. Olivier Blanchard and Jean Tirole, "Major Economic Challenges," France Stratégie, June 2021.

21. *Forbes*, "World's Billionaires List: The Richest in 2023," www.forbes.com /billionaires.

Chapter 10: Foreign Policy

1. Emmanuel Macron, speech, June 2017.

2. Bruno Charbonneau, *Dreams of Empire: France, Europe and the New Interventionism in Africa*, 2008.

3. François-Xavier Verschave, *Mouvements*, May 2002.

4. Nicolas Sarkozy, speech at Cheikh Anta Diop University, July 27, 2007.

5. Emmanuel Macron, *Le Point* interview, October 2017.

6. Nabila Ramdani, "Macron's Algeria Report Isn't Progress. It's a Whitewash," *Foreign Policy*, February 2021.

7. Dan Karenzi, Associated Press interview, July 12, 2021.

8. Entitled "Yemen: Security Situation," a fifteen-page classified report written by France's DRM military intelligence agency includes maps that detail the positioning of French-made weapons inside Yemen and on the Saudi side of the border.

9. Shimon Peres, *No Room for Small Dreams: Courage, Imagination, and the Making of Modern Israel*, 2017.

10. Emmanuel Macron, speech in Paris, February 2022.

Conclusion: The Art of Being French

1. Emmanuel Macron, press conference, Élysée Palace, April 25, 2019.

2. Maximilien Robespierre, *On the Theory of Revolutionary Government*, 1793.

3. Michel Debré, "The Constitution of 1958: Its Raison d'Être and How It Evolved," in *The Impact of the Fifth Republic on France*, eds. William G. Andrews, Stanley Hoffmann, 1981.

4. Michel Debré using the pseudonym Jacquier-Bruère, *Refaire la France: L'Effort d'une Génération*, 1943.

5. Julian Jackson, *A Certain Idea of France: The Life of Charles de Gaulle*, 2019.

6. Figures from Société du Grand Paris, which is in charge of the Grand Paris Express project.

7. Emmanuel Macron, France 2 interview, October 27, 2022.

INDEX

Courtesy of the author

Nabila Ramdani is a French author of Algerian descent who works as a journalist, academic and broadcaster. Nabila began her award-winning journalistic career in the BBC Paris Bureau. She has since broadcast for outlets including Sky News, Al Jazeera and CNN, and has written extensively for *The Guardian, The Daily Mail, The Washington Post* and others. Educated at Paris VII University and the London School of Economics (LSE), Nabila has taught at the University of Oxford and the University of Michigan, Ann Arbor.